13th Conference of the Association for Machine Translation in the Americas (AMTA 2018)

Volume 2: MT Users' Track

Boston, Massachusetts, USA
17-21 March 2018

Editors:

Janice Campbell
Jennifer Doyon

Alex Yanishevsky
Doug Jones

ISBN: 978-1-5108-6727-7

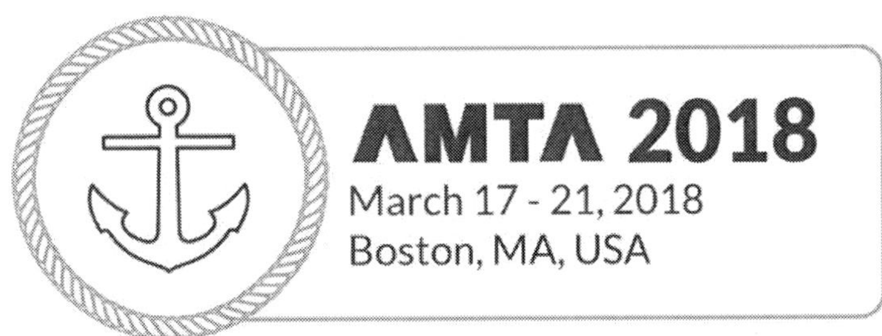

The 13th Conference of
The Association for Machine Translation
in the Americas

www.conference.amtaweb.org

PROCEEDINGS

Vol. 2: MT Users' Track

Editors: Janice Campbell & Alex Yanishevsky *(Commercial Users)*
Jennifer Doyon & Doug Jones *(Government Users)*

Introduction

Commercial Users

The Commercial MT Users and Translators Track at AMTA 2018 features eighteen presentations from worldwide organizations, enterprises, and individuals in the translation and language technology industry, including providers of market research, language services, and commercial and open-source machine translation technologies and services. Many of this year's presentations focus on the wide-ranging applications of artificial intelligence – specifically neural networks – to machine translation and speech, image, video and text processing.

Adopting the latest AI technologies in our industry raises a host of considerations that speakers will address: incorporating adaptive MT, understanding the intersection of humans and machines in augmented translation, creating fair and realistic quality and productivity measures, and calculating the benefits of NMT. New topics presented this year include: automatic conversion of one language variation to another, integration of MT into chatbots, and automatic translation of search queries in data-poor language pairs.

Since machine translation is widely accepted and already applied by default in many business and customer scenarios, a number of presentations will focus on enterprise-level customization, scaling and integration, development of a tiered model for MT application, as well as the shift towards reducing post-editing.

The Commercial MT Users and Translators Track Co-Chairs

Alex Yanishevsky
Janice Campbell

Government Users

The Government and Military MT Stakeholders Track at AMTA 2018 opens with a panel of respected leaders from the commercial world discussing the latest translation workflow systems, which include both neural machine translation and translation memory, and their implications for the government and military. This thought-provoking panel will be followed by sixteen presentations providing insight into MT, MT-related technologies and terminology in government and military settings.

This Government Track is the first since the practical deployment of neural machine translation (NMT), so many of the presentations discuss AI-focused research, development, evaluation and analysis. Topics covered include the impact of NMT on translation workflows, OpenMT model development, challenges in automatic speech recognition and translation and many others.

We are thrilled to have such an impressive set of commercial, research and government experts contributing to the Government Track this year. Please join us in benefiting from their knowledge and being inspired by their creativity.

Government and Military MT Stakeholders Track Co-Chairs

Jen Doyon
Doug Jones

Contents

Government Track

Technology Showcase Presentations

12:30-12:50	**StarMT**
1:00 – 1:20	**XTM International**
1:30 – 1:50	**Translations.com**
2:00 – 2:20	**Plunet**
2:30 – 2:50	**AAMT and Nagoya University**
3:00 – 3:20	**Memsource**
3:30 – 3:50	**MMT Sri**
4:00 – 4:20	**Systran**
4:30 – 4:50	**SDL**
5:00 – 5:20	**SmartCAT**

AMTA
Technology Showcase

Company	Products	Booth	Description	Pres.	First Name	Last Name	Email
Amazon		1			Lexi	Lewis	burnhaml@amazon.com
Asia-Pacific Association for Machine Translation (AAMT) and Nagoya University		2	We will demonstrate our automatic MT output evaluation site based on the AAMT Test-Set Features of the evaluation site opened to the public: (1) on-line automatic evaluation is available from anywhere in the world; (2) results of evaluation are shown on a cobweb chart by grammatical items; (3) average test-set scores of six major Japanese-Chinese MT engines are shown on the same cobweb chart for comparison. Our approach for automatic MT evaluation as established a method of test-set based automatic evaluation using error analysis to clarify the strengths and weaknesses of the current machine translation systems.	2:30-2:50	Hiromi	Nakaiwa	nakaiwa@is.nagoya-u.ac.jp
Common Sense Advisory		3	Common Sense Advisory provides insight for global market leaders to help them gain access to new markets and clients.		Melissa	Gillespie	mgillespie@csa-research.com
eBay	Commerce	4	eBay Inc. (NASDAQ: EBAY) is a global commerce leader including the Marketplace, StubHub and Classifieds platforms. Collectively, we connect millions of buyers and sellers around the world, empowering people and creating opportunity through Connected Commerce. Founded in 1995 in San Jose, Calif., eBay is one of the world's largest and most vibrant marketplaces for discovering great value and unique selection. In 2016, eBay enabled $84 billion of gross merchandise volume. For more information about the company and its global portfolio of online brands, visit www.ebayinc.com.		Yana	Huang	yhuang@ebay.com
Etsy		5					
MateCat	MateCat	6	MateCat is an online open source translation platform. It's the ideal environment for translation and post-editing. MateCat's tight integration with the largest public translation memory (30 billion words and counting) and the best generic and specialized MT systems (including Google Translate, DeepL, ModernMT) make translators from 20 to 30% more productive than with any other CAT tools. As a powerful cloud platform, MateCat can be integrated with translation and content management systems thanks to its comprehensive set of RESTful API		Alessandro	Cattelan	info@matecat.com

Memsource	Memsource Cloud	7	Memsource is an AI-powered, cloud-based translation management system that enables its users to rapidly deploy multilingual content to global markets. Founded in 2010, Memsource is internationally recognized for providing an intuitive, yet powerful translation environment which processes two billion words per month from over 200,000 users around the world. With its combination of REST APIs, automation ability, and robust selection of CMS connectors including Salesforce, Zendesk, and Marketo, Memsource helps global-minded companies achieve a more agile translation process. For more information, visit www.memsource.com	3:00-3:20	Bill John	Lafferty Terninko	bill.lafferty@memsource.com; john.terminko@memsource.gov
MMT Srl	ModernMT Enterprise Edition	8	ModernMT is a new open-source MT software that consolidates the current state-of-the-art of neural MT into a single and easy-to-use product. ModernMT adapts to the context in real-time and is capable of learning from — and evolving through — interaction with users, with the final aim of increasing MT-output utility for the translator in a real professional environment. We will present the Modern Enterprise Edition, which includes pre-trained engines for many languages and many other features not available on the GitHub repository. MMT EE is available to translators as a plug-in of MateCat and to companies in two operating modes: cloud based and on-premise.	3:30 - 3:50	Marcello Davide	Federico Caroselli	marcello@modernmt.eu, davide@modernmt.eu
Plunet Inc.	Plunet BusinessManager	9	Plunet develops and markets a vendor-agnostic business and workflow management software for the translation and localization industry. Plunet BusinessManager provides a high degree of automation and flexibility for professional language service providers and translation departments of multinational organizations. Using a web-based platform, Plunet integrates translation software (CAT Tools), financial accounting, and quality management systems. On-premise or hosted solutions are available.	2:00 - 2:20	Sophie	Halbeisen	sophie.halbaeisen@plunet.com
Prompsit		10			Gema	Ramírez	gramirez@prompsit.com
SDL	ETS	11	SDL ETS (Enterprise Translation Server) is an on-premise neural and statistical machine translation software that automatically translates text, files, and web pages from one language to another. ETS enables organizations to securely translate multilingual content into their languages of interest at high speed and in a cost-effective way. The ETS scalable architecture and multi-server deployment option allows for quick and efficient translation of large volumes of content, while its optimized footprint and single-server deployment option is well-suited for a desktop environment with a low translation volume requirement. ETS can be accessed either via an intuitive Web GUI for an interactive experience or via a rich REST API for easy integration with other applications and workflows. ETS uses state-of-the-art machine learning algorithms and supports a large number of languages.	4:30 - 4:50	Randy	Endemann	www.sdl.com/amta
SmartCat		12		5:00 - 5:20	Jean-Luc	Saillard	jean-luc@smartcat.ai

STAR	STAR MT Translate & integrated Terminology Search	13	STAR MT uses the terminology and writing style of the company's corporate language since the STAR MT engine is based on validated translations and terminology databases from the customer. WebTerm is STAR's web based terminology management system. It can smoothly be integrated in the STAR MT Translate environment. If additional information is needed on the source or the target terms, the user simply highlights the words to search automatically in the company-specific dictionaries. STAR MT Translate, in turn, is integrated in the terminology area, so that it is possible to translate text parts of the dictionary, e.g. definitions, if needed. Users can either translate via the STAR MT Translate web interface or via the STAR MT Translate function that is integrated in the MS office products.		Elke	Fuchs	elke.fuchs@star-group.net
Systran		14	SYSTRAN is an accomplished pioneer in machine translation, and this year we're celebrating our 50th anniversary! Our Pure Neural Machine Translation (PNMT) technology - offered on-premise & in-cloud - will be on display at AMTA 2018. You can find us speaking in four different sessions or visit us at the Showcase to learn more.	4:00 - 4:20	Beth	Flaherty	beth.flaherty@systrangroup.com
Translations.com	GlobalLink	15	Built from the ground up to support a multi-vendor, multi-national approach to translation management, GlobalLink Enterprise lets you pick your translators, combine multiple vendors and internal linguistic resources, customize your workflows with or without machine translation, integrate with back-end systems, and automate manual processes associated with launching and maintaining global content—both online and offline. And since everything is managed from your central workflow platform, your organization will enjoy complete transparency into all of your translation efforts.	1:30- 1:50	Diego Mark	Bartolome Ambrose	dbartolome@translations.com, mambrose@translations.com
XTM International	XTM Cloud	16	XTM Cloud is a cloud-based enterprise translation management system (TMS). It is an all-in-one solution integrating workflow management, TM/terminology management, and an online CAT tool. XTM includes built-in connectors to 14 different machine translation (MT) providers, including several NMT systems, and where available sends post-edited translations back to the MT provider to further train the system. The flexible translation settings in XTM enable everything from dedicated MT+post-editing workflows to merely offering MT as a suggestion when no better TM match is available. These various configurations can be saved is Project templates for automation and easy reuse to support the different requirements of all the departments or content types across the entire enterprise. XTM can track when MT is used in a translation and automatically track both the post-editing changes as well as the time spent editing a segment. XTM also features a built-in integration with TAUS DQF, so MT usage and post-editing metrics along with LQA results can be seamlessly shared in DQF for benchmarking etc.	1:00-1:20	John	Weisgerber	jweisgerber@xtm-intl.com

Augmented Translation:
A New Approach to Combining Human and Machine Capabilities

March 18, 2018
Arle R. Lommel, Ph.D.
Senior Analyst

Background

- In 2016, CSA research predicted that post-edited machine translation (PEMT) will be the fastest-growing segment of the *enterprise* translation market (36% CAGR from 2016–2019 vs. 25% for raw MT and 7% for HT)
- Human linguists do not like PEMT:
  - It leaves them at the end of the chain with no way to fix things: They see the same mistakes over and over
  - Prices tend to be 65% of the total for HT, but do not account for effort, so many translators feel they are getting paid less for the same amount of work
- Traditional CAT tools have embraced MT as an optional information source
  - This is **not** post-editing: Linguists can use MT or not as they see fit
  - Most implementations are one-way: The MT provides segments, but only learns from changes if/when the engines are retrained

Common Sense Advisory

Business challenge

- Human linguists alone cannot scale to meet demand
  - Enterprise content volumes are growing much more quickly than the supply of human translators is
  - Much of the growth is in on-demand content where traditional human processes are too slow and expensive
- Current-generation technology treats various technologies as discrete entities and cannot deliver needed efficiencies
- Language service providers (LSPs) that embrace MT grow more quickly than those that take a "wait and see" approach, but struggle to define their MT-centric business models

Large LSPs that adopted MT grew 3.5 times faster than others

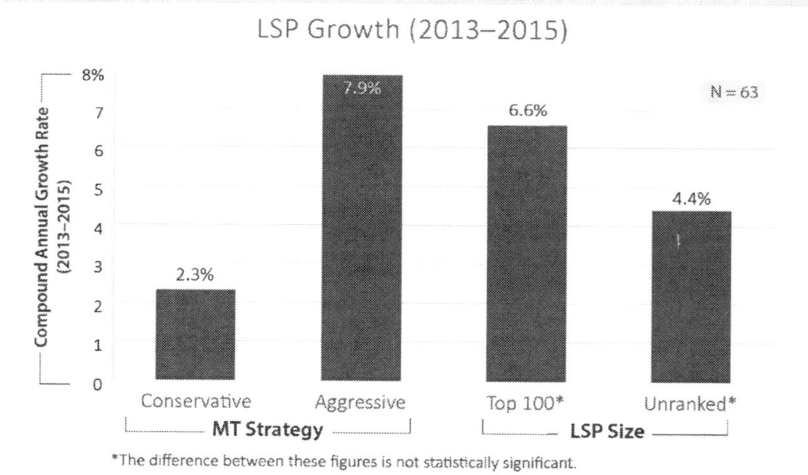

Source: "Fast-Growing LSPs Turn to Machine Translation," © Common Sense Advisory, Inc.

Agenda

In the presentation, based on more than a decade of independent research and analysis on machine translation, CSA Research discusses and analyzes:

1. Overview of current technology approaches to MT in human-translation centric environments
2. Defining "augmented translation" and its components: sub-segment TM, adaptive (neural) MT, automated content enrichment (ACE), improved terminology management, AI-driven project management
3. Detailed discussion of adaptive MT and ACE
4. Overview of technology providers in this space
5. Discussion of the future of augmented translation

Common Sense Advisory

Augmented translation overview

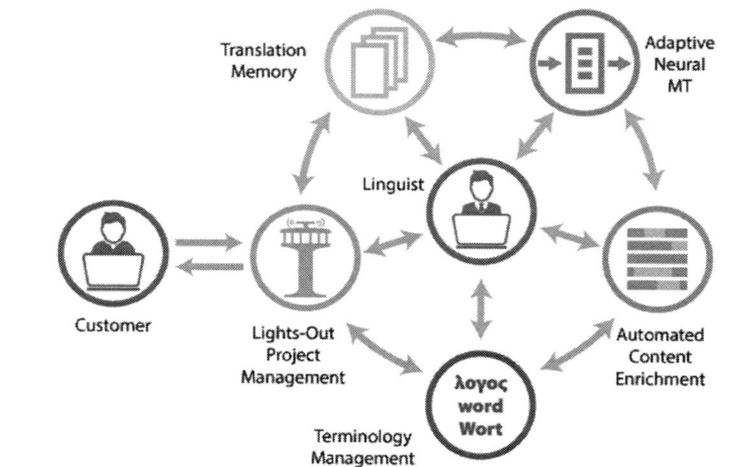

Source: "How AI Will Augment Human Translation," © Common Sense Advisory, Inc.

Common Sense Advisory

Research referenced in this presentation

- "How AI Will Augment Human Translation"
- "The Calculus of Global Content"
- "MT's Journey to the Enterprise"
- "The Language Services Market: 2017"
- "Fast-Growing LSPs Turn to Machine Translation"
- "TechStack: Automated Content Enrichment"
- "TechStack: Machine Translation"
- "TechStack: Terminology Management Tools"
- "Neural MT: Sorting Fact from Fiction"
- "The Winds of Content Are Changing"

Common Sense Advisory

11

Thank you.

Arle Lommel

alommel@csa-research.com

+1.978.275.0500 x1114

- Research: www.csa-research.com
- Twitter: @CSA_Research

To request a copy of this presentation, e-mail media@csa-research.com.

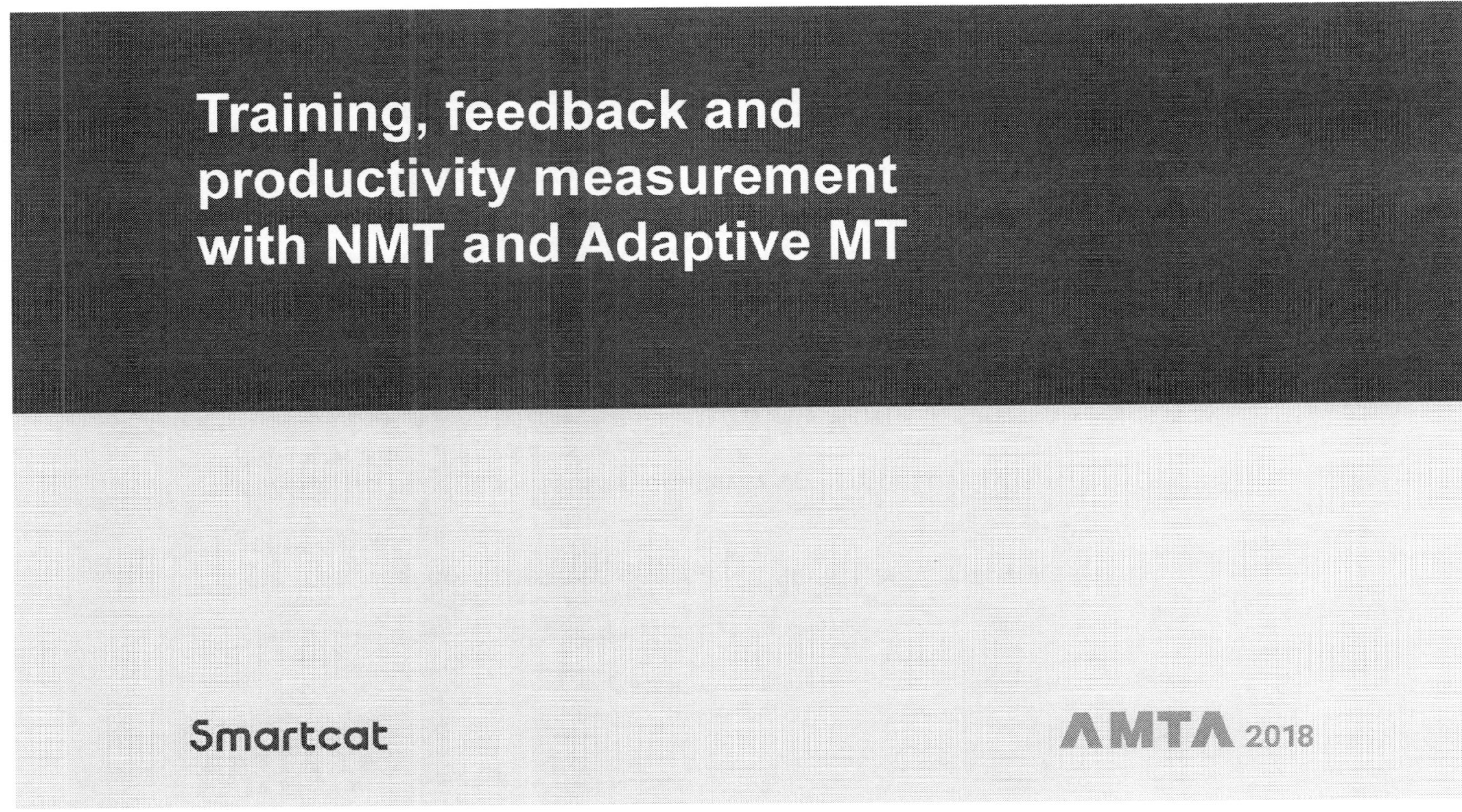

Training, feedback and productivity measurement with NMT and Adaptive MT
Smartcat
AMTA 2018

Why?

- Why MT — does it make sense for everybody?

- And if so, why do companies choose to train MT engines over existing generic ones?

- Why do we need to measure productivity and collect other data and does it impact our processes?

Smartcat

AMTA

Industry Challenges

- **Many MT providers**
- **Lack of integrated benchmarks**
- **Little usable feedback to project participants**
- **Small organizations (LSPs and End-Users) left behind**
  - Generally no in-house expertise
  - Training engines takes time and data, and is expensive!

Smartcat

AMTA

Many MT Providers – Decisions, decisions...

- Various technologies each with their own advantages and flaws
  - RBMT
  - SMT
  - NMT
  - Adaptive MT
- Some MT providers add the option to train or customize engines
- CAT Tools do a low level integration of many of these MT engines of don't support them at all

Smartcat

AMTA

How do we choose?

- Most process participants simply default to the easiest option in their CAT tools

- Other rely on the opinion or preferences of their post-editors – but how reliable is that when for example NMT's fluency can distort an evaluation?

- Pricing is important!

Smartcat

AMTA

Lack of Integrated Scoring

- **Multiple MT scoring systems**
  - BLEU
  - METEOR
  - LEPOR
- **These scores are not available in CAT tools.**
- **Scores for engine trained on an unknown corpus can be unreliable and scores for generic engines vary with time.**

Smartcat

AMTA

Or Benchmarks!

- **Quality evaluation approaches used for human translation cannot be used for quality evaluation of the machine translation.**
  - Do we create new rating systems (MQM comes to mind)
  - How do we make them available to participants?
- **What other metrics could assist project participants?**
  - Effort/Productivity/Prices
  - QA reports

Smartcat

AMTA

Solutions

- **Integration of benchmark in the CAT tool interface**
  - Display standard scores
  - And possible custom scores
  - Add pricing calculations to the mix!
- **Calculate and display PEMT productivity numbers:**
  - For each MT engine integrated in the CAT tool
  - For individual translators on various MT engines
- **Produce after-action reports**

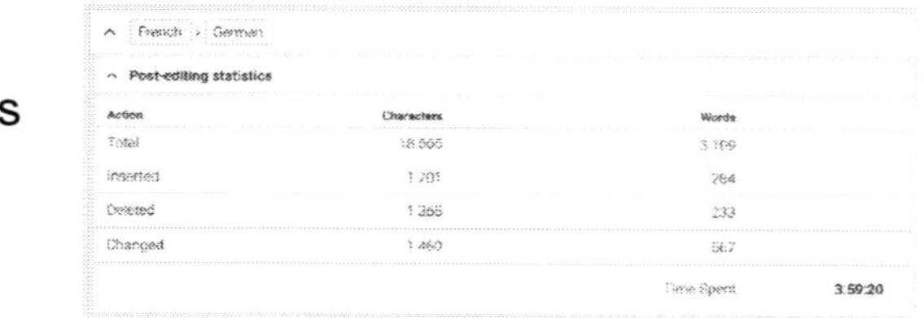

Smartcat

AMTA

The Adaptive MT Conundrum

- **Standard scoring system cannot score the adaptiveness of the engine.**
- **Productivity metrics can still be produced but should vary more than with other engine types.**
- **Can we devise a new metrics**
  - Adaptive Factor?
  - Other methods

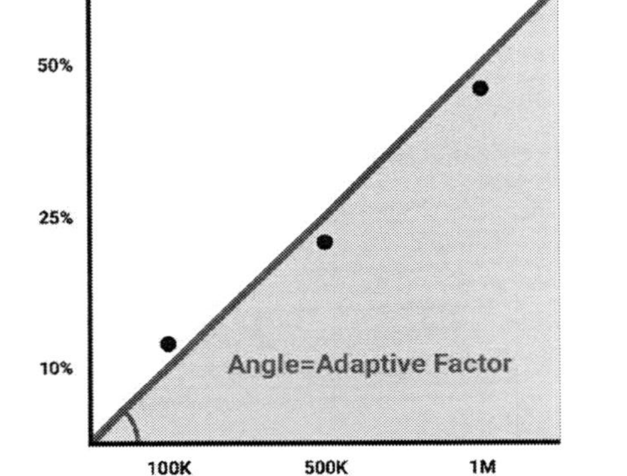

Smartcat

AMTA

Feedback – Project Managers

How useful could the access to these metrics be for project managers?

- Select the best potential MT engine for each language pair/topic at the best price
- Use productivity and QA reports to assist in task assignment
- More accurate costs analysis around MT and PEMT
- Better deadline predictions

Smartcat

AMTA

Feedback – Translators

How about for the translators?

- Lower reluctance to use MT when presented with updated productivity numbers

- A new evaluation of the per word pricing

- In the context of a marketplace, more information for the potential buyers or higher ranking for the translator

- Improve training using reviewed "after action" reports and productivity benchmarks

Source text	Unhide column to see translators → Translation	Unhide columns to see editors and distance → Editing	Unhide columns to see proofreaders and distance → Proofreading
In the town where I was born lived a man who sailed to sea.	In der Stadt, in der ich geboren wurde, lebte ein Mann, der zur See gefahren war.	In der Stadt, in der wo ich geboren wurde, lebte ein Mann, der zur in See gefahren gestochen war.	In der Stadt, wo ich geboren wurde, meiner Heimatstadt lebte ein Mann Seemann, der in See gestochen ausgesegelt war.

Smartcat

AMTA

Next Steps

Additional process automation – not only can project be created automatically but:

- The best possible MT resources can be allocated automatically by the system.

- Translators can be assigned to the tasks without human interaction to match deadline and cost requirements.

- Real-time productivity numbers can be used to re-allocate translation resources as needed

Smartcat

AMTA

Small Organization Access

- Generally no in-house experience
- Training performant engines takes data, time and expenses
- Not practical for temporary needs

Smartcat

AMTA

Solutions

Utilize the marketplace model:

- **Trained MT engine marketplace**
    - Real-time scores and productivity benchmarks
    - Data source information
- **Training data marketplace – already in place**
- **PEMT vendors marketplace – partially in place**
    - Real-time productivity benchmarks
    - QA reports and feedback

Smartcat

AMTA

Thank you!

Jean-Luc Saillard
Jean-luc@smartcat.ai
smartcat.ai

Smartcat

AMTA

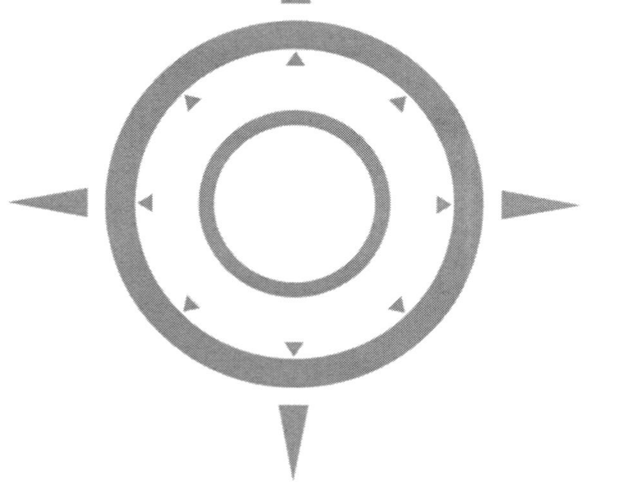

The Collision of Quality and Technology with Reality

March 19, 2018
Donald A. DePalma, Ph.D.
Chief Strategy Officer

Background

- With broad reach comes great expectations.

- The publishing requirements for most organizations ballooned as online channels dominated their outreach.

- Everyone expects an all-you-can-eat buffet of information in a form they can readily consume on demand − on computers, mobile devices of any sort, smart TVs, Alexa, and car dashboards − wherever and however they need it. And most expect to receive in in their language(s).

- Organizations struggle with the practicalities tied to this newfound role as a publisher of multilingual content as they deal with a dozen strategic languages, consider a hundred long-tail markets, and ponder what to do with the massive volumes of content their organizations generate every day. We talk with and advise many of these "accidental publishers" who are in the process of defining, renovating, or expanding their global content strategies.

Common Sense Advisory

Business challenge

- This presentation addresses the business challenge of how commercial enterprises and government agencies meet that expectation for locally digestible content using their available but frequently limited resources.
- As they develop their global content strategies, they encounter conflicting agendas and mandates:
  - An internal requirement for absolute linguistic quality in all publications
  - Arguably usable and ever improving automated translation
  - The reality of declining information consumer expectations for language perfection

Common Sense Advisory

Agenda

In the presentation, based on more than a decade of independent research and analysis on machine translation, CSA Research discusses and analyzes:

1. How non-publishing organizations became accidental publishers
2. Global content tiering strategies that involve human, machine, and comingled translation modalities
3. How those strategies will be affected by advances in machine translation and supporting technologies
4. Lowered expectations for language quality among information consumers
5. How these phenomena intersect with traditional and evolving quality metrics.

The challenge continues:
2027 total online market and audience shares

All Tiers
with Tier One broken
down by language

Sources: *"Forecasting Global Language Priorities: 2022 and 2027,"*
© *Common Sense Advisory, Inc.*

Common Sense Advisory

Research referenced in this presentation

- "The Calculus of Global Content"
- "MT's Journey to the Enterprise"
- "The Language Services Market: 2017"
- "The Winds of Content Are Changing"
- "How AI Will Augment Human Translation"
- "The ROI of Customer Engagement"
- "Neural MT: Sorting Fact from Fiction"
- "TechStack: Machine Translation"
- "Fast-Growing LSPs turn to Machine Translation"

Thank you.

Don DePalma

don@csa-research.com

+1.978.275.0500 x1001

- Research: www.csa-research.com
- Twitter: @CSA_Research

To request a copy of this presentation, e-mail media@csa-research.com.

Common Sense Advisory — **Insight for global market leaders**

Same-language MT for local flavours/flavors

Janice Campbell - Adobe
Gema Ramírez - Prompsit

Proceedings of AMTA 2018, vol. 2: MT Users' Track

Intro: brief history of AltLang 1/3

A call from the industry:

not Prompsit's idea but Autodesk's

Intro: brief history of AltLang 2/3

Based on FOSS Apertium technology and data: easy to reuse, extend and adapt

Automatic, reliable conversion for language varieties

Intro: brief history of AltLang 3/3

www.altlang.net

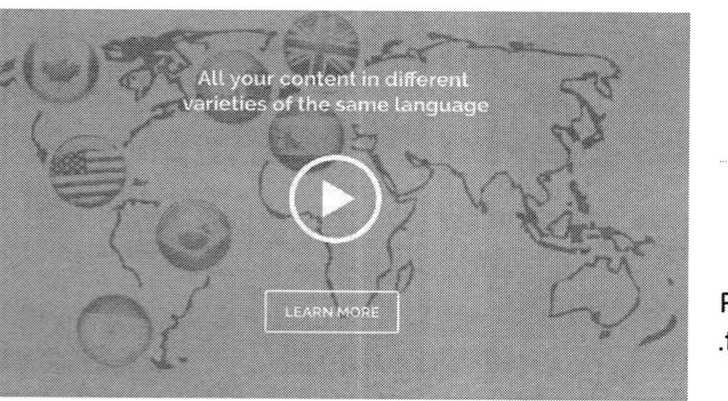

prompsit

Languages and formats

EN	FR	ES	PT
American English ↓↑ British English	Canadian French ↓↑ European French	LATAM Spanish ↓↑ European Spanish	Brazilian Portuguese ↓↑ European Portuguese
Plain text .txt, .latex	(Libre)Office .odt, .docx .odp, .pptx .ods, .xslx	Website .html, .xml	Localisation .xliff, .po

prompsit

Adobe Business Case

Personalize the international customer experience by delivering local language variants to Adobe.com country sites.

Avoid time-consuming, costly manual editing of high-volume, constantly-changing content.

Requested by UK field sales & marketing.

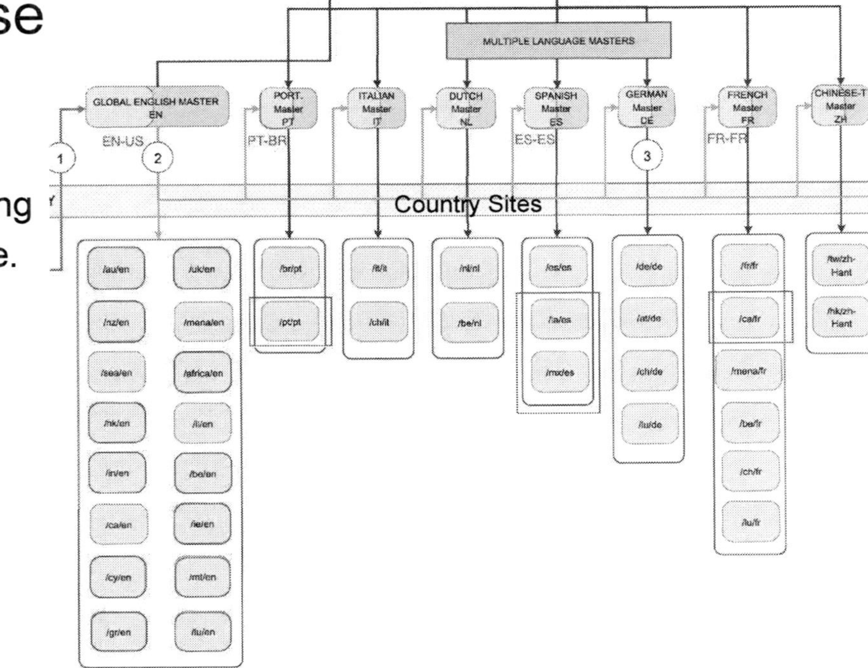

How does AltLang work? The basics… 1/3

- **automatically** and **quickly replaces differences** among two variants of the same language → nice for dynamic content
- performs **only controlled changes** → no (or low) risks
- highly **customisable** → can adapt to DNT, lexical choices, etc.
- easily **accessible** → full integration (JSON API), out-of-the-box testing (web-based demo), professional use (CAT tools and CMS)
- AltLang is **SaaS, a GPLv2- based service**

Variants is all about letters, words, some local changes…

It looks like we can automate it!

How does AltLang work? prompsit It deals with… 2/3

spelling differences

en_GB (-ise)	en_US (-ize)
customise	customize
realise	realize
wise	wize
advertise	advertize

word choices

a lift!

Please, give me an elevator!

Proceedings of AMTA 2018, vol. 2: MT Users' Track

How does AltLang work? It deals with… 3/3

prompsit

grammar structures

CAN YOU PLEASE...

help + pronoun + infinitive =
help + pronoun + **to** + infinitive

style/numeric conventions

Deliver by ~~28~~ **February 28**

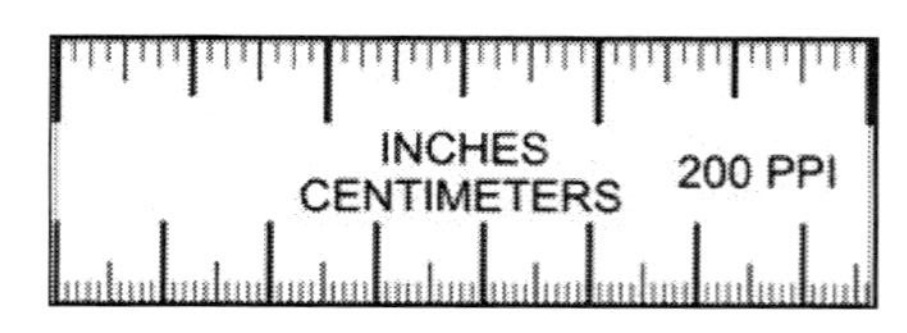

2.5" = 6.4 cm (2.5")

Proceedings of AMTA 2018, vol. 2: MT Users' Track

AltLang all together... in its web-based demo

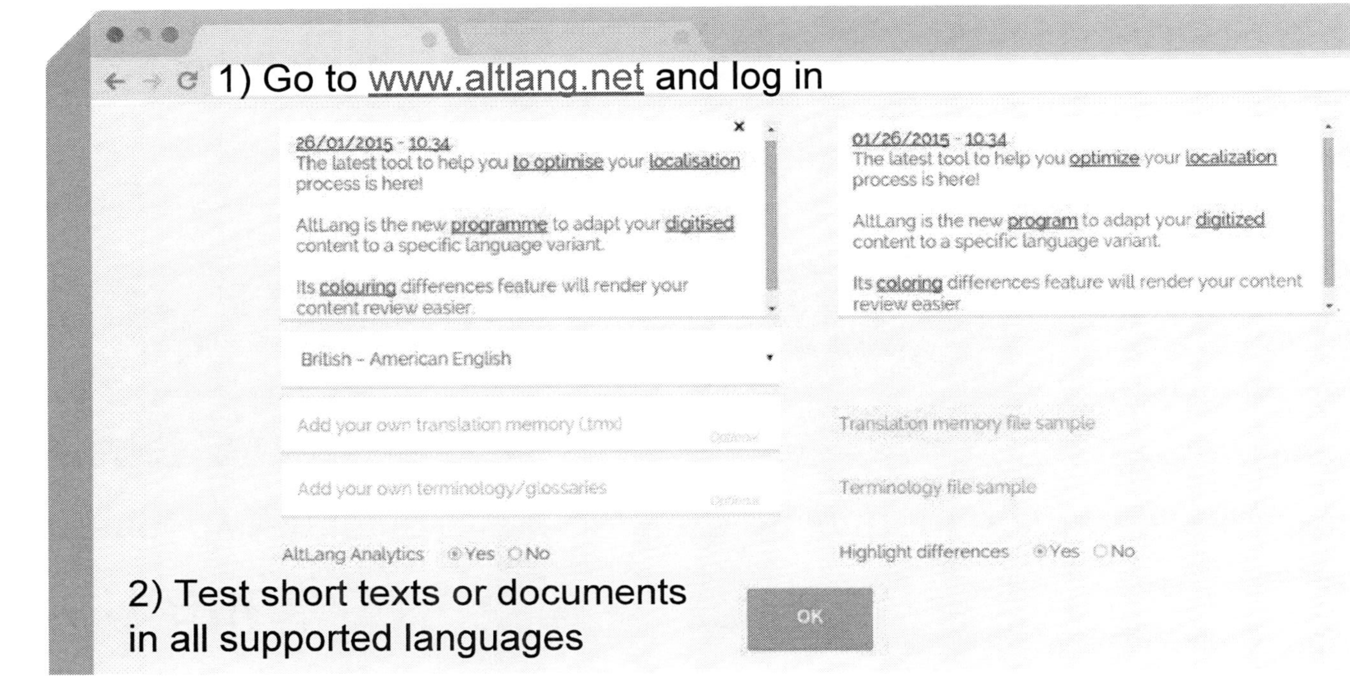

2) Test short texts or documents in all supported languages

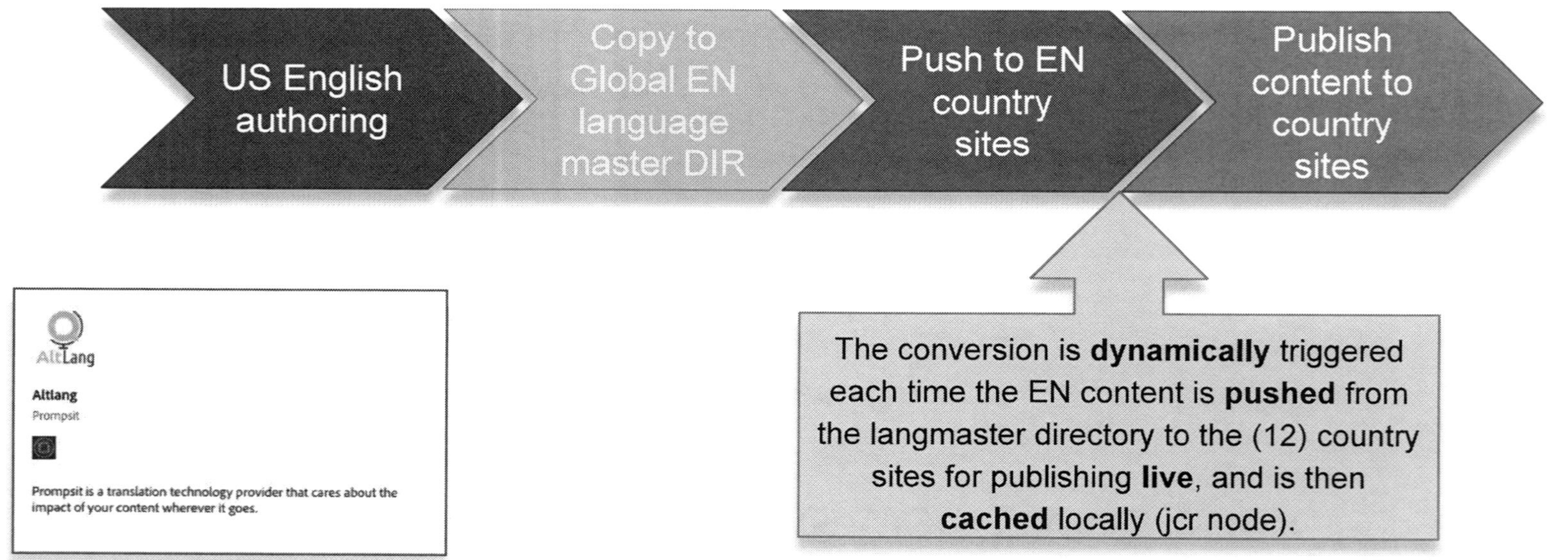

Implementation

Goal: Automatic, dynamic, low-risk conversion without any human intervention.

AltLang cloud service is delivered through integration with the CMS (AEM) as a connector available on the Adobe Exchange.

https://www.adobe.io/apis/marketingcloud/aem/aemconnectors.html

Challenges - Customization

- DNT - Adobe product & brand names
  - Lumetri Color
  - Media Optimizer (Media Manager in Japan)

English (United Kingdom)	English (United States)
Adobe Stock	Adobe Stock
Xpress	Xpress
Elements Organizer	Elements Organizer
ActionScript for Flash Lite	ActionScript for Flash Lite
Acrobat 8	Acrobat 8
Adobe Photoshop	Adobe Photoshop
Adobe Media Server Extended	Adobe Media Server Extended
Adobe Media Gateway	Adobe Media Gateway
Adobe Media Optimizer	Adobe Media Optimizer
Adobe Eazel	Adobe Eazel
Adobe Eazel for Photoshop	Adobe Eazel for Photoshop
Adobe Color	Adobe Color

- No Adobe-specific aligned bilingual corpus
  - zero target language content for language variations
- Adobe Style Guides lack language variations

45

Test Strategy

- Three test cycles to customize for Adobe
  - Review staged content based on test cases
    - Conversion is working correctly and consistently
    - Check for over/under conversions via search and diff
    - Check for regionalisms (state vs county)
    - Check for anomalies
      - "leveraging" > "leverage";
        "resizable" > "resisable", but "sizable" did not convert, as expected
  - Create dummy content pages (with sample test cases) for troubleshooting & debugging

Challenges - Post-Testing

- Language conversion for multiple countries not applicable to all; too many "exceptions" can create other issues.
  - [EN-US] "state" (administrative division) <> [EN-GB] "county" applies to just a few of the 12 country sites that prefer UK English.
  - [EN-US] "advertising dollars". How to deal with currencies? Best to change the source to "advertising budget", for example.
- How to scale fixing one-off feedback from web producers, field
- Website Architecture/Infrastructure Issues
  - Pulling and aligning source/converted content directly from the CMS so quality scoring can be performed.
  - Only a page with a change made to it, will trigger the conversion. (Bug fixes to AltLang)

Metrics

Language Quality

- Prompsit scoring (BLEU, WER, Edit Distance)

Customer Impact

- 12 of 16 Global English country sites prefer UK English
  (Africa, BE_EN, CY_EN, GR_EN, IE, LU_EN, MT, UK, AU, NZ, HK_EN, IN)
- ~15K pages converted in the initial launch
- Traffic: Avg. 77% VISITS/MONTH UK English/Global English-language websites

Customer Engagement - SEO (Future)

on converted pages since the change from EN-US to EN-GB

- Bounce rate
- CTR
- Time/pages per visit

Language quality evaluation: general numbers

- American to British English
- 190 web pages (HTML)
- 5k translation units (after deduplication)

General numbers			
	# of words	# of lines that change from source to...	# of words that change from source to...*
source (US)	65,857	-	-
Altlang UK, before customisation	65,956	1,257 (≈25%)	1,618
AltLang UK, after customisation	66,025	1,535 (≈31%)	1,957

*sum of substitutions + insertions + deletions

Language quality evaluation: automatic metrics

- BLEU is almost 1 (between 0 -- worst and 1 -- best)
- WER is lower than 1% (between 0% -- best and 100% -- worst)
- Edit distance (character level, between before and after customisation):

Automatic metrics	
BLEU	0,98
WER	0,82%
EDIT DISTANCE	541

Are these differences good or bad?
Need for an qualitative evaluation

Language quality evaluation: a human insight

- sampling of 500 sentences with 84 changes
- human inspection of changes classified as correct, incorrect and missing

Qualitative results	UK before	UK after
Correct changes	62	72
Missing changes	20	10
Incorrect changes	1	2

- DNT (Adobe Color, Acrobat Catalog)
- -ising → - izing, offline → off-line, specialty → especiality, right away → straightaway

- Add "segment", "harness" and "retarget" as verbs to apply "help + pron. + to + infinitive" rule
- Adobe Experience Cloud → Adobe Marketing Cloud (7 times)

- a useful → an useful
- Facebook Customised Audience

Conclusions about AltLang @ Adobe

- Easy integration through the AltLang connector for AEM
- Hands-off automation from authoring to publishing
- Cost-effective and "sim-ship" geo customization
- Customi[z|s]ation is key but not an obstacle
  - With no training corpora, customization is done post-implementation
- Metrics creation is a journey

Thanks!
Questions & Comments
Welcome

Same-language MT
for local flavours/flavors

Janice Campbell - Adobe
Gema Ramírez - Prompsit

Thinking of Going Neural?

Factors Honda R&D Americas is Considering before Making the Switch

Phil Soldini

Language Services

Honda R&D Americas, Inc.

Contents

1. Introduction
2. Honda R&D MT Overview
3. Factors to Consider when Upgrading
4. Takeaway
5. Questions?

Introduction

Phil Soldini

- Translator/interpreter at Honda R&D Americas, Inc.
- Certified translator Ja-En
- MT/CAT tool administrator

Mission

Corporate Objective

As an integral part of Honda Motor Co., we sell product designs and drawings that are created in a unique system that is highly suited to incorporation of leading-edge research from a wide range of fields.

With that end in mind, we encourage everyone at Honda R&D to develop their individual ability to its fullest potential.

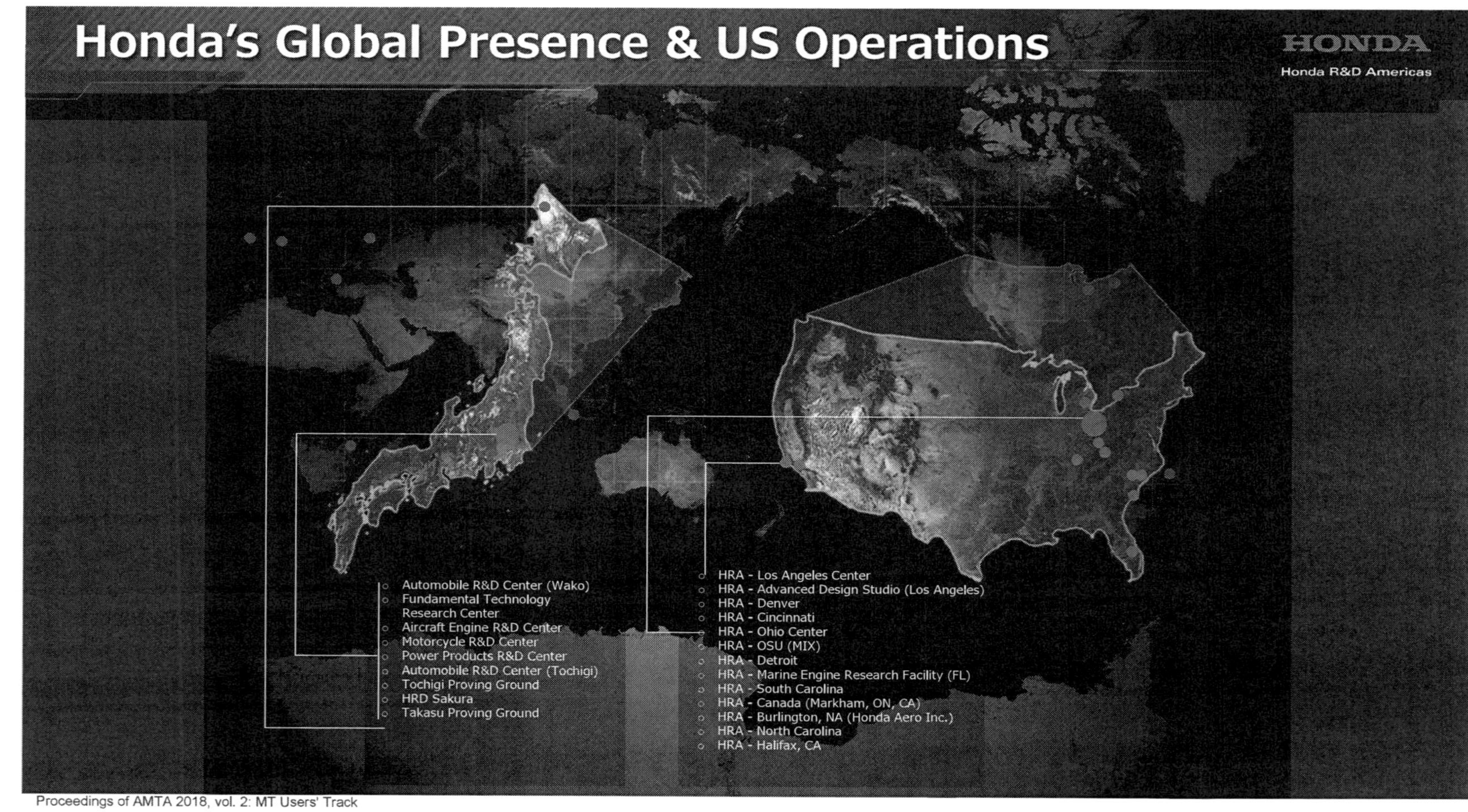

Honda's Global Presence & US Operations
HONDA
Honda R&D Americas
Automobile R&D Center (Wako)
Fundamental Technology Research Center
Aircraft Engine R&D Center
Motorcycle R&D Center
Power Products R&D Center
Automobile R&D Center (Tochigi)
Tochigi Proving Ground
HRD Sakura
Takasu Proving Ground
HRA - Los Angeles Center
HRA - Advanced Design Studio (Los Angeles)
HRA - Denver
HRA - Cincinnati
HRA - Ohio Center
HRA - OSU (MIX)
HRA - Detroit
HRA - Marine Engine Research Facility (FL)
HRA - South Carolina
HRA - Canada (Markham, ON, CA)
HRA - Burlington, NA (Honda Aero Inc.)
HRA - North Carolina
HRA - Halifax, CA

Honda=Mobility Company

Automobiles | Powersports | Power Equipment | Marine | Racing | Robotics Technology | HondaJet

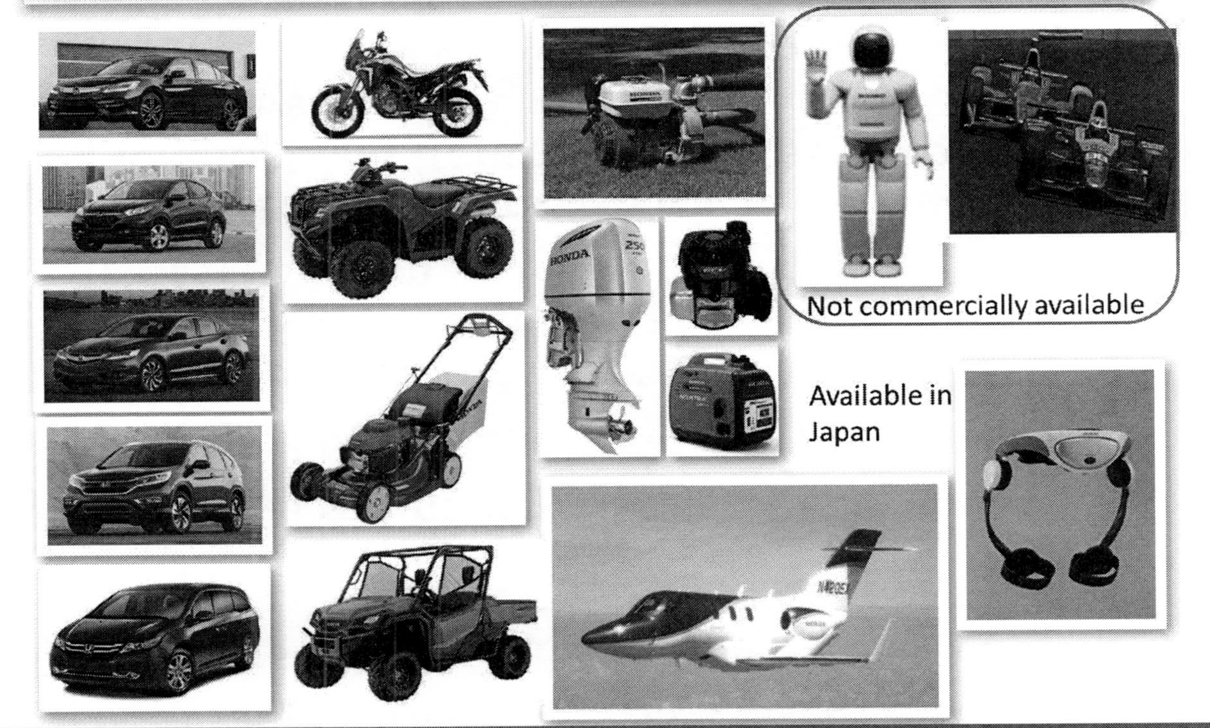

Honda R&D MT Overview

- Japanese to English, English to Japanese
- Technical documents written by engineers
- For the past decade, Honda R&D has been using a Rule-based Machine Translation (RBMT) system
- In-house translators use MT to translate and then post edit translation requests from engineers
- Engineers also use MT to directly translate documents and emails

Honda R&D MT Overview

- Honda terminology dictionaries categorized and added to MT, unifying terms among all R&D facilities around the world.

- Dictionaries updated monthly

- Better communication with accurate technical terms

- A feedback function has been added to the web-based MT for mistranslations/ unregistered terms to keep the dictionaries up-to-date

Honda R&D MT Overview

- In-house translations reduced and outsourcing costs cut by half
- Significant translation speed increase

Honda R&D MT Overview

Example Of Comments

LINGO
Critical Feedback 1/1

Accuracy/
Low output Quality

- Accuracy needs improved.
- Lingo is often outperformed by other machine language tools in terms of accuracy and readability. I typically need to ask a Japanese speaker in my group to 'fix' the Lingo translation.
- Lingo is a pain to upload/download – feel Atlas style plug-in nicer. Accuracy is improved, but I use Lingo less because it isn't convenient.
- Some improvements in machine translation through Lingo for readability be appreciated, but not much.
- LINGO is helpful, but could be better.
- Still have format issues with LINGO (largely running the format macro).
- I'm reluctant to use these, due to cost. How significant is this? LINGO is kind of suffering in comparison to an actual translation.
- OK for rough understanding but not for detailed application.
- It is very hit or miss. Sometimes it is understandable other times it makes no sense.
- [illegible] rarely works for Me. LINGO translation doesn't seem any better/worse than standard internet services.
- Haven't used much but if didn't seem working well to me.
- lingo website is difficult to find (typing in lingo doesn't work) and use (it doesn't remember defaults, so I have to change [illegible] every time).
- Doesn't work too well with technical documentation.
- [illegible]

Factors to Consider when Upgrading

Cost & Quality

Source (Japanese)

そんなメーカーが高級車の分野に進出するという計画に、見通しを危ぶむ声が少なくなかったのは当然だろう。

Target (NMT)

It seems natural that there were not ~~many~~ a few voices of doubts about the prospects in such a plan that such manufacturers will advance into the field of luxury cars.

Target (RBMT)

Naturally plan under which such a maker advances to field of luxury car did not have at little voice which is doubtful of prospect.

Factors to Consider when Upgrading

Consistent Use of Terminology

Factors to Consider when Upgrading

Preserve
Original
Format

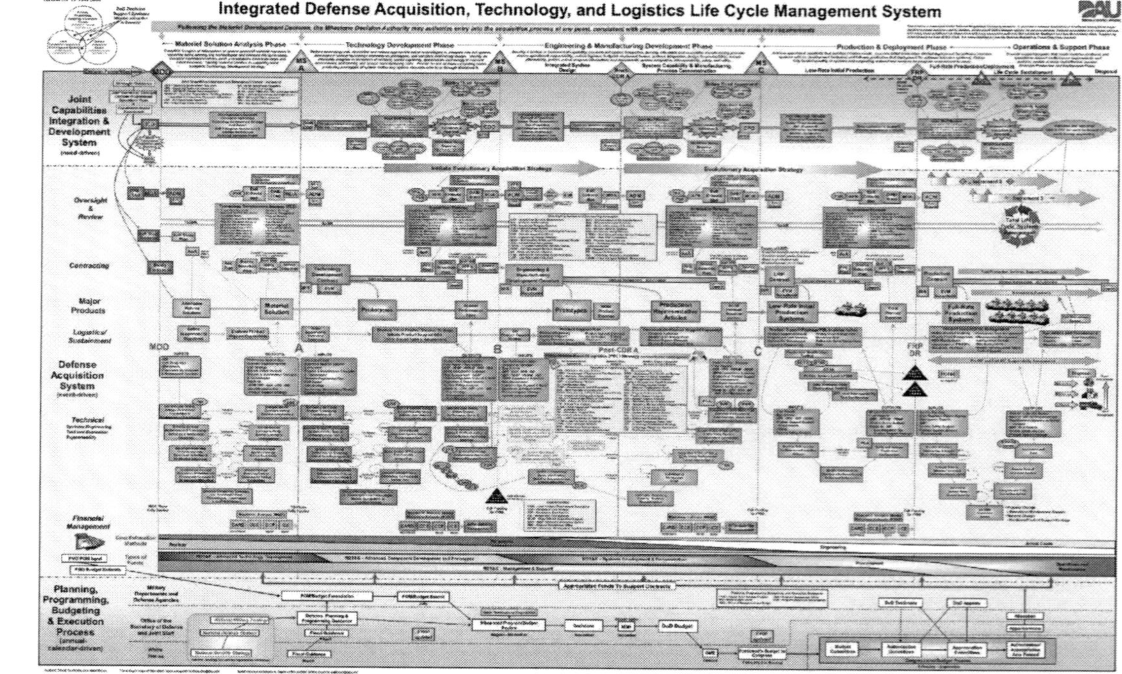

Factors to Consider when Upgrading

Speed

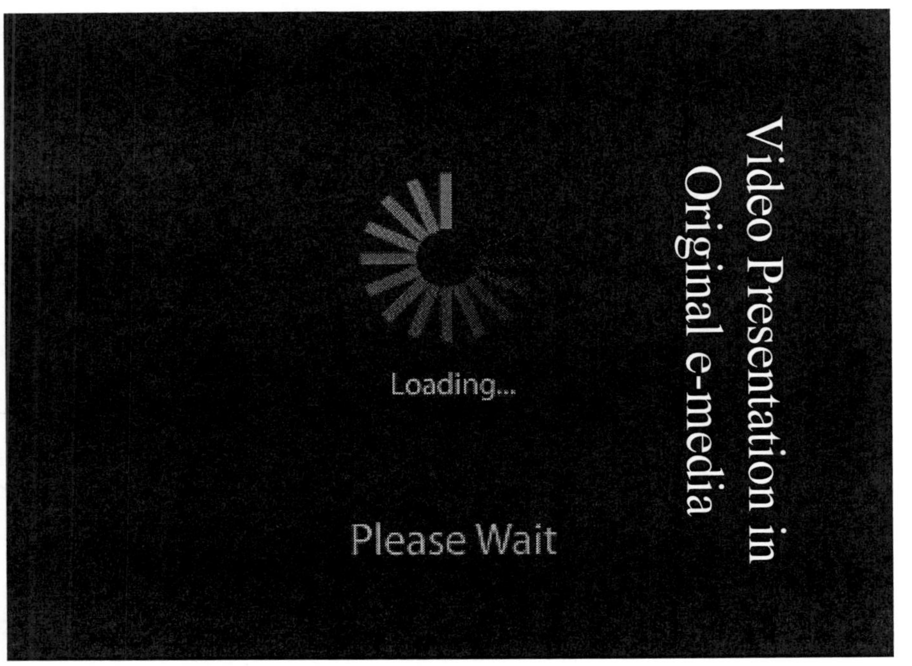

Factors to Consider when Upgrading

Confidentiality

Factors to Consider when Upgrading

Other Considerations

- Maintenance
- Plugin for MS Office/Outlook
- CAT tool compatibility
- User feedback button
- Cell phone app
- OCR
- Languages

Takeaway

Corporate users:
Be sure to consider these and other factors important to you when purchasing an MT system or upgrading your existing system.

MT developers:
Please take into account these corporate user needs when developing MT systems.

Thank you

Questions?

Developing a Neural Machine Translation Service for the 2017-2018 European Union Presidency

Mārcis Pinnis
Rihards Kalnins
Tilde, Vienības gatve 75A, Riga, Latvia, LV-1004

marcis.pinnis@tilde.com
rihards.kalnins@tilde.com

Abstract

The paper describes Tilde's work on developing a neural machine translation (NMT) tool for the 2017-2018 Presidency of the Council of the European Union. The tool was developed by combining the European Commission's eTranslation service with a set of customized, domain-adapted NMT systems built by Tilde. The central aim of the tool is to assist staff members, translators, EU delegates, journalists, and other visitors at EU Council Presidency events in Estonia, Bulgaria, and Austria. The paper provides details on the workflow used to collect, filter, clean, normalize, and pre-process data for the NMT systems; and the methods applied for training and adaptation of the NMT systems for the EU Council Presidency. The paper also compares the trained NMT systems to other publicly available MT systems for Estonian and Bulgarian, showing that the custom systems achieve better results than competing systems.

1 Introduction

The administrative work of the European Union (EU) is led by the Presidency of the Council of the EU, which is hosted by a different EU Member State every six months. During its half-year term, the hosting country is tasked with organizing hundreds of high-level events, including conferences and administrative meetings. As the EU Council Presidency brings together delegates and journalists from 28 EU Member States – home to the EU's 24 official languages – the issue of language barriers becomes a major challenge for the politically important event.

To overcome language barriers during the EU Council Presidency in 2017-2018, the Northern Europe-based language technology company Tilde developed a multilingual communication tool that enables automated translation at scale by combining customized neural machine translation (NMT) systems and the Connecting Europe Facility (CEF) eTranslation service for the EU's official languages, developed by the European Commission's Directorate-General for Translation.[1] Tilde first developed a prototype version of the EU Council Presidency Translator for the 2015 EU Council Presidency in Latvia.

eTranslation is a building block of the European Commission's CEF program, which "supports trans-European networks in the sectors of transport, telecommunications and energy"[2] with building blocks that "facilitate the delivery of digital public services across borders."[3] According to the European Commission's CEF Digital website[4],

"the central aim of [the CEF eTranslation service] is to help European and national

---

[1] https://ec.europa.eu/cefdigital/wiki/display/CEFDIGITAL/eTranslation

[2] https://ec.europa.eu/digital-single-market/en/connecting-europe-facility

[3] https://ec.europa.eu/cefdigital/wiki/display/CEFDIGITAL/About+CEF+building+blocks

[4] https://ec.europa.eu/cefdigital/wiki/display/CEFDIGITAL/What+is+eTranslation+-+MT@EC+and+eTranslation

public administrations exchange information across language barriers in the EU, by providing machine translation capabilities that will enable all Digital Service Infrastructures to be multilingual. CEF eTranslation builds on the existing machine translation service of the European Commission, MT@EC, developed by the Directorate-General for Translation (DGT). MT@EC translation engines are trained using the vast Euramis translation memories, comprising over 1 billion sentences in the 24 official EU languages, produced by the translators of the EU institutions over the past decades."

By combining the CEF eTranslation service with custom NMT engines developed by Tilde, the EU Council Presidency Translator is used to translate text snippets, documents, and websites using a responsive online translation website and a computer-assisted translation (CAT) tool plugin. The main users for the translation tools include EU Council Presidency staff members, public sector translators in the hosting country of the Presidency, EU delegates, and international journalists covering the events. The service was first utilized during the 2017 EU Council Presidency in Estonia[5], from July-December 2017, and featured NMT systems for Estonian, a highly inflected, agglutinative language with just 1.5 million native speakers.

The customized NMT systems for Estonian were built utilizing Tilde's methods for developing state-of-the-art NMT systems for complex languages. The methods include extensive data collection, corpus filtering (i.e., noise removal), data pre-processing, unknown phenomena modelling, and training of NMT models with state-of-the-art recurrent neural network architectures. Additionally to the custom NMT systems, the EU Council Presidency Translator provides access to all of the machine translation (MT) systems from the CEF eTranslation service, for translation between the 24 official languages of the EU and English.

In 2018, the EU Council Presidency Translator has been expanded to feature customized NMT systems for Bulgarian[6], to support the Bulgarian EU Council Presidency in January-June of 2018. The tool has been integrated directly into the official website of the Bulgarian EU Council Presidency, eu2018bg.bg, where the site's many users from throughout the world can find the translation tool in the main menu under the heading "Media." The tool will be further expanded and adapted to include customized NMT systems for German to support the upcoming Austrian EU Council Presidency, in the second half of 2018.

To date, the EU Council Presidency Translator has been used to translate over 4.5 million words. This encompasses translation requests made in the last three months of the Estonian EU Council Presidency (following the launch of the tool in late September 2017) and the first two months of the Bulgarian EU Council Presidency (from January 1 to February 19, 2018). 95% of translation requests were made for the customized NMT systems developed by Tilde for Estonian and Bulgarian.

Since its launch in September 2017, the EU Council Presidency Translator has received accolades from the European Commission[7], from staff translators at the EC's translation directorate, from the Ministry for the 2018 Bulgarian EU Council Presidency[8], as well as from the prime ministers of Italy and Greece[9], who were introduced to the tool at the EU Digital Summit in Tallinn, Estonia.

In this paper, we describe the unique multilingual challenges faced by the EU Council Presidency, the Presidency's stated requirements for a multilingual communication tool, and

---

[5] https://www.translate2017.eu

[6] https://eu2018bg.bg/en/translation

[7] https://ec.europa.eu/cefdigital/wiki/display/CEFDIGITAL/2018/01/26/Official+Website+of+2018+EU+Council+Presidency+Integrates+CEF+eTranslation

[8] https://eu2018bg.bg/en/news/354

[9] https://tilde.com/news/eu-council-presidency-begins-using-ai-powered-translation-tool

Tilde's methods for developing NMT engines for complex languages.

The paper is further structured as follows: Section 2 describes the challenges and requirements for the EU Council Presidency Translator; Section 3 provides a general overview of the EU Council Presidency Translator; Section 4 describes the interfaces that can be used by users to access the MT systems of the EU Council Presidencies; Section 5 describes the methods used to develop the custom NMT systems; and Section 6 concludes the paper.

2 Challenges and Requirements for the EU Council Presidency Translator

The numerous EU delegates, international journalists, and foreign visitors at the events organized by each hosting country of the EU Council Presidency represent speakers of (at least the) 24 official languages of the EU. Preparation of documents, press releases, event information, cultural programmes, and other texts in all 24 languages would be a costly endeavour for the hosting country. Therefore, the EU Council Presidency requires machine translation systems that can allow the participating parties to consume all the information produced by the hosting country in its own official language.

In addition, the hosting country gathers these thousands of visitors in its own capital city, where local news and information is produced in the language of the hosting country. Therefore, the EU Council Presidency also required machine translation systems that produced highly fluent translations for the official language of the hosting country (Estonian in 2017, Bulgarian and German in 2018).

To make these systems available for the wide variety of individuals attending official EU Council Presidency events the EU Council Presidency also required the above-mentioned machine translation systems to be made as easily usable as possible, i.e., integrated into user-friendly online tools, including the official website of the EU Council Presidency. These tools should allow for the translation of various types of content: text snippets, full documents (e.g., various OpenDocument[10] or Office Open XML[11] formats), websites, and professional translation files (e.g., Translation Memory eXchange (TMX)[12], XML Localisation Interchange File Format (XLIFF)[13], etc.).

The main challenges posed by these requirements were as follows:

- Integration of CEF eTranslation service for all 24 official EU languages.

- Development of customized NMT systems for the official languages of the hosting countries in 2017-2018 (Estonian, Bulgarian, German).

- Development of user-friendly tools for utilizing the machine translation systems (responsive online interface, integration in the official website of the EU Council Presidency, etc.).

- Development of text, document, website translation functionality.

- Development of a MT plugin for staff and public sector translators in the hosting country to utilize in CAT tools.

3 Infrastructure for the EU Council Presidency Translator

To facilitate translation needs of the EU Council Presidencies, the EU Council Presidency Translator has been developed as a toolkit (see Figure 1 for an overview) that utilizes services

---

[10] http://opendocumentformat.org/

[11] See ISO/IEC 29500 at http://standards.iso.org/ittf/PubliclyAvailableStandards

[12] http://www.ttt.org/oscarstandards/tmx/tmx13.htm

[13] http://docs.oasis-open.org/xliff

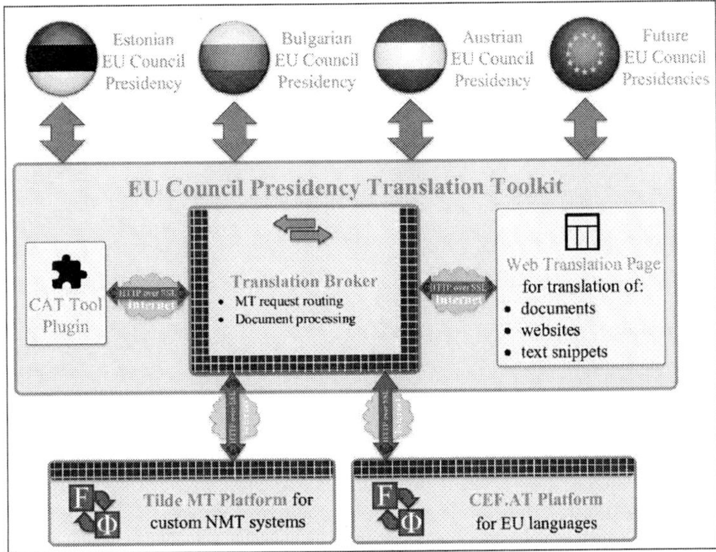

Figure 1: Architecture of the EU Council Presidency Translator

of both the Tilde MT platform (Vasiļjevs et al., 2012) and the CEF eTranslation service. The Tilde MT platform performs two tasks:

1. Serves as an MT system broker that receives translation requests (text snippets, translation segments, documents, and websites) from the two main translation interfaces (the translation website and the CAT tool plugin) and routes the requests to specific MT systems for translation. This architecture allows not only to utilise Tilde MT and eTranslation systems in one user interface, but it also allows to integrate other external MT provider systems within the MT broker in a way that no changes have to be made to the EU Council Presidency Translator's user interfaces.

2. Provides access to the customized EU Council Presidency NMT systems that have been trained and adapted to better translate texts specific to the topics covered by each of the EU Council Presidencies.

4 Translation Interfaces for the EU Council Presidencies

Translators of the EU Council Presidencies, as well as journalists, EU delegates, and other visitors, can use two types of MT interfaces to translate texts, documents, and websites written in the local language of the hosting country into English or content written in English into their own language.

4.1 EU Council Presidency Translation Website

The EU Council Presidency Translator is available online, in a special website linked to the main page of the official EU Council Presidency website.[14] The website is an online translation workspace that allows users to translate texts, full documents (preserving document formatting), and websites in the 24 official EU languages. The portal is customized for each EU Council

---

[14]https://eu2018bg.bg/en/translation

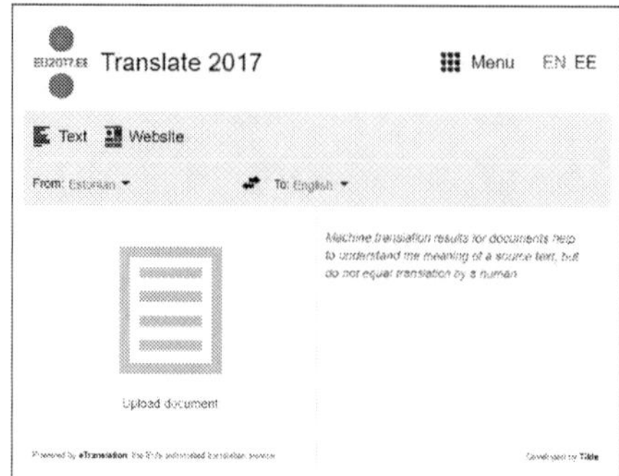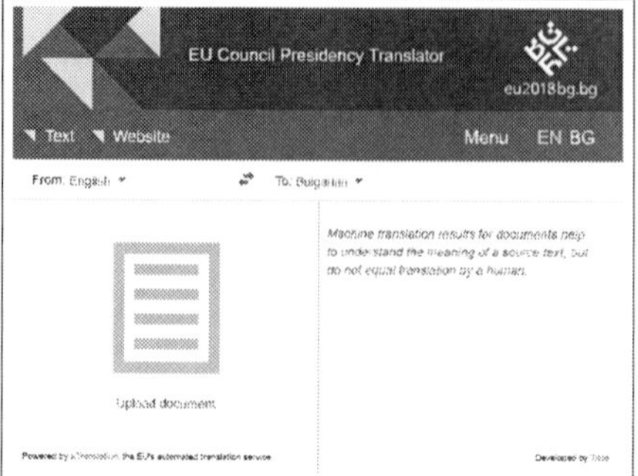

Figure 2: Examples of the Estonian (left) and Bulgarian (right) EU Council Presidency Translator websites

Presidency, featuring the local Presidency branding and other custom elements. An example of the document translation form for both Estonian and Bulgarian EU Council presidencies is depicted in Figure 2.

4.2 CAT Tool Plugin

The EU Council Presidency Translator is also available for professional translators who use the SDL Trados Studio[15] CAT tool with the help of a plugin. The plugin enables users specifically, public administration translators and staff of the EU Council Presidency to utilize the eTranslation service and the custom NMT systems in their everyday work. The plugin provides functionality for translation task pre-translation or translation suggestion preparation in a segment-by-segment translation scenario.

5 Customized NMT Systems

Customized NMT systems for the EU Council Presidencies were developed using the Tilde MT platform, which provides the necessary functionality for corpora cleaning, data pre-processing, and post-processing, as well as allows to deploy NMT systems in a scalable cloud-based infrastructure. The following processing steps were performed to train each of the NMT systems:

- First, parallel and monolingual corpora were collected. The EU Presidency systems have two main goals: 1) to help EU Council Presidency staff members to prepare translations of documents related to the EU Council presidency, and 2) to help visitors of the hosting country to get acquainted with current events taking place in the hosting country. Therefore, the MT systems have two broad target domains - EU Council Presidency and news content. To ensure that the NMT systems are capable of translating such content, focussed web crawling was performed to collect parallel and monolingual data from government and media websites. Additionally, parallel and (in-domain) monolingual data were selected from the Tilde Data Library[16] or supplied by the project's partners.

- Then, the parallel corpora were filtered, cleaned, and normalized using corpora processing tools from Tilde MT. The filtering procedure identifies and removes sentence pairs with the following issues: equal source and target content (i.e., source-source or target-target

---

[15]http://www.sdl.com

[16]https://tilde.com/products-and-services/machine-translation/features/data-library

entries), sentence splitting issues (e.g., a part of a sentence aligned to a full sentence), foreign (neither source, nor target) language sentences, words, or phrases in source or target sentences, sentence alignment (i.e., non-parallel sentence pair) issues, data redundancy issues, and data corruption issues (e.g., due to errors caused by optical character recognition or wrong formatting of documents). For more details on the filtering procedures, see the paper by Pinnis et al. (2017b). The data were further cleaned and normalized by removing HTML and XML tags, byte order marks, control symbols, escaped characters (e.g., "\n", "\r"), empty braces and curly tags (specific to some CAT tools), decoding XML entities, normalizing whitespace characters and punctuation marks (e.g., quotation marks, apostrophes, dashes, etc.), and separating ligatures (specific to data that are acquired using OCR methods).

- The normalized data were further pre-processed using language-specific tools for non-translatable entity (e.g., e-mail address, file or URL address, various tag and alphanumeric code, etc.) identification, tokenization, and truecasing.

- Following the methodology by Pinnis et al. (2017a), for the Bulgarian EU Presidency we trained NMT models that are more robust to unknown phenomena than vanilla NMT models. To do this, we supplemented the parallel corpus with a synthetic version of the same parallel corpus, which had content words replaced with unknown word tokens in a random manner. To make sure that the same words were replaced on both (source and target) sides, we performed word alignment of the corpus using fast-align (Dyer et al., 2013) and restricted the replacement to only those content words that had non-ambiguous (one-to-one) word alignments.

- Once the data were pre-processed, NMT models were trained using the Nematus (Sennrich et al., 2017) toolkit. All NMT models were sub-word (Sennrich et al., 2015) level attention-based encoder-decoder models with multiplicative long short-term memory units (MLSTM; Krause et al. (2016)). For training, we used the MLSTM model implementation and the NMT training configuration defined by Pinnis et al. (2017b). More specifically, the NMT models were trained using a vocabulary of 25,000 word parts, an embedding layer of 500 dimensions, recurrent layers of 1024 dimensions, dropout rate of 0.2 for recurrent layers and 0.1 for input and output embedding layers, and gradient clipping with a threshold of 1. For parameter updates, the Adadelta (Zeiler, 2012) optimizer with a learning rate of 0.0001 was used.

- When the baseline systems were trained (i.e., they reached the Nematus early stopping criterion of not improving for more than 10 times on validation data), we performed back-translation of in-domain monolingual data in order to prepare synthetic corpora for domain adaptation. The synthetic corpora were filtered, cleaned, normalized and pre-processed using the same workflow that was used to process the parallel corpora. This allowed ensuring that excess noise (i.e., possible NMT mistranslations) was filtered out before performing domain adaptation.

- Finally, NMT model domain adaptation was performed using new training corpora that consisted in balanced proportions (i.e., one-to-one) of the initial training data and the synthetic back-translated data. The one-to-one proportion allows the NMT model to adapt to the required domain, but, at the same time, it allows the model to remember what it had learned during the initial training phase.

Further, we will analyse the data used for training of the NMT systems and the evaluation results of the Estonian (see Section 5.1) and Bulgarian (see Section 5.2) EU Council Presidency NMT systems.

Corpus	English-Estonian	Estonian-English
Cleaned parallel corpus		18,937,780
Cleaned back-translated in-domain corpus	1,716,618	734,417
1-to-1 training data (for domain adaptation)	3,433,236	1,468,834

Table 1: Statistics of the parallel corpora (in terms of unique sentence pairs) used for training of the Estonian EU Council Presidency NMT systems

5.1 NMT Systems for the Estonian EU Council Presidency

The Estonian EU Council Presidency NMT systems were trained on a mixture of publicly available and proprietary corpora. The largest corpora among the publicly available corpora were the Open Subtitles (Tiedemann, 2009) (release of 2016), DTG-TM (Steinberger et al., 2012), Tilde MODEL (Rozis and Skadiņš, 2017), DCEP (Hajlaoui et al., 2014), Microsoft Translation Memories and UI Strings Glossaries (Microsoft, 2015), and Europarl (Koehn, 2005) parallel corpora. The public corpora amounted to approximately half of all the training data. The other half was comprised of proprietary data from the Tilde Data Library.

For domain adaptation, we collected parallel and monolingual corpora from the Estonian EU Council Presidency website[17] and monolingual corpora from various local news agencies. The crawling was restricted to only local resources as the main goals of the EU Council Presidency systems are to enable better translation for content specific to the topics covered by the EU Council Presidency and the topics covered in the news of the hosting country (and not to cater for general translation tasks).

Statistics of the data used for training of the NMT systems are given in Table 1. The data show that for training of the Estonian-English and English-Estonian NMT systems, a substantial amount of data (almost 19 million sentence pairs) were used. The table also shows that the in-domain Estonian monolingual corpus that was used for domain adaptation of the English-Estonian system was more than two times larger than the English monolingual corpus. This is due to the fact that local content in English is much harder to obtain as it is available in much smaller quantities.

The training progress of the baseline NMT systems, as well as the NMT system adaptation process, is depicted in Figure 3. The figure shows that domain adaptation did improve translation quality for the English-Estonian NMT system (by more than one BLEU point), however, the quality increase for the Estonian-English system was rather insignificant (only 0.15 BLEU points). This may be partially explained by the significantly smaller amount of in-domain monolingual data that were available for the creation of the synthetic parallel corpus.

After training and adaptation, we performed automatic evaluation of all NMT systems (both baseline and adapted systems) using BLEU (Papineni et al., 2002), ChrF2 (Popović, 2015), and CharacTER (Wang et al., 2016) (one standard and two newer evaluation metrics that show higher correlation scores to human judgements compared to BLEU for Slavic and Finno-Ugric languages (Bojar et al., 2017)). The results of the evaluation are given in Table 2. The table includes also evaluation results for Google Translate[18] and the English-Estonian and Estonian-English CEF eTranslation systems.

The evaluation was performed using two different evaluation sets: 1) the ACCURAT balanced evaluation set (Skadiņa et al. (2012); a broad domain evaluation set), and 2) an evaluation set created from the parallel corpora of the Estonian EU Council Presidency website (covering also news on various events and topics concerning the Presidency). The results show that both

---

[17]https://www.eu2017.ee/

[18]https://translate.google.com

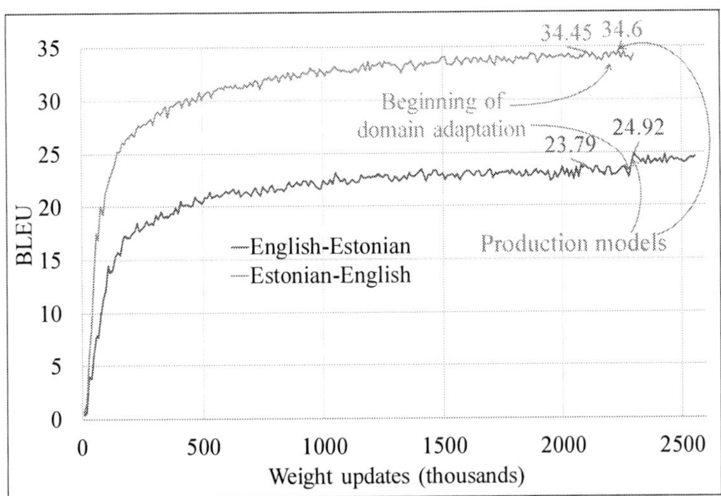

Figure 3: Training progress of the Estonian EU Council Presidency NMT systems

adapted NMT systems achieve the best translation quality on the in-domain evaluation set. I.e., the adapted systems are better suited for translation of texts that cover EU Council Presidency related topics than other compared systems. The results also show that the baseline NMT system for English-Estonian achieves better quality than all competing systems with the adapted system still outperforming other systems also on the broad domain evaluation set. This shows that the adapted NMT systems are also highly competitive broad domain NMT systems.

5.2 NMT Systems for the Bulgarian EU Council Presidency

Similarly to the Estonian NMT systems, the Bulgarian EU Council Presidency NMT systems were also trained on a mixture of publicly available and proprietary corpora. The largest corpora among the publicly available corpora were the DTG-TM, Tilde MODEL, Microsoft Translation Memories and UI Strings Glossaries, DCEP, and Europarl parallel corpora. The public corpora amounted to approximately 79% of all the training data. Slightly over 14% of the data for training of the baseline systems were provided by the project's partners, the Department of Computational Linguistics (DCL) of the Institute for Bulgarian Language (IBL) of the Bulgarian Academy of Sciences.[19] The remaining 7% of the data comprised of proprietary data from the Tilde Data Library. For domain adaptation, monolingual corpora were collected by DCL from various local (for the Bulgarian and English monolingual corpus) and also international (for the English monolingual news corpus) news websites. For the English data, only documents with explicit mentions of Bulgaria were selected.

Statistics of the data used for training of the NMT systems are given in Table 3. The data show that for training of the Bulgarian NMT systems, we used a corpus that was almost 3 times smaller than the parallel corpus that was used to train the baseline NMT systems for the Estonian EU Presidency. However, for the Bulgarian NMT systems, we supplemented the data with synthetically generated data (see Section 5 for details on the synthetic data). Therefore, the total number of sentence pairs that were used for training was almost two times larger than in the initial training data. Because the in-domain monolingual data comprised of approximately the same amount of sentences as the initial training data, the data sets for domain adaptation

---

[19]http://ibl.bas.bg

System	Broad domain evaluation set			Presidency evaluation set		
	BLEU	**ChrF2**	**Charac-TER**	**BLEU**	**ChrF2**	**Charac-TER**
Estonian-English						
Google Translate	**37.85±1.83**	**0.7003**	**0.4592**	31.84±1.26	0.6594	0.5945
eTranslation	37.36±2.76	0.6820	0.4994	28.07±1.21	0.6272	0.6134
PNMT	36.94±1.80	0.6944	0.4604	29.31±1.18	0.6401	0.6014
Adapted PNMT (last model)	35.89±1.84	0.6884	0.4690	**32.46±1.20**	**0.6641**	**0.5410**
Adapted PNMT (best BLEU model)	35.47±1.90	0.6896	0.4665	31.19±1.21	0.6569	0.5592
English-Estonian						
Google Translate	23.23±1.75	0.6553	0.5192	22.72±1.44	0.6409	**0.5063**
eTranslation	24.19±2.15	0.6206	0.5925	20.82±1.40	0.6025	0.5768
PNMT	**25.58±1.66**	**0.6643**	**0.4931**	20.34±1.24	0.6223	0.5420
Adapted PNMT (last model)	24.28±1.64	0.6637	0.4981	**23.18±1.42**	**0.6471**	0.5072
Adapted PNMT (best BLEU model)	23.92±1.60	0.6597	0.5061	22.3±1.29	0.6384	0.5162

Table 2: Automatic evaluation results of the Estonian EU Council Presidency NMT (PNMT) systems

Corpus	English-Bulgarian	Bulgarian-English
Cleaned parallel corpus		6,236,963
Partner data in the parallel corpus		886,416
Parallel corpus with synthetic data (for training of the baseline NMT models)		12,116,548
Cleaned back-translated in-domain corpus	6,188,194	6,098,572
Back-translated corpus with synthetic data	12,068,573	12,209,291
1-to-1 training data (for domain adaptation)	24,325,838	24,185,120

Table 3: Statistics of the parallel corpora (in terms of unique sentence pairs) used for training of the Bulgarian EU Council Presidency NMT systems

reached even 24 million sentence pairs (where approximately 75% amount for all the synthetic data).

The training and adaptation progress for the Bulgarian NMT systems is depicted in Figure 4. The figure shows that (similarly to the trend visible for the Estonian NMT systems) domain adaptation did improve translation quality for the English-Bulgarian NMT system (however, in this case, the improvement was by almost three BLEU points). However, the domain adaptation failed for the Bulgarian-English NMT system. We believe that this may be the result of a too broad coverage of the English monolingual corpus. Because the system has to translate from Bulgarian into English, the English monolingual corpus (for the domain adaptation to work) has to represent what texts in Bulgarian will cover (and not what foreigners may want to write about Bulgaria in English).

The automatic evaluation was performed using two evaluation data sets: 1) a current news evaluation data set, and 2) an EU Council Presidency evaluation data set that covers texts re-

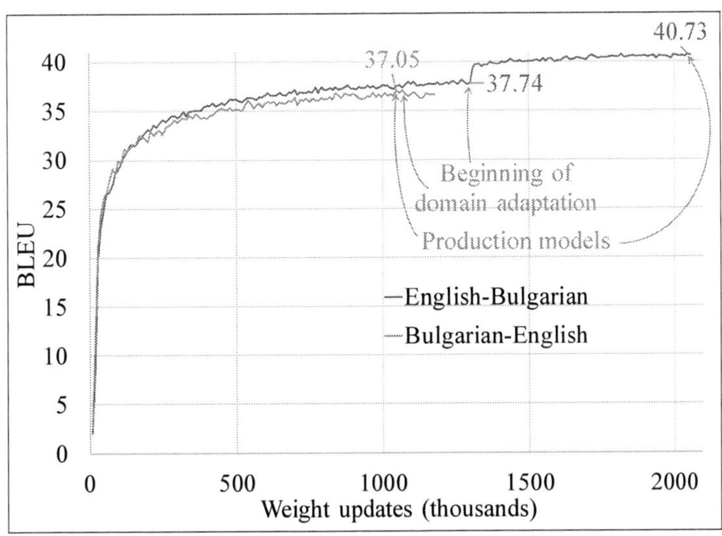

Figure 4: Training progress of the Bulgarian EU Council Presidency NMT systems

System	News evaluation set			Presidency evaluation set		
	BLEU	**ChrF2**	**Charac-TER**	**BLEU**	**ChrF2**	**Charac-TER**
Bulgarian-English						
Google Translate	**38.29±1.15**	**0.6964**	**0.4458**	**46.85±0.91**	**0.7727**	**0.3798**
eTranslation	24.61±0.81	0.6140	0.5725	37.97±0.84	0.7223	0.4565
PNMT	30.84±0.92	0.6579	0.4933	42.68±0.85	0.7486	0.4064
English-Bulgarian						
Google Translate	**38.08±1.32**	**0.6887**	**0.4393**	46.35±0.91	**0.7681**	0.3621
eTranslation	23.36±0.75	0.5977	0.5584	38.03±0.88	0.7230	0.4253
PNMT	31.40±0.96	0.6507	0.4822	44.38±0.85	0.7515	0.3788
Adapted PNMT (best BLEU model)	33.63±1.03	0.6657	0.4659	**46.97±0.90**	0.7672	**0.3620**

Table 4: Automatic evaluation results of the Bulgarian EU Council Presidency NMT (PNMT) systems

lated to the topics covered by the Bulgarian EU Council Presidency. Both evaluation sets were prepared by DLC for evaluation of the EU Council Presidency NMT systems. The results in Table 4 show that for Bulgarian-English the best results are achieved by the Google Translate systems. As mentioned above, domain adaptation for this language pair did not produce better results, which may be the result of domain adherence issues of the monolingual data. However, our baseline NMT systems show significantly better results than the eTranslation systems. This tendency is evident also if we look at the results for the English-Bulgarian systems. However, according to BLEU, the English-Bulgarian adapted NMT system does outperform all other systems on the EU Council Presidency data set. This means that for content covering the EU Council Presidency, the adapted NMT system will be the most suited system.

6 Conclusion

In this paper, we presented the EU Council Presidency Translator developed by Tilde for the 2017-2018 EU Council Presidency. We discussed the architecture of the translation tool and the two main user interfaces - the translation website and the CAT tool plugin. The translation tool is available to all translators, EU delegates, journalists, and other visitors of the EU Council Presidencies in Estonia and Bulgaria. It will also be available for the Austrian EU Council Presidency in the second half of 2018.

In the six months since its launch in September 2017, the EU Council Presidency Translator has helped to translate content amounting to over 4.5 million words (or approximately 470 thousand sentences). The main translation directions for both the Estonian and Bulgarian EU Council Presidencies so far have been between English and the official languages of the hosting countries (amounting to approximately 95% of all translated words).

By applying Tilde's own methods for developing domain-specific NMT systems for complex languages, we were able to create customized NMT systems that outperformed the general eTranslation systems by up to 4 BLEU points for Estonian, and by up to 8 BLEU points for Bulgarian. Tilde's customized NMT systems for Estonian and Bulgarian outperformed Google Translate's general domain NMT engines for the respective language pairs by up to 1 BLEU point.

The tool proves that, when integrated into user-friendly tools, NMT can be successfully applied to enable multilingual communication at high-profile, politically important international events gathering thousands of visitors. The tool also shows that NMT is useful not only for professional translators to boost their productivity, but also as a reading and document analysis tool for a wide range of users in their everyday work, such as EU delegates and international journalists. By applying NMT to their work, users can access information in multiple languages and enjoy better understanding of information, thus helping to promote the aims of goals of high-level events such as the Presidency of the Council of the EU.

7 Acknowledgements

The research has been supported by the European Regional Development Fund within the research project "Neural Network Modelling for Inflected Natural Languages" No. 1.1.1.1/16/A/215.

References

Bojar, O., Graham, Y., and Kamran, A. (2017). Results of the wmt17 metrics shared task. In *Proceedings of the Second Conference on Machine Translation, Volume 2: Shared Task Papers*, pages 489–513, Copenhagen, Denmark. Association for Computational Linguistics.

Dyer, C., Chahuneau, V., and Smith, N. A. (2013). A simple, fast, and effective reparameterization of ibm model 2. In *Proceedings of the Conference of the North American Chapter of the Association for Computational Linguistics: Human Language Technologies (NAACL HLT 2013)*, number June, pages 644–648, Atlanta, USA.

Hajlaoui, N., Kolovratnik, D., Väyrynen, J., Steinberger, R., and Varga, D. (2014). Dcep-digital corpus of the european parliament. In *LREC*, pages 3164–3171.

Koehn, P. (2005). Europarl: a parallel corpus for statistical machine translation. In *MT summit*, volume 5, pages 79–86.

Krause, B., Lu, L., Murray, I., and Renals, S. (2016). Multiplicative lstm for sequence modelling. *arXiv preprint arXiv:1609.07959.*

Microsoft (2015). Translation and ui strings glossaries.

Papineni, K., Roukos, S., Ward, T., and Zhu, W.-J. (2002). Bleu: a method for automatic evaluation of machine translation. In *Proceedings of the 40th annual meeting on association for computational linguistics*, pages 311–318. Association for Computational Linguistics.

Pinnis, M., Krišlauks, R., Deksne, D., and Miks, T. (2017a). Neural machine translation for morphologically rich languages with improved sub-word units and synthetic data. In *Proceedings of the 20th International Conference of Text, Speech and Dialogue (TSD2017)*, Prague, Czechia.

Pinnis, M., Krišlauks, R., Miks, T., Deksne, D., and Šics, V. (2017b). Tilde's machine translation systems for wmt 2017. In *Proceedings of the Second Conference on Machine Translation (WMT 2017), Volume 2: Shared Task Papers*, pages 374–381, Copenhagen, Denmark. Association for Computational Linguistics.

Popović, M. (2015). chrf: Character n-gram f-score for automatic mt evaluation. In *Proceedings of the Tenth Workshop on Statistical Machine Translation*, pages 392–395.

Rozis, R. and Skadiņš, R. (2017). Tilde model-multilingual open data for eu languages. In *Proceedings of the 21st Nordic Conference on Computational Linguistics*, pages 263–265.

Sennrich, R., Firat, O., Cho, K., Birch, A., Haddow, B., Hitschler, J., Junczys-Dowmunt, M., Läubli, S., Barone, A. V. M., Mokry, J., et al. (2017). Nematus: a toolkit for neural machine translation. *arXiv preprint arXiv:1703.04357.*

Sennrich, R., Haddow, B., and Birch, A. (2015). Neural machine translation of rare words with subword units. In *Proceedings of the 54th Annual Meeting of the Association for Computational Linguistics (ACL 2015)*, Berlin, Germany. Association for Computational Linguistics.

Skadiņa, I., Aker, A., Mastropavlos, N., Su, F., Tufi, D., Verlic, M., Vasijevs, A., Babych, B., Clough, P., Gaizauskas, R., Glaros, N., Paramita, M. L., and Pinnis, M. (2012). Collecting and using comparable corpora for statistical machine translation. In Calzolari, N. C. C., Choukri, K., Declerck, T., Doan, M. U., Maegaard, B., Mariani, J., Odijk, J., and Piperidis, S., editors, *Proceedings of the Eight International Conference on Language Resources and Evaluation (LREC'12)*, pages 438–445, Istanbul, Turkey. European Language Resources Association (ELRA).

Steinberger, R., Eisele, A., Klocek, S., Pilos, S., and Schlter, P. (2012). Dgt-tm: a freely available translation memory in 22 languages. In *Proceedings of the Eight International Conference on Language Resources and Evaluation (LREC'12)*, pages 454–459.

Tiedemann, J. (2009). News from opus - a collection of multilingual parallel corpora with tools and interfaces. In *Recent advances in natural language processing*, volume 5, pages 237–248.

Vasiļjevs, A., Skadiņš, R., and Tiedemann, J. (2012). LetsMT!: A Cloud-Based Platform for Do-It-Yourself Machine Translation. In Zhang, M., editor, *Proceedings of the ACL 2012 System Demonstrations*, number July, pages 43–48, Jeju Island, Korea. Association for Computational Linguistics.

Wang, W., Peter, J.-t., Rosendahl, H., and Ney, H. (2016). Character : Translation edit rate on character level. In *Proceedings of the First Conference on Machine Translation (WMT 2016), Volume 2: Shared Task Papers*, volume 2, pages 505–510, Berlin, Germany.

Zeiler, M. D. (2012). Adadelta: an adaptive learning rate method. *arXiv preprint arXiv:1212.5701.*

March **2018**

Neural Won:

Now What?

Alex Yanishevsky

Senior Manager

MT and NLP Deployments

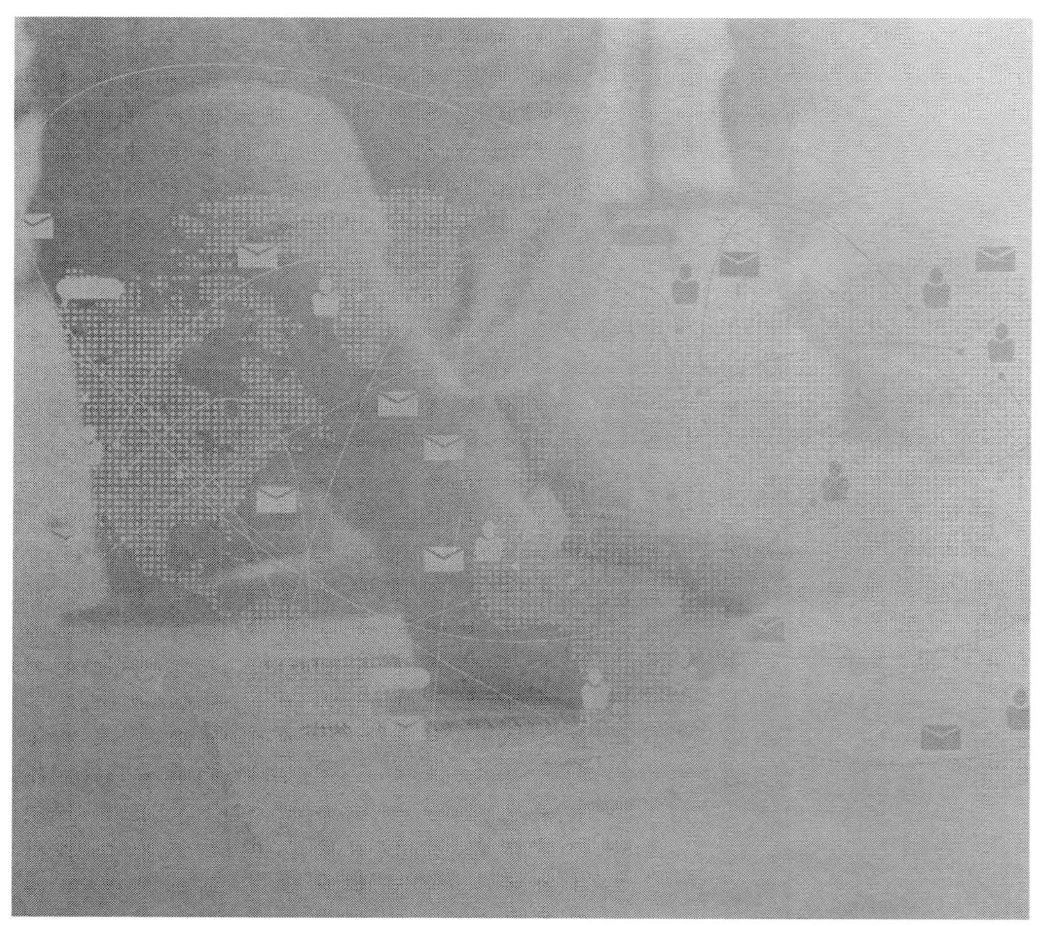

welocalize
doing things differently

Our **History**

1997.	2000.	2005.	2006.	2007.	2008.	
Company Started	Expanded Market into Germany (Acquisition)	Established European Headquarters in Dublin (Acquisition)	Opened APAC Services in Jinan and Beijing, China (Acquisitions)	US Acquisitions Including Global Sight Technology, Leading Open Source Training Management System	Added to APAC Presence with Tokyo Office (Acquisition)	

2010.	2012.	2014.	2015.	2016.
Major Expansion in Europe with UK Acquisition of Lloyd International	Added Legal Services with Market Leader Park IP Translations (Acquisition)	Acquired CD Language Solutions in Houston, TX Acquired Agostini Associati in Milan, Italy	Significant Investment from Norwest Equity Partners Acquired Adapt Worldwide (Traffic Optimiser) in London, United Kingdom 11th Year on Inc. 5000 Fastest Growing Private Companies	Nova Language Services Acquisition Expands Regulated Industry Solutions in Life Sciences (Acquisition) Global Language Solutions (GLS) Acquisition Strengthens Life Sciences Market Leadership (Acquisition)

welocalize
doing things differently

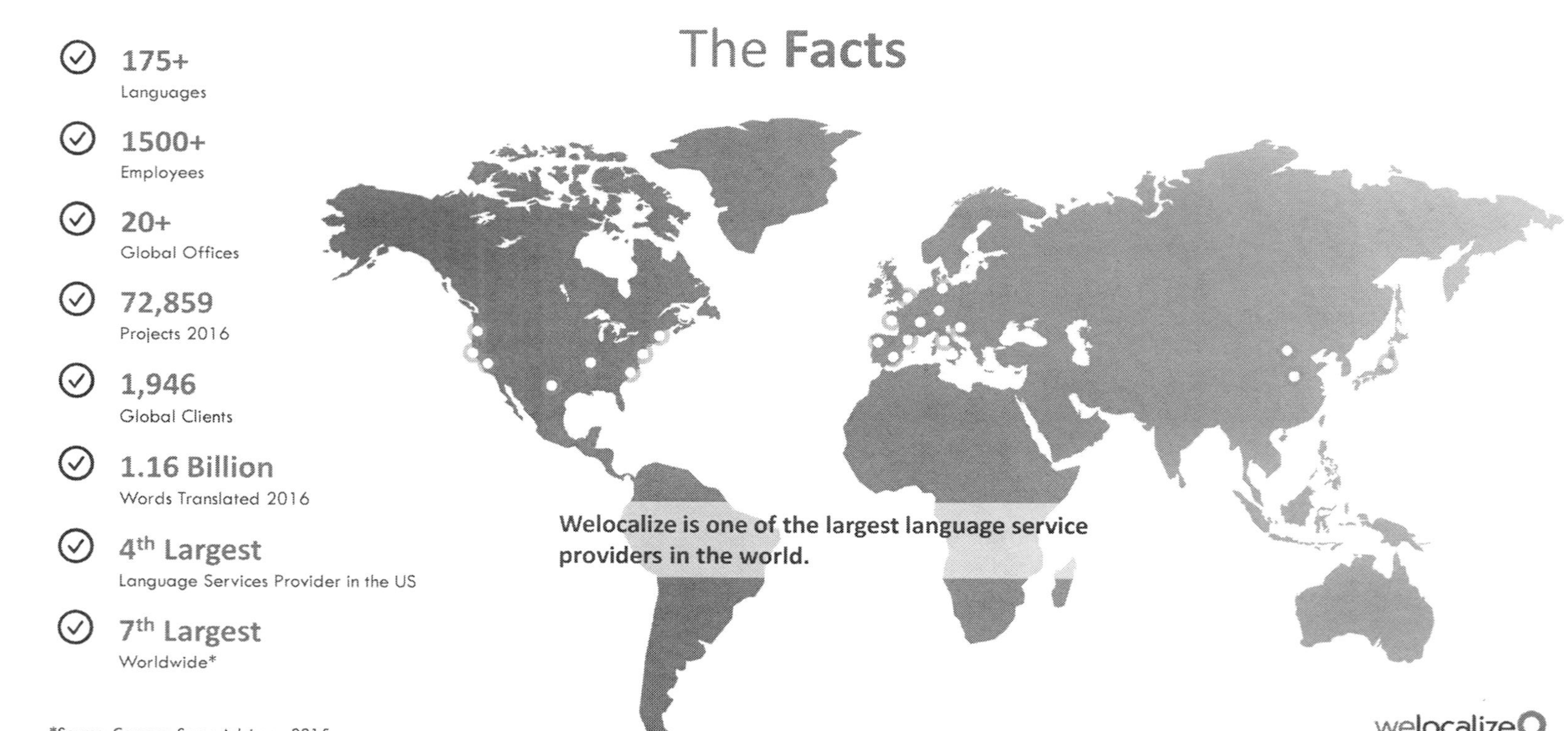

Proceedings of AMTA 2018, vol. 2: MT Users' Track

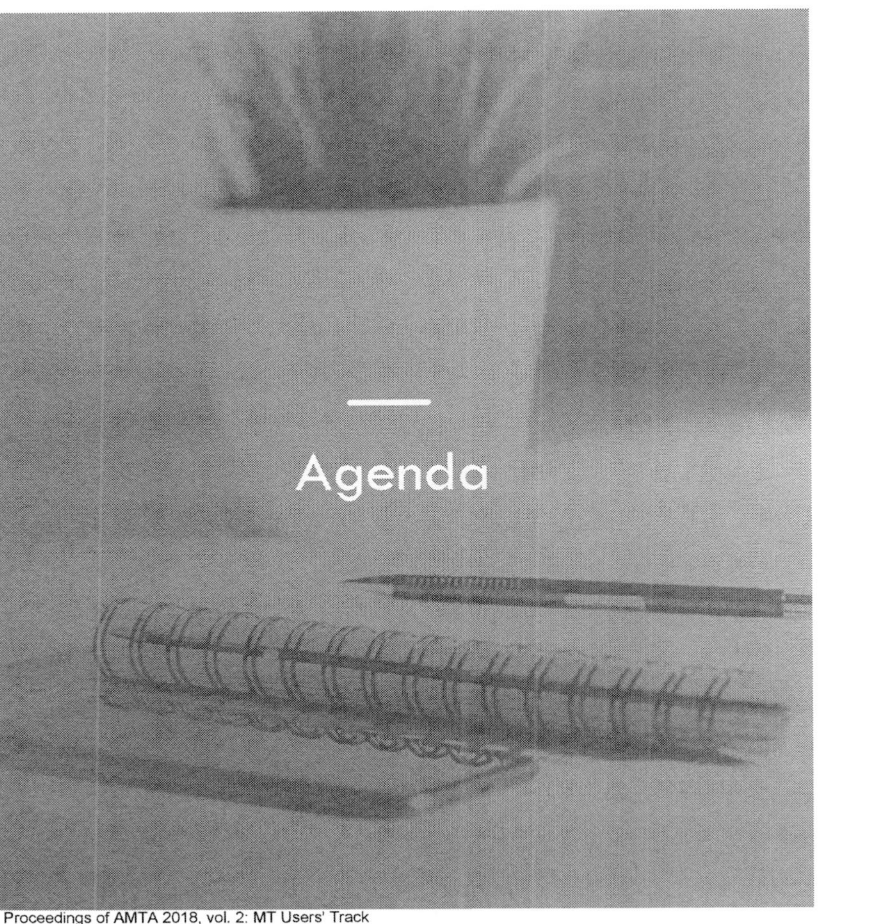

- **Did NMT really win?**

- **Migration path**

  - Build or buy?
  - Infrastructure and Cost
  - TMS and Connectors
  - Additional Use Cases – CMS, applications using MT such as chat, KB, forums
  - Training and Maintenance
  - Supply Chain

- **Case studies**

- **What else can we do with neural technology?**

Did NMT Really Win?

Proceedings of AMTA 2018, vol. 2: MT Users' Track

Did NMT Really Win? /1

Generally, yes, and the future lies in NMT, but…

- ⊙ **Locale variants such as ES-ES>ES-MX: consider transformation tables or Apertium (RBMT)**
- ⊙ **Related language pairs such as ES-ES>PT-PT: consider Apertium (RBMT) or SMT**

- ⊙ **Rare, long-tail language translation directions: consider SMT**
- ⊙ **In some cases, well trained SMT engine in Romance languages can be preferred to NMT**
- ⊙ **In some cases, SMT better at short sentences**

Did NMT Really Win? /2

Locale	Evaluation	Light Marketing				Technical Documentation			
		Generic NMT1	Generic NMT2	Customized SMT	Diff Best NMT & SMT	Generic NMT1	Generic NMT2	Customized SMT	Diff Best NMT & SMT
de-DE	Ranking	√	2	3	6.02 pp	2	√	3	7.38 pp
	Accuracy			√	0.06		√		0.08
	Fluency		√		0.07		√		0.45
	Edit Distance	2	3	√	3.32 pp	√	3	2	1.12 pp
	Edit Distance (PE)	2		√	1.55 pp				
fr-FR	Ranking	√	3	2	1.97 pp	√	2	3	7.29 pp
	Edit Distance	2	3	√	2.02 pp	2	3	√	0.62 pp
ja-JP	Ranking	√	2	3	12.96 pp	√	2	3	10.51 pp
	Accuracy		√		0.32		√		0.76
	Fluency		√		0.2		√		0.49
	Edit Distance	√	3	2	8.17 pp	√	3	2	5.79 pp
	Edit Distance (PE)	√		2	21.07 pp				
pt-BR	Ranking	√	3	2	4.59 pp	√	2	3	6.65 pp
	Accuracy		√		0.09		√		0.26
	Fluency		√		0.45		√		0.28
	Edit Distance	2	3	√	1.68 pp	√	3	2	0.28 pp
	Edit Distance (PE)	2		√	3.62 pp				
zh-CN	Ranking	√	2	3	10.57 pp	√	2	3	10.40 pp
	Edit Distance	√	3	2	5.87 pp	√	3	2	3.12 pp
ru-RU	Ranking	√	2	3	5.95 pp				
	Edit Distance	2	3	√	1.58 pp				

- SMT better for DE for accuracy and edit distance
- SMT better for PTBR for edit distance
- SMT better for RU for edit distance

Did NMT Really Win? /3

Engine	Content	BLEU	NIST	METEOR	GTM	PE Dist	TER	Precision	Recall	Length (Hyp./Ref.)	Segs.	Words	PE Diff	Ranking 1	Ranking 2
NMT	Test set	64.10	10.33	73.72	80.11	37.05%	30.93	0.82	0.79	0.96	2460	33322	17.11%		
MS Hub	Test set	60.22	9.75	71.64	78.96	54.16%	36.61	0.79	0.79	0.99	2500	33863			
NMT	Aug-projects	63.07	8.00	73.28	77.57	50.44%	38.84	0.76	0.79	1.03	513	3852	-5.77%		
MS Hub	Aug-projects	72.38	9.34	81.98	86.89	44.67%	23.41	0.88	0.86	0.97	559	4201			
NMT	Oct-projects	54.90	7.91	66.81	72.63	59.63%	45.65	0.71	0.74	1.04	940	7265	-4.65%	43%	37%
MS Hub	Oct-projects	60.96	8.84	72.95	79.79	50.78%	34.49	0.80	0.80	1.00	1057	8395		33%	26%

- The NMT engines scores better in human ranking
- NMT engine has a lot of omissions, duplications and unusual mistranslations
- Results for auto-scoring are mixed

welocalize
doing things differently

Did NMT Really Win? /4

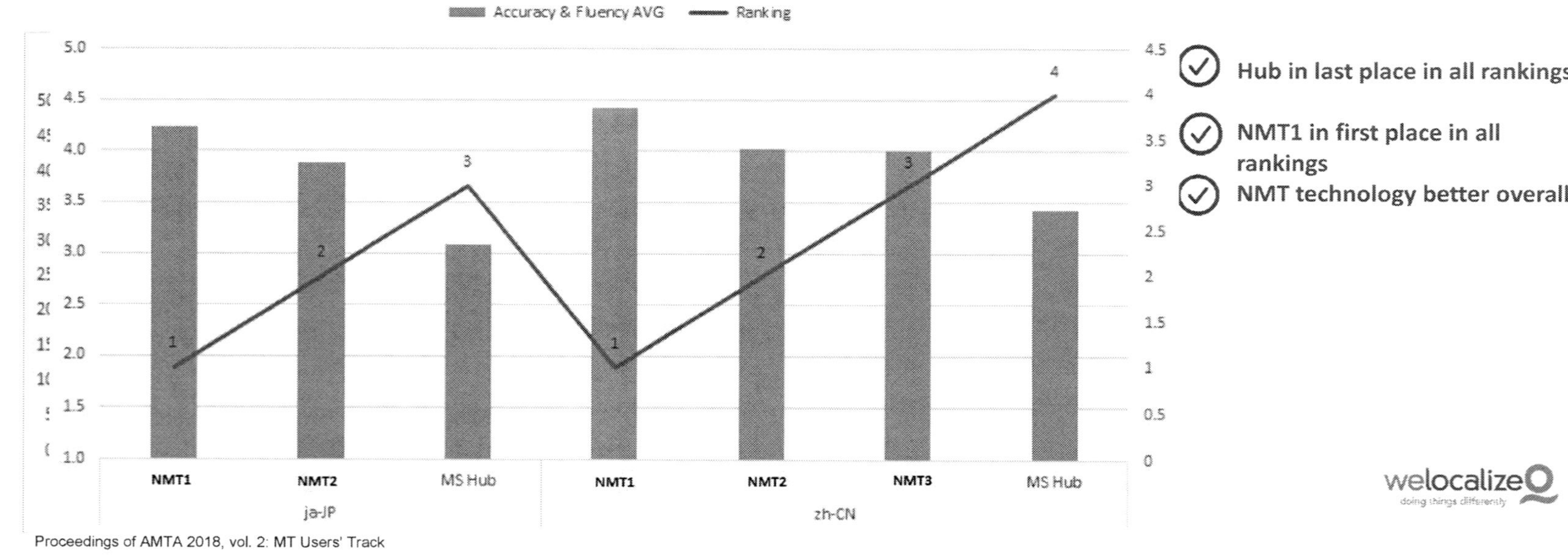

Proceedings of AMTA 2018, vol. 2: MT Users' Track

Now What?

 **PAIN POINTS**
Raw MT, PE, both

 **NUMBER OF ENGINES**
How many domains and engines do you have and for how many languages?

 **STRATEGY**
What is your migration path and strategy?

Migration Path

welocalize
doing things differently

Migration Path

Build or Buy /1

BUILD

- Customized needs
- Internal expertise
- Flexibility

BUY

- Lack of time
- Lack of expertise
- Lack of customizability

BUILD

- Competitive advantage
- Build from scratch or adapt open source solutions

BUY

- Lack of influence over product roadmap
- Reliable tech support
- Reliable solutions available out of the box

welocalize
doing things differently

Build or Buy /2

BUILD

- Modern MT
- Open NMT
- Tensor Flow
- Nematus
- Marian
- Moses

BUY

- Google, Amazon, Bing — not customizable
- MS Hub SMT, Globalese, Kantan, Omniscien, SDL, Systran, Iconic, etc. - customizable

BUILD

- Limited baseline
- Difficult to enforce terminology

BUY

- Robust or limited baseline based on provider
- Generally difficult to enforce terminology, but based on provider

Proceedings of AMTA 2018, vol. 2: MT Users' Track

Build or Buy /3

BUILD

- More options to control (epochs, layers, baseline vs domain data)
- Quality of documentation and code samples may be more uneven

BUY

- Less options to control
- Very good documentation and code samples

BUILD

- Unlimited usage
- $3/hr for cloud for processing MT requests
- 2K per engine for training per month for 20 epochs at 4 hours an epoch

BUY

- $10-20 for 1 million characters – not customizable and MS Hub SMT
- Several hundred to several thousand per engine – customizable

Proceedings of AMTA 2018, vol. 2: MT Users' Track

TMS and CAT Tool Considerations

- Availability and additional cost of connectors depends on TMS or CAT tool
- Tag handling
- Pre and post processing scripts
- Tags as sentence breakers
- Capabilities for providing feedback
- Interacting with Adaptive MT

Ideally, the TMS has several MT connectors so you can pick and choose and migrate when results are conclusive and/or run several MT providers in parallel.

99

Additional Use Cases of MT

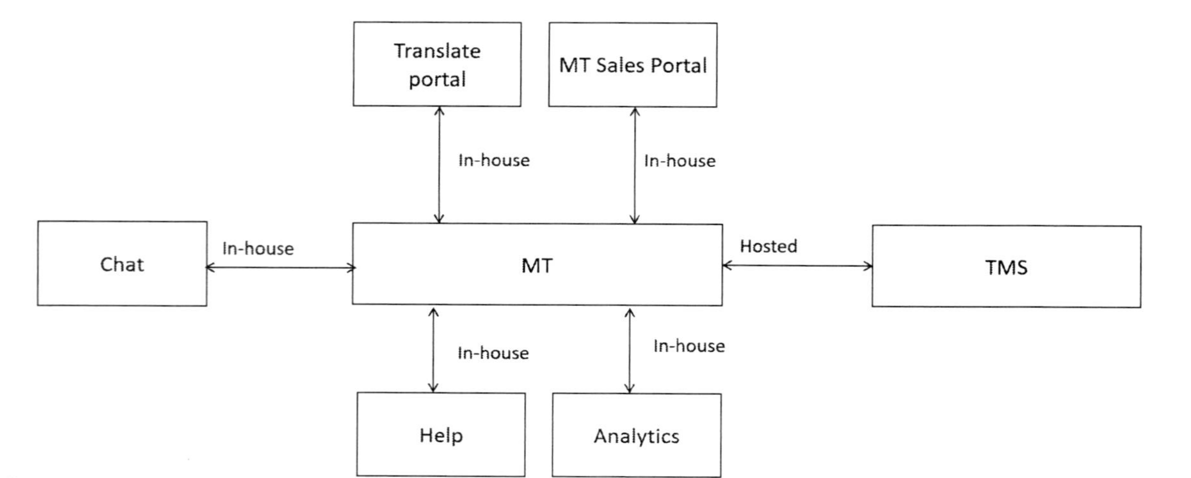

Rewrite connectors for
- KB
- Forums
- Chat
- Any other applications

6 points of MT integration!

Training and Maintenance /1

Initial training
Computational costs of building NMT vs SMT are higher

Maintenance
Computational cost of enforcing specific patterns from linguistic feedback
is higher; it's not a matter of modifying phrase tables or language models
as with SMT or rules/dictionaries with RBMT.

Training and Maintenance /2

- Data availability
  - ✓ Some NMT systems with restricted options require a lot more training data than comparable SMT or RBMT systems
  - ❑ 5-7 million TUs (sometimes 10-11 million) overall to match the quality of an SMT engine in MS Hub with 500-600K TUs and MS Models
  - ❑ Client data ranged from 50K to 700K TUs
  - ✓ Possible to train decent engine with 1-2 million TUs in a different framework with more options available

Training and Maintenance /3

Data Quality
Bad for both
- Uneven or misaligned TUs
- Wrong target language
- Poor, unreliable or inconsistent translations
- Really long segments (NMT – attention mechanism keeps track for only so long due to vanishing gradients, SMT – can't focus on long term dependencies, e.g. English with relative clauses)

Bad for NMT only
- Short segments (1-3 words)
- High ratios of DNT if you do not have method to enforce dictionary

Training the Supply Chain

- NMT output is remarkably more fluent.
- However, **this fluency does not guarantee accuracy**. The cognitive load can be higher for a post-editor to review the source and suggested target.
- OOVs and DNT mistranslations

59805384	Arianna Fontana ha vinto al fotofinish la medaglia d'Oro nella finale dei 500m di short track ai Giochi olimpici invernali di PyeongChang.	59805384	Arianna Fontana won the medal's medal on the end of the short track of short track listeners at the Olympic Olympic Games of the FIFA Winter.

Source	Hypothosis	Reference
6 Div(Low)	6、、	6 分割(低)

Source	Hypothosis	Reference
a04JwiqW9El4hce/Z3+nOHOckWJ0VSCFoqox1FVpYW4fXSeHfuQ0ktVn ylyMz/vYTAWrnj493YlY Examples: file:///remote/file/system/mount/point, \\\\server\\path or nfs://server:/path	X/Z3+Delete/bbr 示例：、或更高版本	a04JwiqW9El4hce/Z3+nOHOckWJ0VSCFoqox1FVpYW4fXSeHfuQ0kt VnylyMz/vYTAWrnj493YlY 示例: file:///remote/file/system/mount/point、 \\\\server\\path 或 nfs://server:/path

Source	Hypothosis	Reference
<proxyAddress:port> GuestRpc:	<> :	<proxyAddress:port> GuestRpc:

welocalize
doing things differently

Case Studies

Case Study 1: Internal Dept, MTPE

- MemoQ as CAT tool
  Numerous MT connectors
- Currently on MS Hub SMT
  EN<>FR, IT, DE, ES, PTBR
- One domain, life sciences
  Any SMT or NMT solution must be customizable
- OpenNMT adaptation shows markedly improved scores

Case Study 1
ROI
Calculations

ITEM	COST	SAVINGS
Connector	0	
MT Usage	0	
Engine Cost ($1000 per locale pair per year)	$8000	
Vendor discounts (100K new words per year* 8 locale pairs* .01 per word)		$8000

- By how much does NMT need to win in order to move now?

- How can we put a price on this?

- How much volume? What languages?
  NOTE: How likely is additional .01 per word for each locale pair? What additional discount does it represent? For rate of .15, that's an additional 7%.

Case Study 2, Tech Support, Raw MT

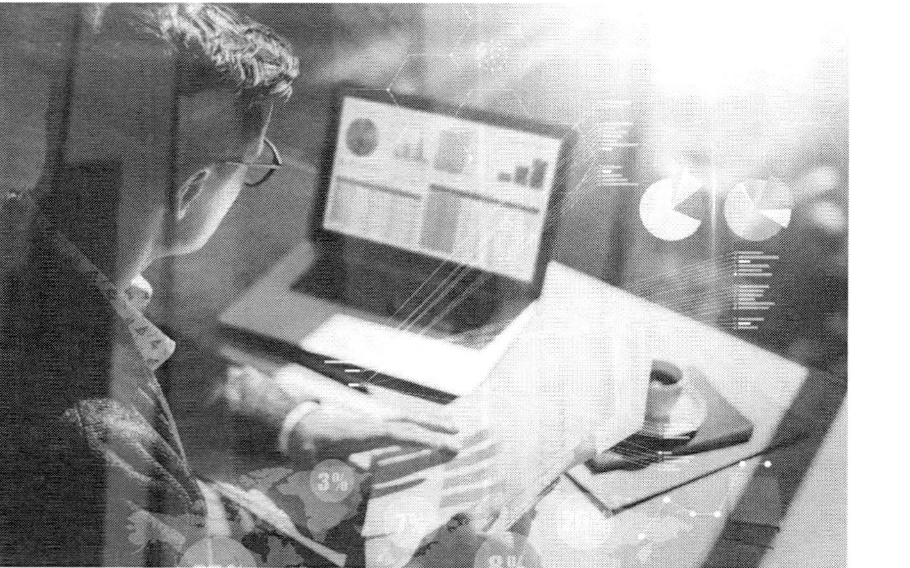

- All possible language combinations, i.e. over 50 languages
- UGC – prone to slang, typos, incorrect formatting
- MT embedded into chat application
- How important is lexical coverage?
- How many MT connectors does the chat application support?
- If several, can you mix and match?
- If you deploy several, what's the administrative overhead of licensing and retraining from several different MT providers?
- Is normalization taking place?

What is the minimum allowable level of quality for the lowest cost?

Proceedings of AMTA 2018, vol. 2: MT Users' Track

Case Study 3, Enterprise, MTPE

- Enterprise level TMS
- Currently on MS Hub
- Each MT connector costs money and has to be vetted by TMS provider
- Many (but not all) languages do better in NMT

- What business problem are we solving – TAT, quality, cost of delivery? How will the move to NMT be a game changer?
- Split the languages amongst the connectors or only move when you can do all of them?
- As in case study 1, what's the cost of each connector relative to the expected volume, increased quality and expected discount by moving to neural?

What Else Can We Do with Neural Technology?

Proceedings of AMTA 2018, vol. 2: MT Users' Track

What Else Can We Do?

- NLG (Natural Language Generation) with subsequent NMT
- Sentiment analysis
- Predictive analytics for localization program management and linguist selection
- Predictive input
- Virtual assistants
- Machine learning for LQA and evaluation of source
- Document summarization

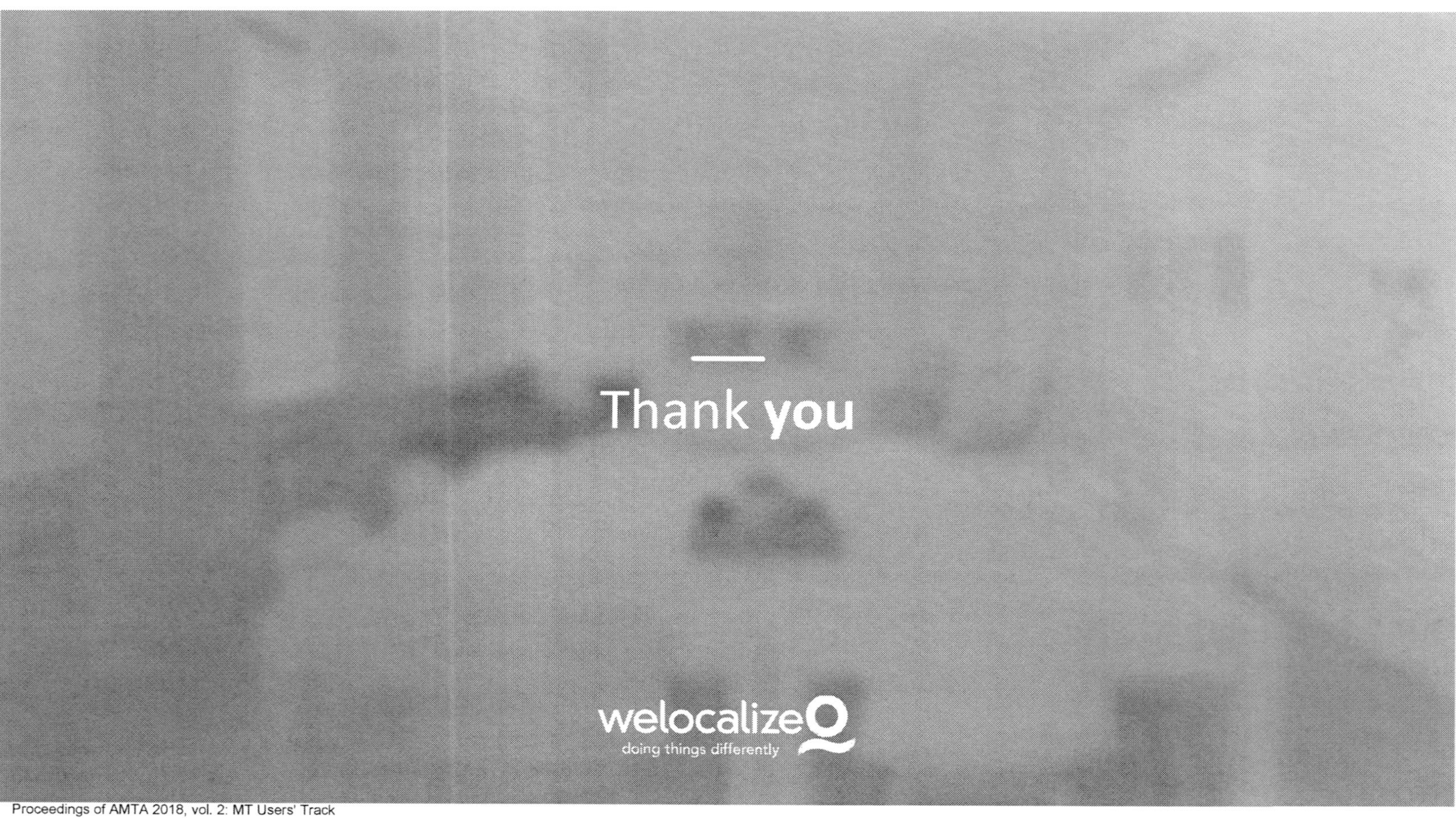
Thank you
welocalize
doing things differently

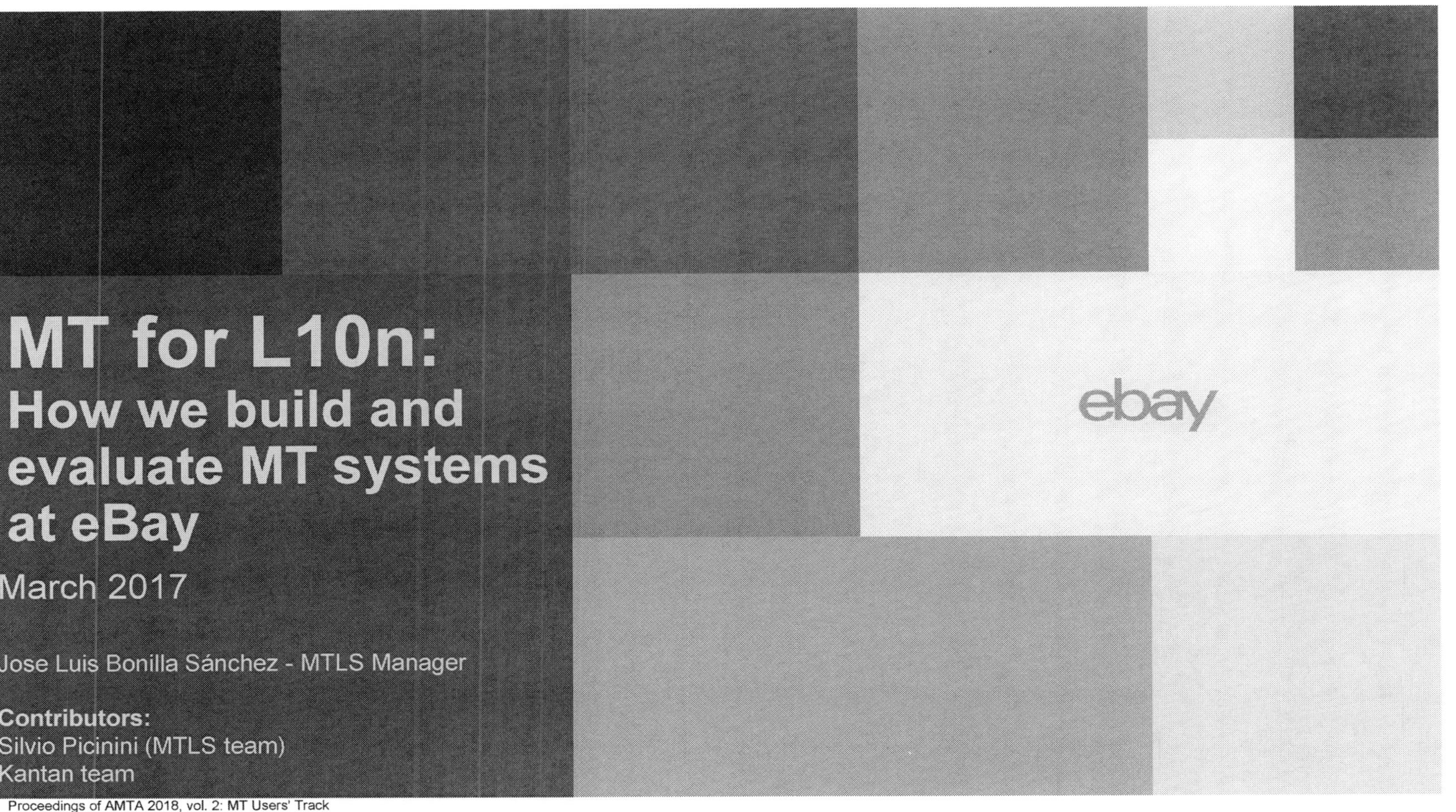

MT for L10n:
How we build and evaluate MT systems at eBay
March 2017
Jose Luis Bonilla Sánchez - MTLS Manager
Contributors:
Silvio Picinini (MTLS team)
Kantan team
ebay

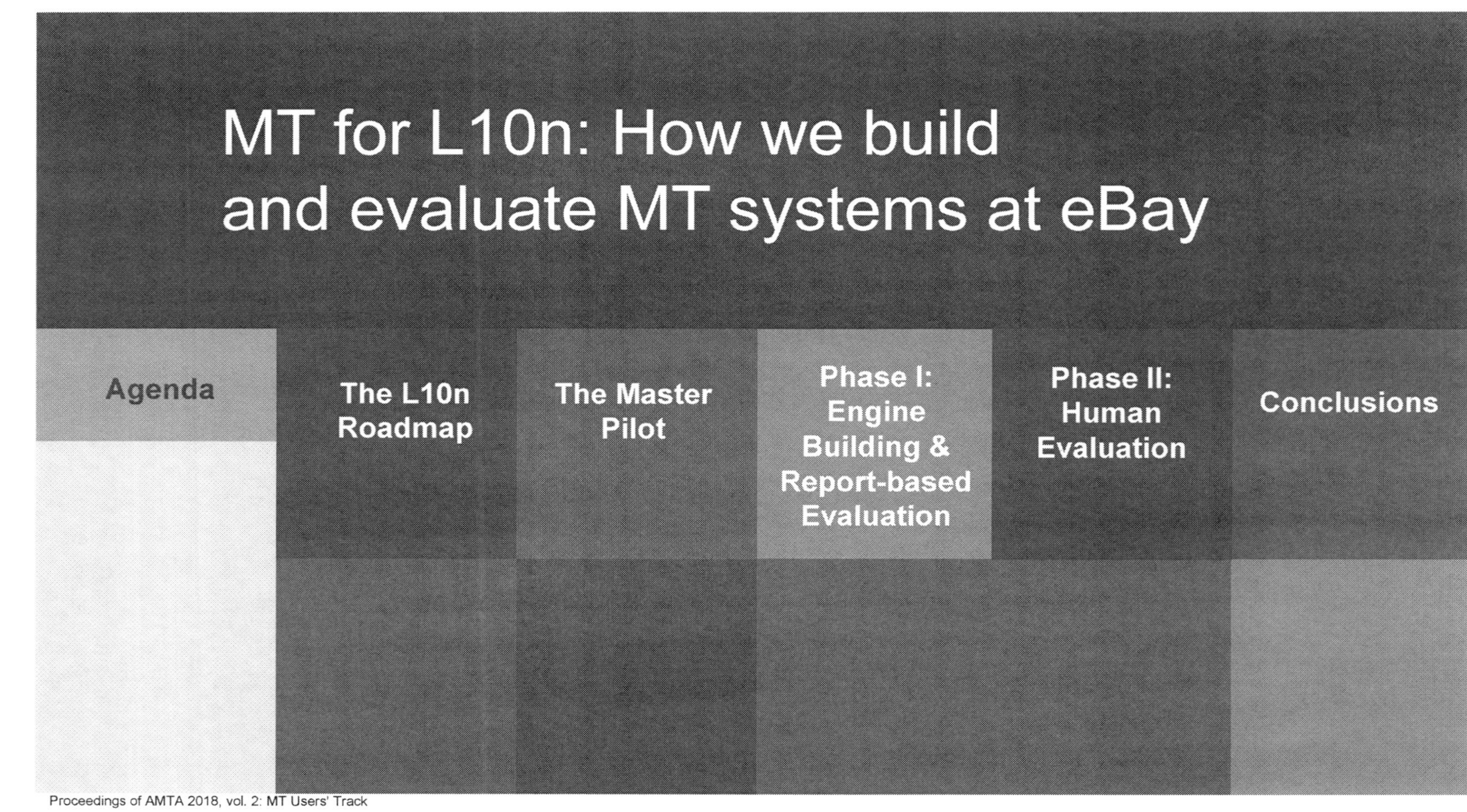

MT for L10n: How we build and evaluate MT systems at eBay
Agenda
The L10n Roadmap
The Master Pilot
Phase I: Engine Building & Report-based Evaluation
Phase II: Human Evaluation
Conclusions

The eBay L10n Roadmap

L10n Roadmap: MT for All eBay-created content (Help, UI, CS…)

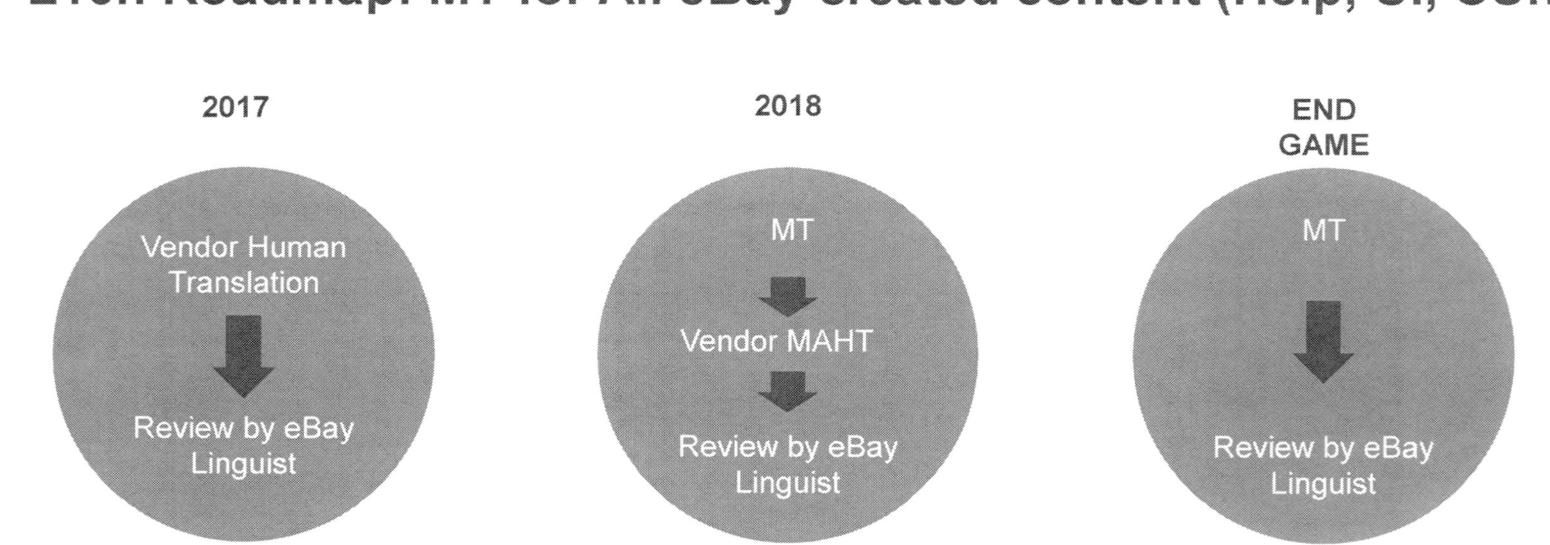

Our Roadmap's Keystone: Building a reliable Master Pilot for all future projects

ebay

Proceedings of AMTA 2018, vol. 2: MT Users' Track

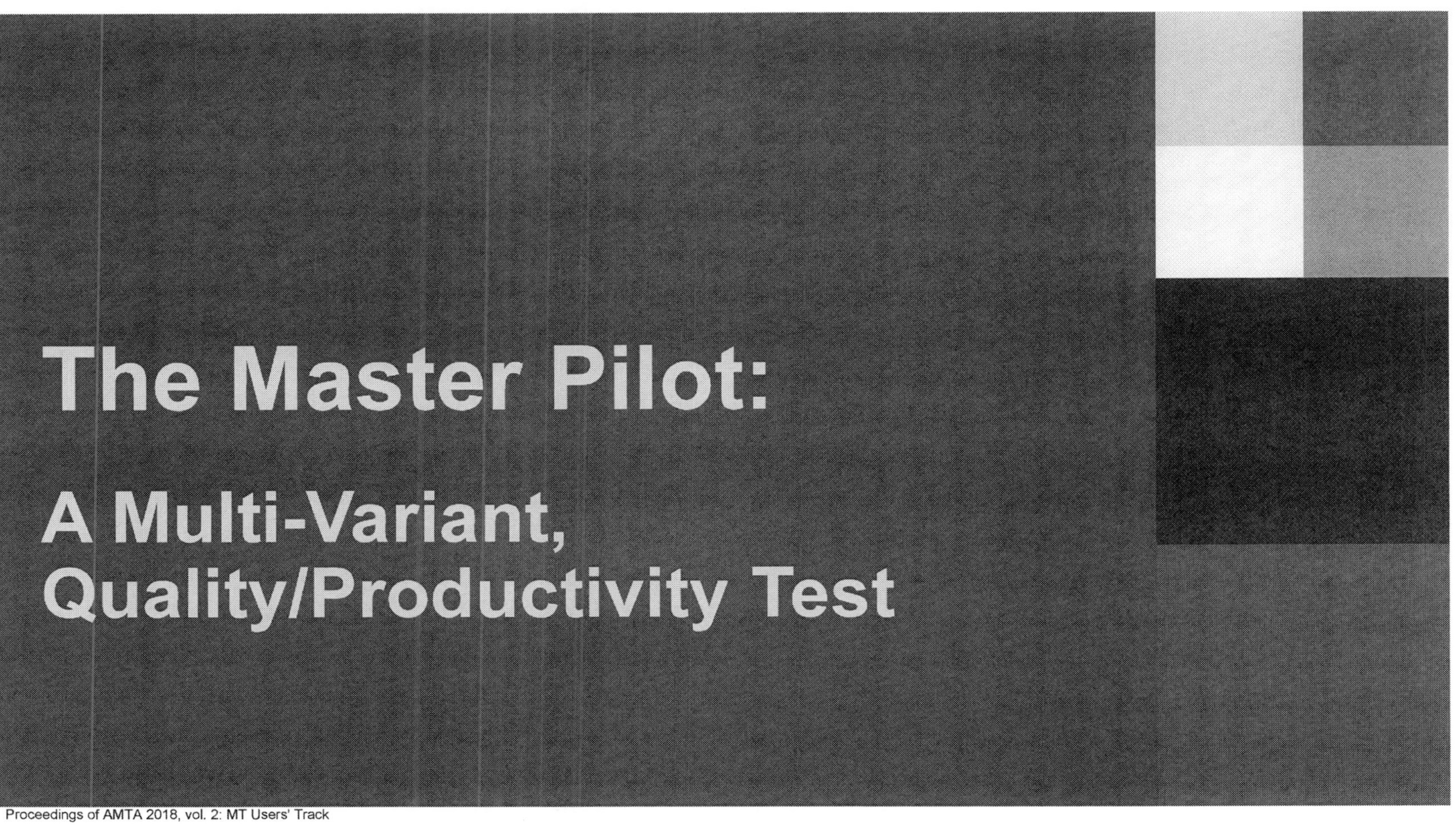

The Master Pilot:
A Multi-Variant,
Quality/Productivity Test

Master Pilot for MT Evaluation

Build Stage

- Partnering with our internal client (Customer Support) and external vendors (Kantan)

- Building and tuning SMT and NMT systems

Evaluation Stage

Principles:

Multi-dimensional:
- Error Analysis
- Quality and Productivity
- Data Correlation

Conclusions

For the pilot: Best engine?
For future pilots: Best process & KPIs?
For the industry:
- Best evaluation method? (Or combination thereof)
For eBay L10n:
How to engage linguists and best leverage their skills?

Factors that Decided Us for Our Partner - KantanMT

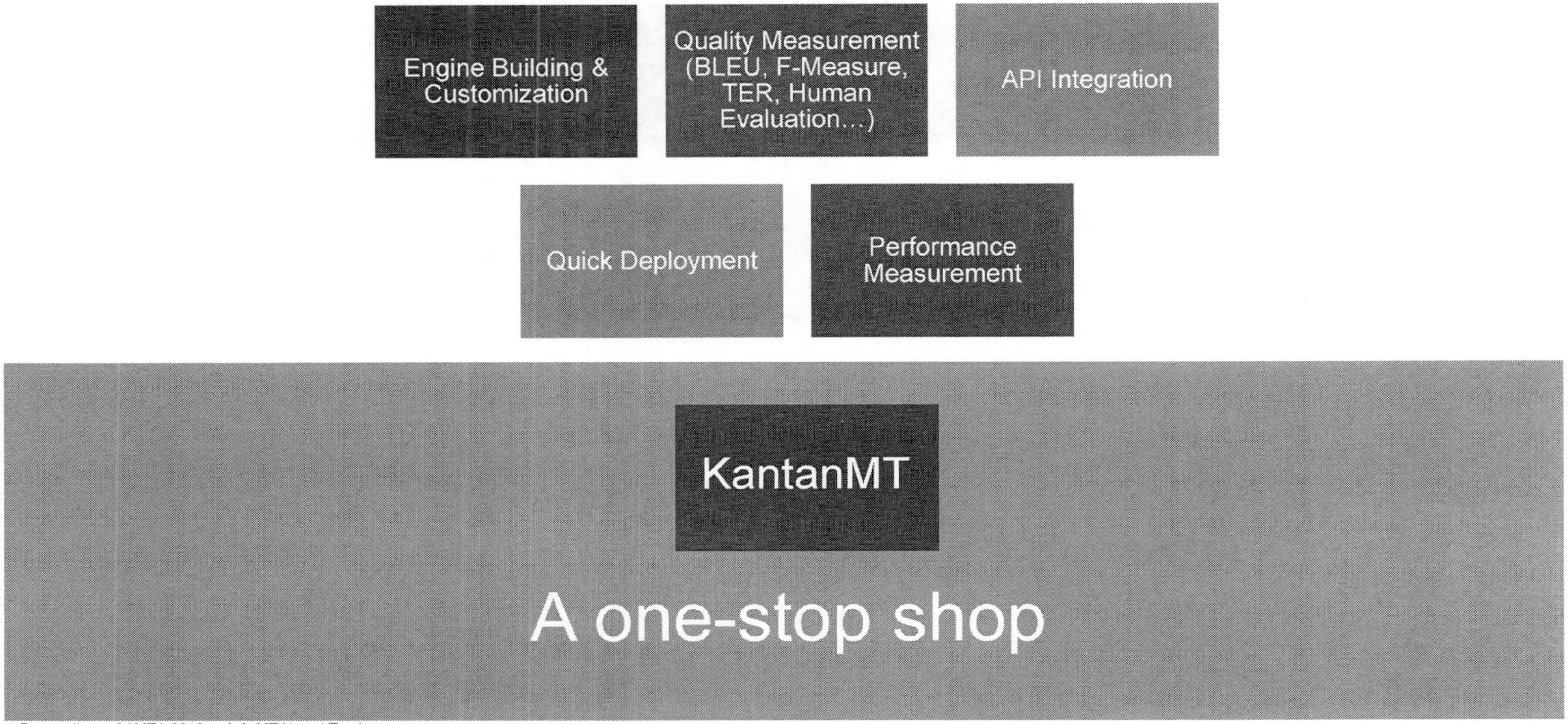

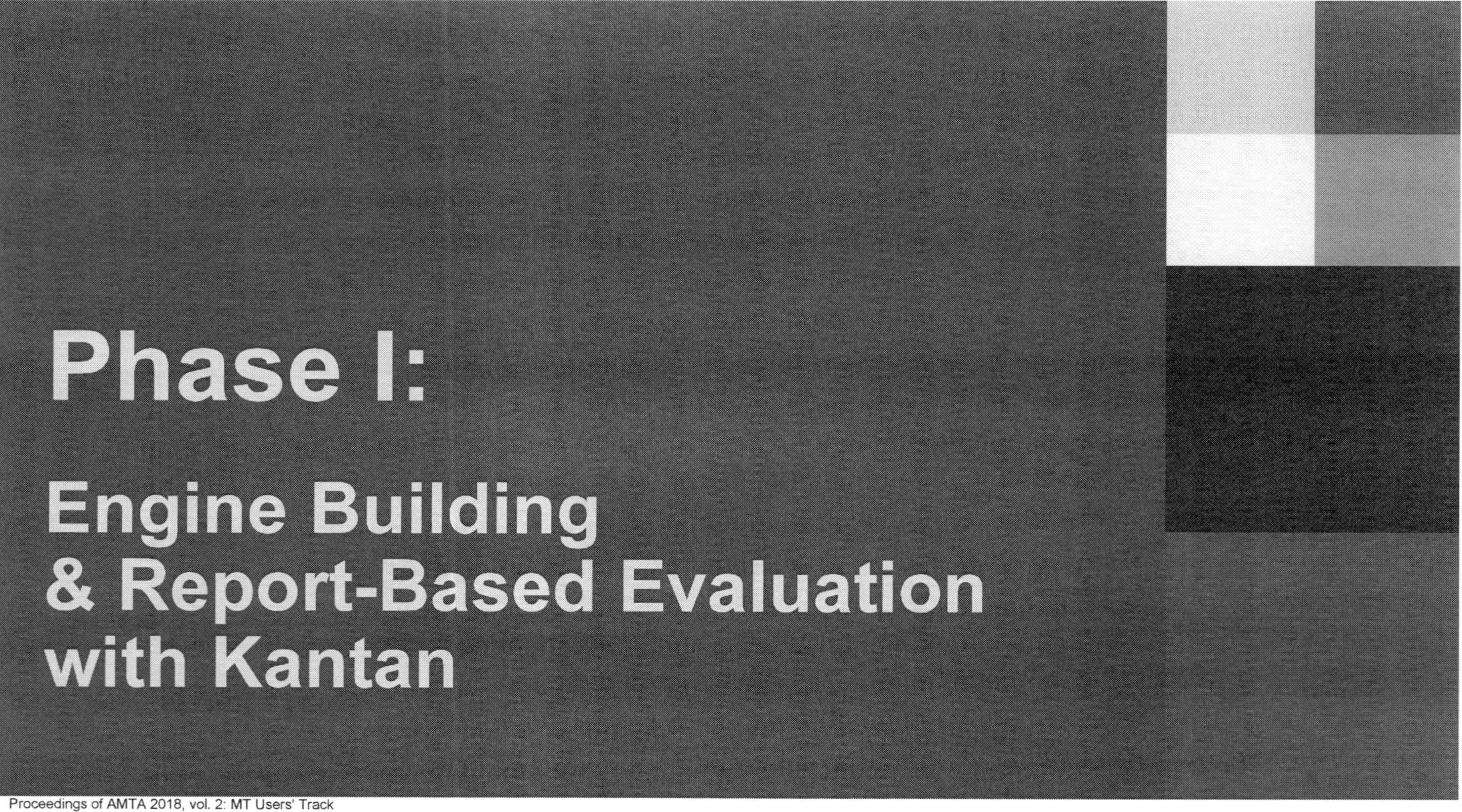

Phase I:
Engine Building
& Report-Based Evaluation
with Kantan

Building & Evaluating Engines – The Workflow

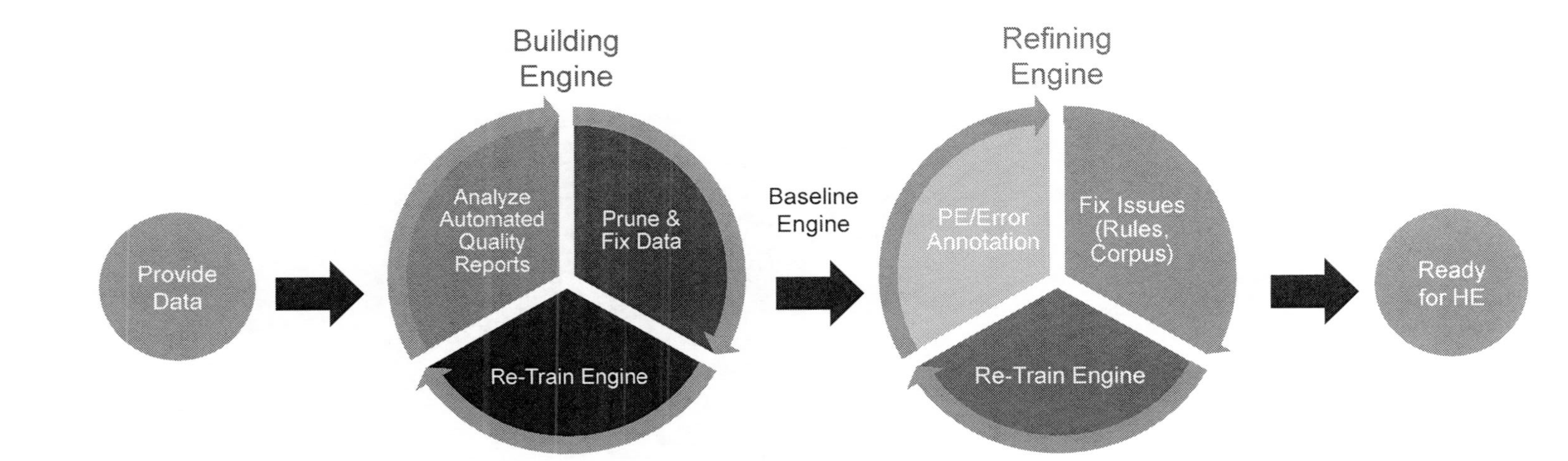

Baseline Engine – Evaluation Based on Automated Reports

Reports produced by:
- Vetting training corpora
- Comparing MT output with the human-translated Reference.

Goal: Finding and fixing major errors to reach threshold scores for Baseline Engine.

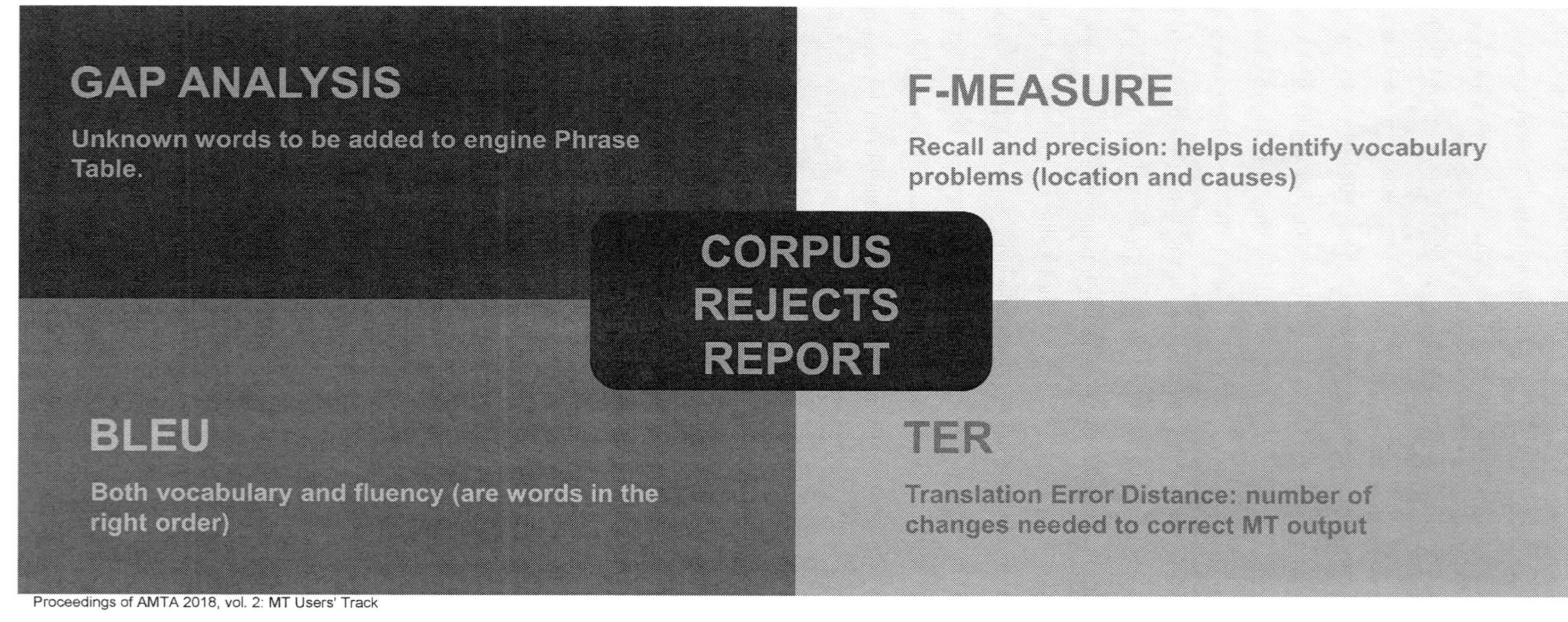

Engine Refinement – Linguistic Quality Review

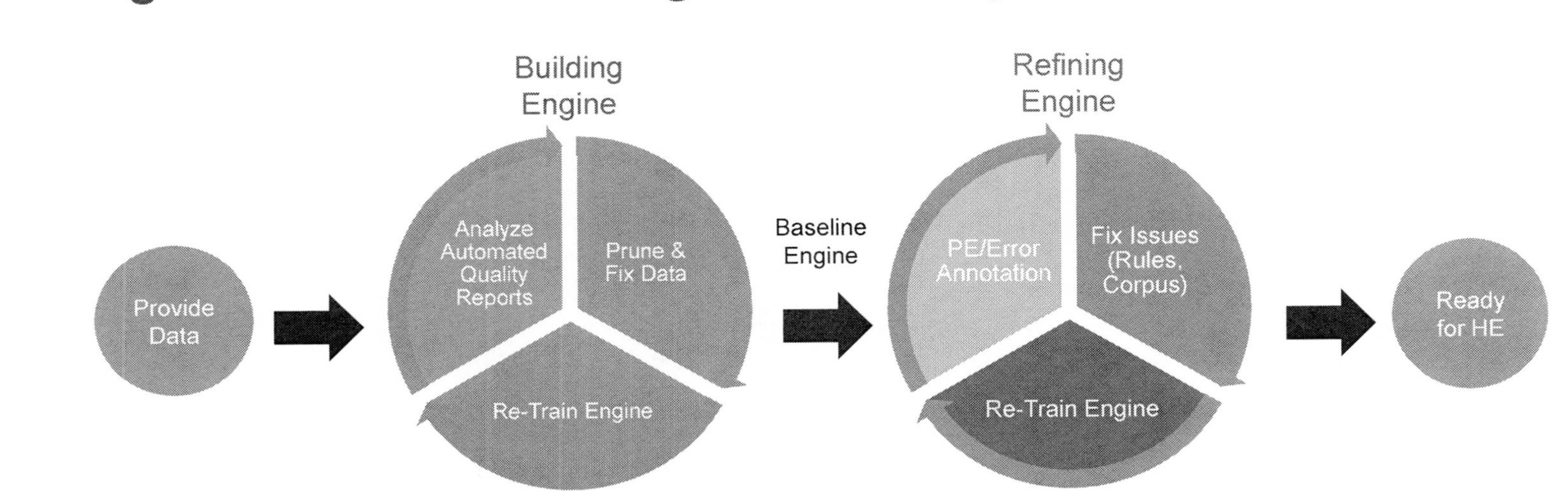

Engine Refinement - Details

First "Real World" MT translation

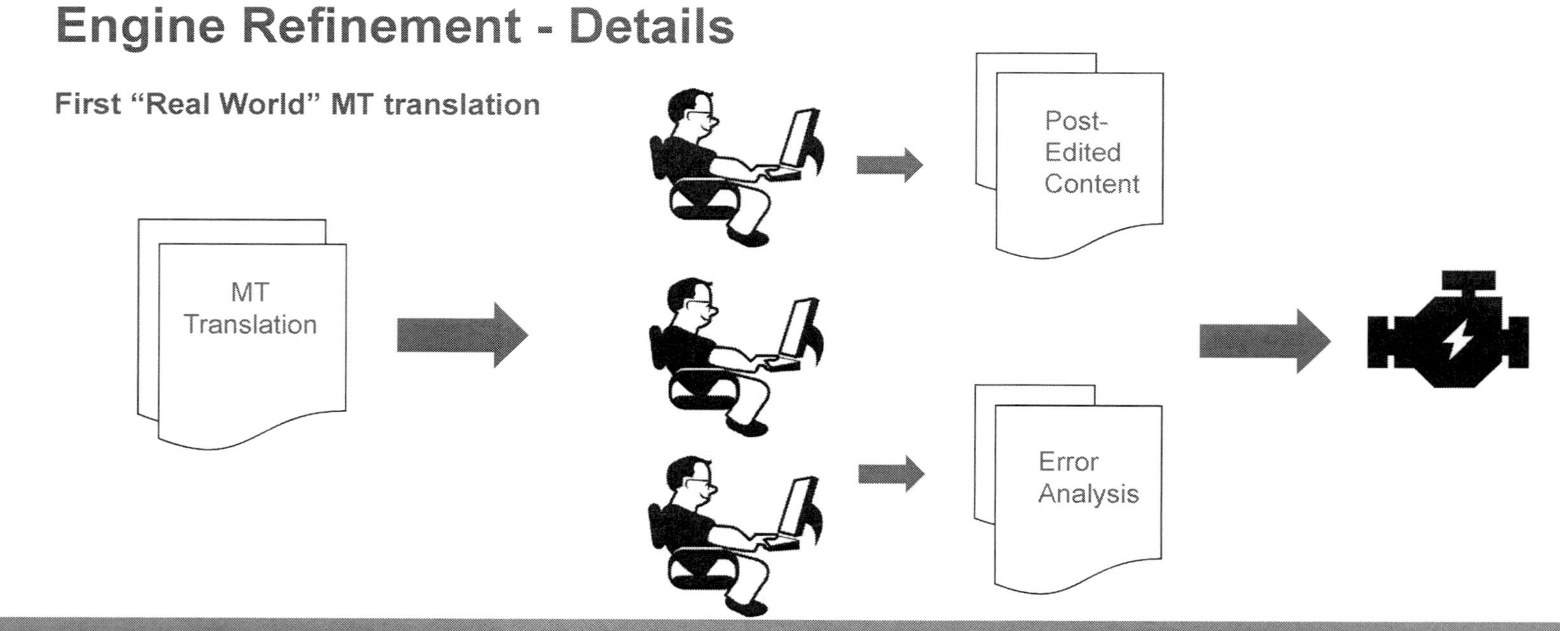

- 3 EVALUATORS: 2 L10N LINGUISTS AND 1 FINAL CLIENT (CS) REPRESENTATIVE

- 2 ROUNDS TO REACH ACCEPTABLE OUTPUT FOR BENCHMARKING

Engine Refinement – An Effective Error Typology

Error Typology for <u>MT-translated</u> content (DQF-MQM customized subset)

Category	Sub-category	Definition	Action
Terminology		Terminology issues relate to the use of domain- or organization-specific terminology	Add more terms to glossary / add new glossaries
Accuracy	Omission	Translation omits source information	Find out why MT omits information
	Do-not-translate	Term that should stay untranslated is translated	Add terms to NTA list /Tag them in pre-processing
	Untranslated	Term that should be translated stays untranslated	Find out in what areas; we may need additional corpora (what kind?)
	Mistranslation	Term incorrectly translated	Find out whether there is a pattern
Fluency	Grammar - word form	Morphological problem - E.g. "has becomed" instead of "became".	Fix in corpora / with PEX rules
	Grammar - word order	Bad word order	Fix in engine / with PEX rules
Locale	Format problems - measurement, currency, date/time, address, telephone...	The text does not adhere to locale-specific mechanical conventions and violates requirements for the presentation of content in the target locale.	Fix with PEX rules

ebay

Proceedings of AMTA 2018, vol. 2: MT Users' Track

Engine Refinement – An Effective Error Typology

Error Typology for <u>Source</u> Content (DQF-MQM customized subset)

Category	Sub-category	Definition	Action
Ambiguity		The text is ambiguous in its meaning.	Look for a pattern – always identify the error cause when possible. Examples: - Misused punctuation (e.g. "we had problems, coming home" vs "we had problems; coming home"; "high end designer item" vs "high-end designer item") - Overuse of the -ing form ("I will want you to study after watching TV" can mean "after I watch TV" or "after you watch TV") - Wrong capitalization (e.g. with a UI element: "Employment Fraud" vs "employment fraud". Makes it difficult to recognize if this is a UI element (and should stay in English) or not) - Others
Grammar		Function words, word-form, word-order. Typos affecting MT translation.	Look for a pattern (gender/number disagreements, incorrect word order that may cause MT problems) Examples: - high end designer item vs high-end designer item -> Missing hyphen - 3day duration -> Missing space grammar error
Terminology		Inconsistency - multiple words for one concept. Lack of consistency may produce incorrect MT translations, especially in Neural MT.	Provide recommended term.
Design - Markup	Markup	Issues related to "markup" (codes used to represent structure or formatting of text, also known as "tags"). Wrong markup can cause tags to be exposed for translation, or missing, which causes a loss of meaning.	Report for content creators to fix. When in doubt as to whether the missing content is a placeholder, use the Ambiguity error type. Examples: - Full URLs: "ATO %20UK%20Communication%20Preferences%20Change.png" />" - Missing placeholders: "Actively selling when occurs"

Proceedings of AMTA 2018, vol. 2: MT Users' Track

Engine Refinement Results – SMT vs NMT Errors

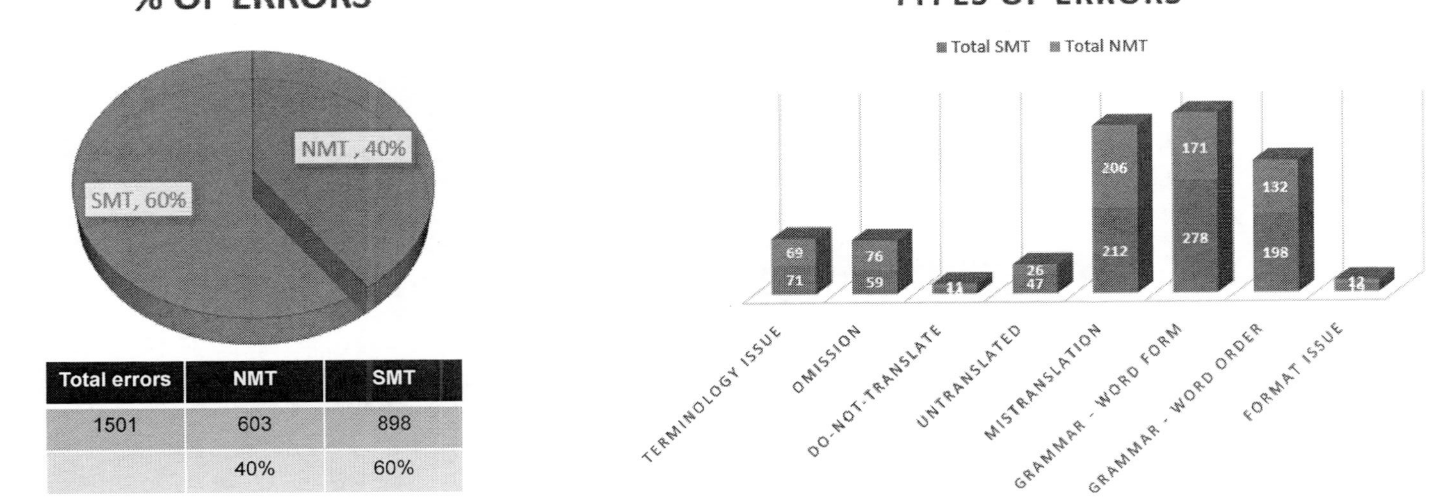

Total errors	NMT	SMT
1501	603	898
	40%	60%

CONCLUSIONS:
NMT produces considerably less errors than SMT
NMT matches or beats SMT in all areas except omissions
NMT performs specially well in grammar (morphology, word order), i.e. Fluency

ebay

Proceedings of AMTA 2018, vol. 2: MT Users' Track

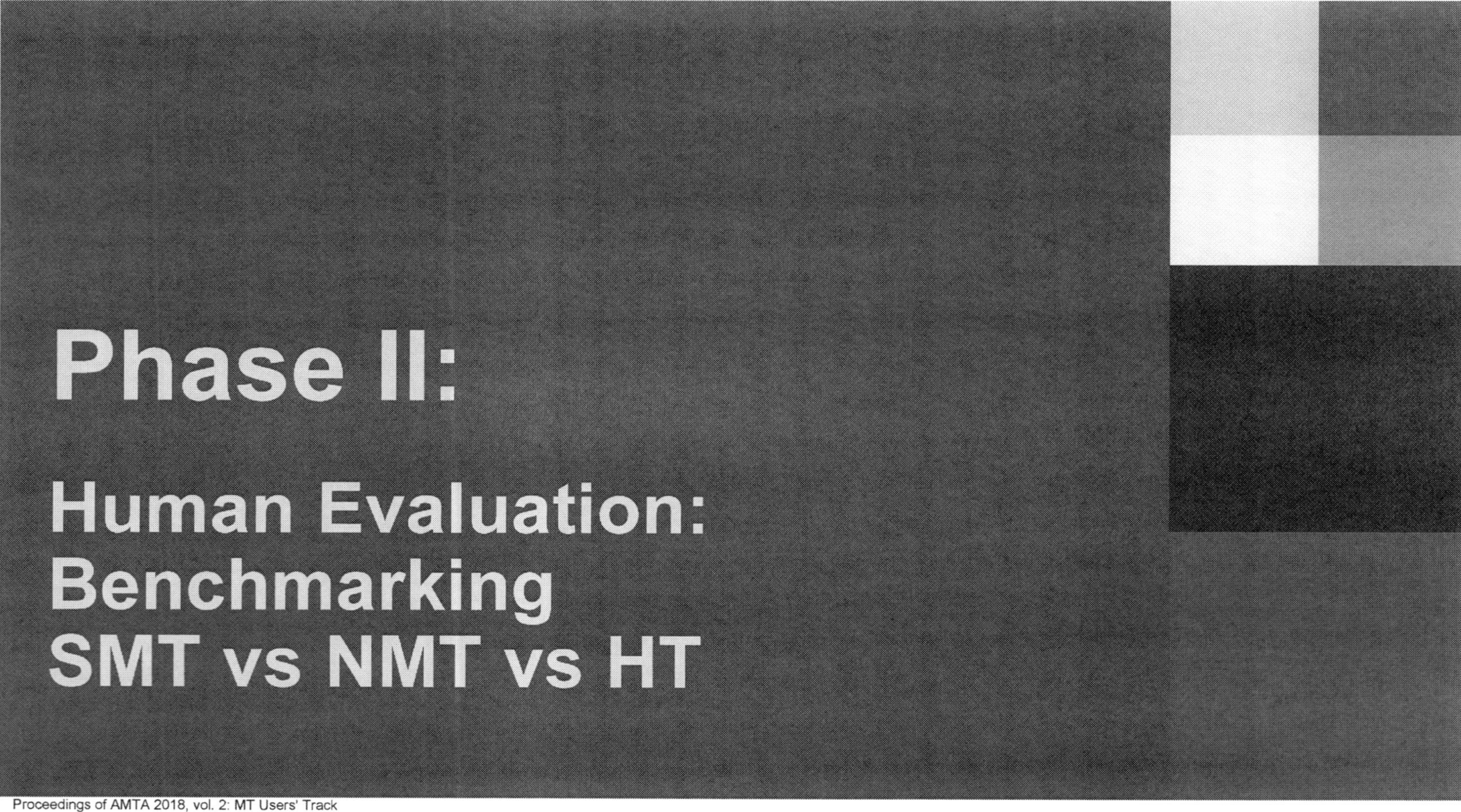

Phase II:
Human Evaluation:
Benchmarking
SMT vs NMT vs HT

Benchmarking Flow – SMT, NMT and HT

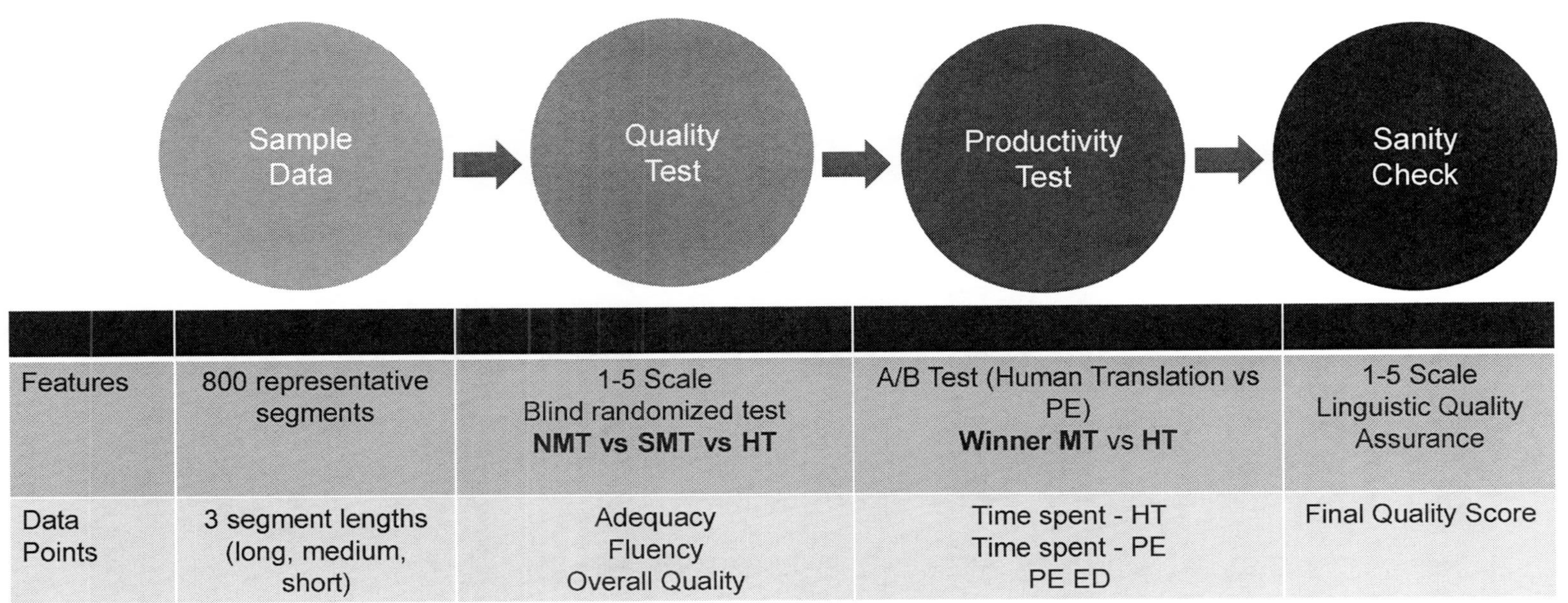

	Sample Data	Quality Test	Productivity Test	Sanity Check
Features	800 representative segments	1-5 Scale Blind randomized test **NMT vs SMT vs HT**	A/B Test (Human Translation vs PE) **Winner MT vs HT**	1-5 Scale Linguistic Quality Assurance
Data Points	3 segment lengths (long, medium, short)	Adequacy Fluency Overall Quality	Time spent - HT Time spent - PE PE ED	Final Quality Score

ebay

Data for Quality and Productivity: A Representative Sample

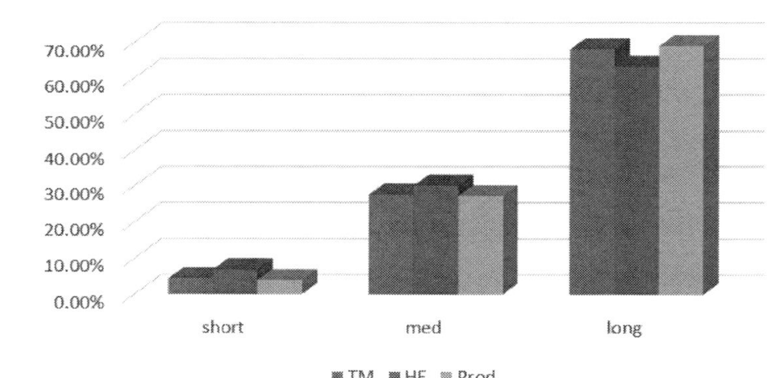

By Silvio Picinini, eBay BPT MTLS

Our sample mirrors the CS TM length distribution:
- Short segments (1-4 words): little context
- Medium segments (6-12 words) simple full sentences
- Long segments (13-35 words) complex sentences

5 sets of short-medium-long segments:
- 2 for post-editing
- 1 for human translation (to compare with PE)
- 1 for human evaluation

Proceedings of AMTA 2018, vol. 2: MT Users' Track

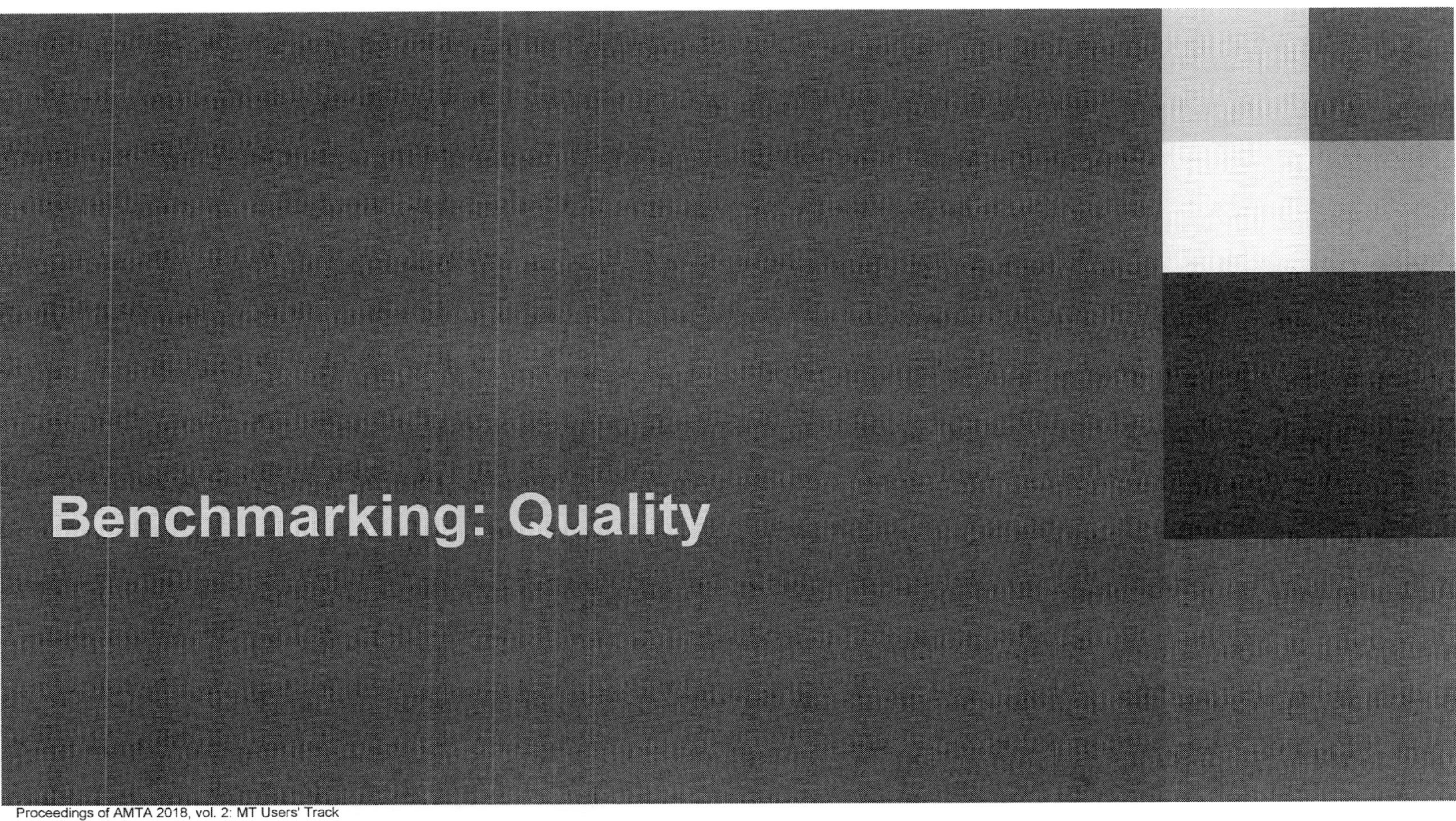
Benchmarking: Quality

Quality Evaluation Stage

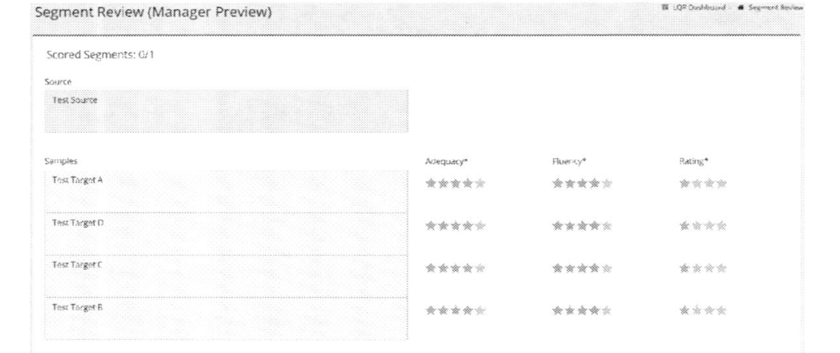

WHO

4 Linguists: - 1 External Vendor
- 2 eBay In-House Linguists
- 1 Customer Support

WHAT   - NMT vs SMT vs Human Translation
- Adequacy: How much of the source meaning is preserved in the translation
- Fluency: To what extent is the translation grammatical and natural-sounding.
- Overall: General impression

WHERE

Kantan AB Test Tool:
- Simple, easy-to-use ranking and rating features

Adequacy Results: Quality per Segment Length

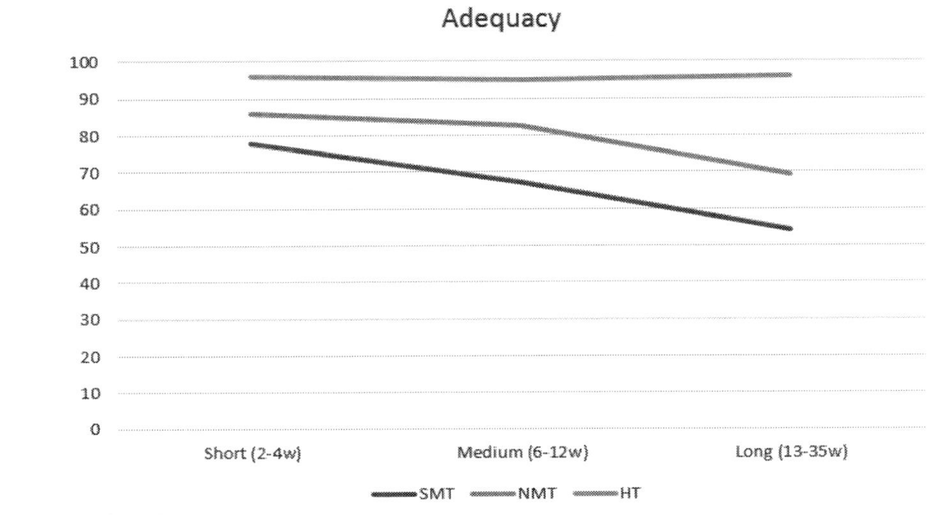

1-100 Scale
- HT Stable high quality (as expected)
- On average, **NMT 22% better than SMT** (79% vs 65%)
- SMT and NMT adequacy declines with longer segments
- NMT is (surprisingly) better **even in shorter segments**

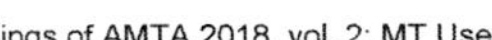

ebay

Proceedings of AMTA 2018, vol. 2: MT Users' Track

Fluency Results: Quality per Segment Length

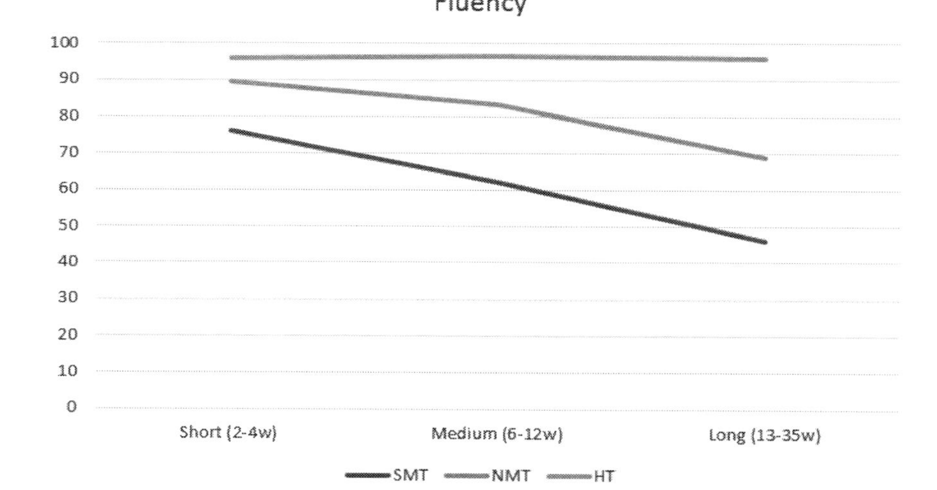

1-100 Scale
HT Stable
On average, **NMT 33% better than SMT** (80% vs 60%)
SMT and NMT adequacy also declines with longer segments **(but NMT holds better - expected)**

Proceedings of AMTA 2018, vol. 2: MT Users' Track

Overall HE Ranking

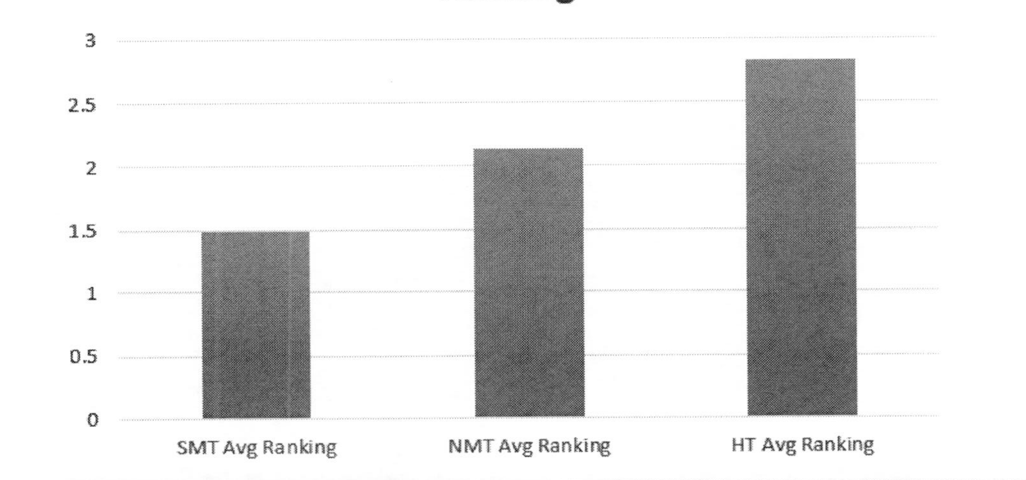

SMT Average Ranking	NMT Average Ranking	HT Average Ranking
1.49 (50%)	2.13 (71%)	2.83 (94%)

By including HT in test set, we determine ideal baseline is 94% of a perfect score

Benchmarking: Productivity

Productivity Evaluation Stage

NMT vs HT – Time Gains

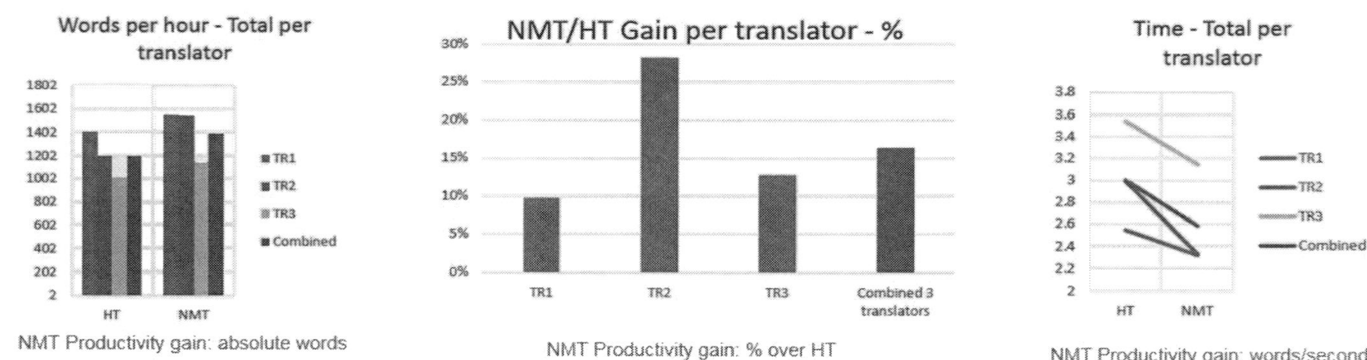

PENMT consistently increases productivity (10-27%)

2 in-house translators (1 in particular) leverage greatest gains

ebay

Proceedings of AMTA 2018, vol. 2: MT Users' Track

NMT vs HT – Correlation Time-Edit Distance

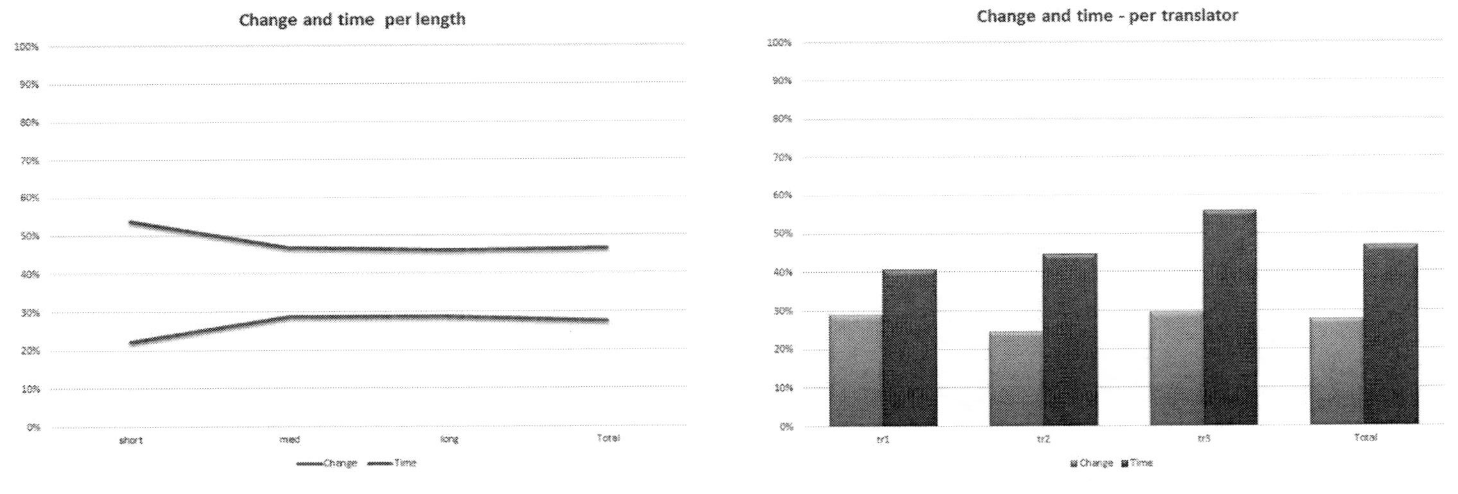

PER SEGMENT LENGHT

A uniform ratio between edit distance and time to edit, **except** for very short segments, that require proportionally more time (likely significant terms, requiring more research)

PER TRANSLATOR

ED and time are mostly aligned, with one exception. one of the linguists's (vendor) time to edit is an outlier.

ebay

Proceedings of AMTA 2018, vol. 2: MT Users' Track

NMT vs HT–Correlation Time-Edit Distance vs Adequacy-Fluency

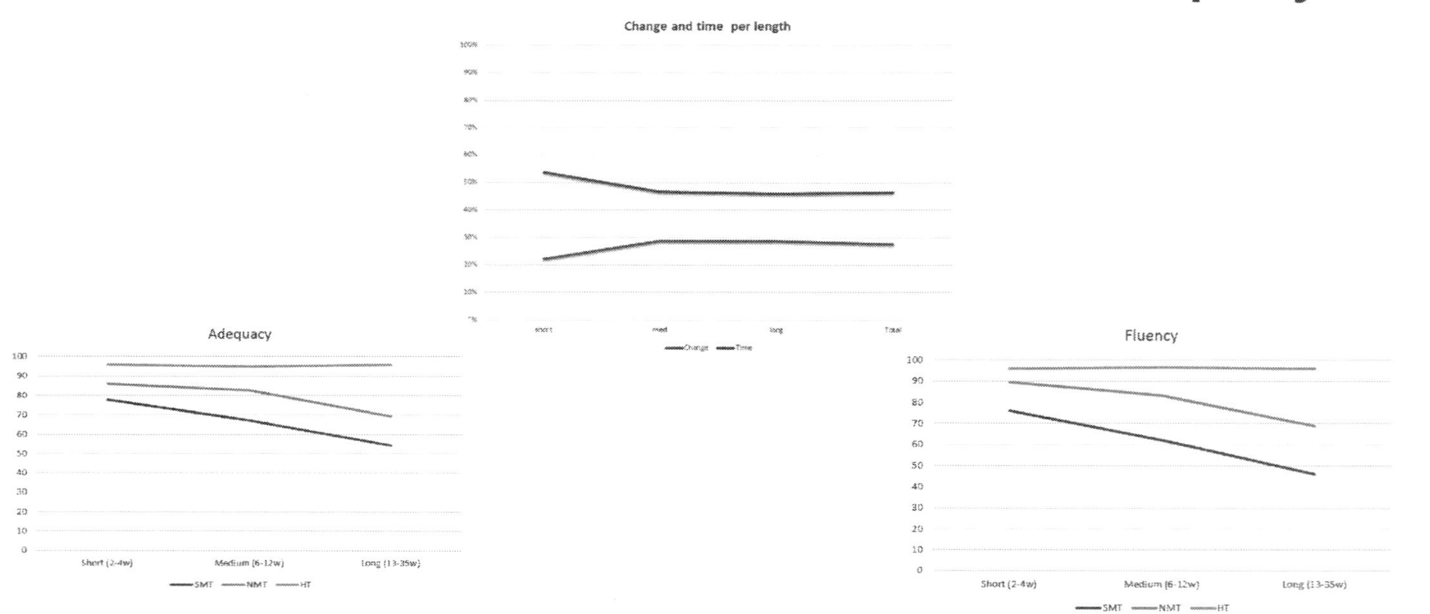

Interestingly, the perceived decline in Adequacy and Fluency for long segments is not reflected in a higher ED or longer time to edit.

Quality Assessment: The Sanity Check

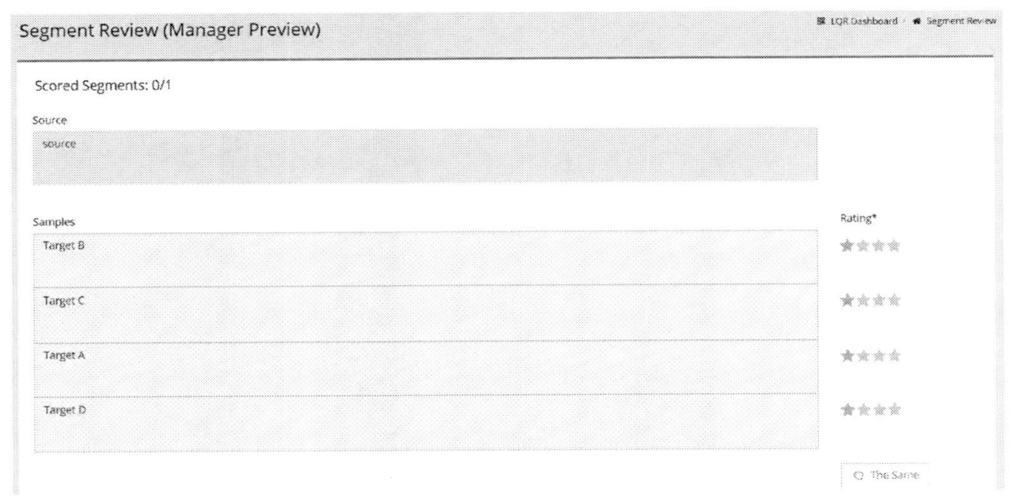

From KantanLQR

A Quality Assessment of post-editors' final quality

Quality Assessment: Results

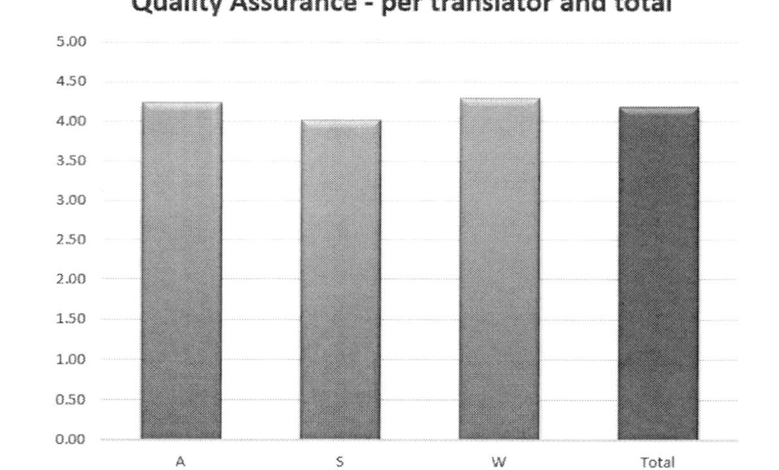

A linguist reviewed a sample of the post-edit work of the evaluators

Quality was very similar: 4.24 - 4.01 - 4.29

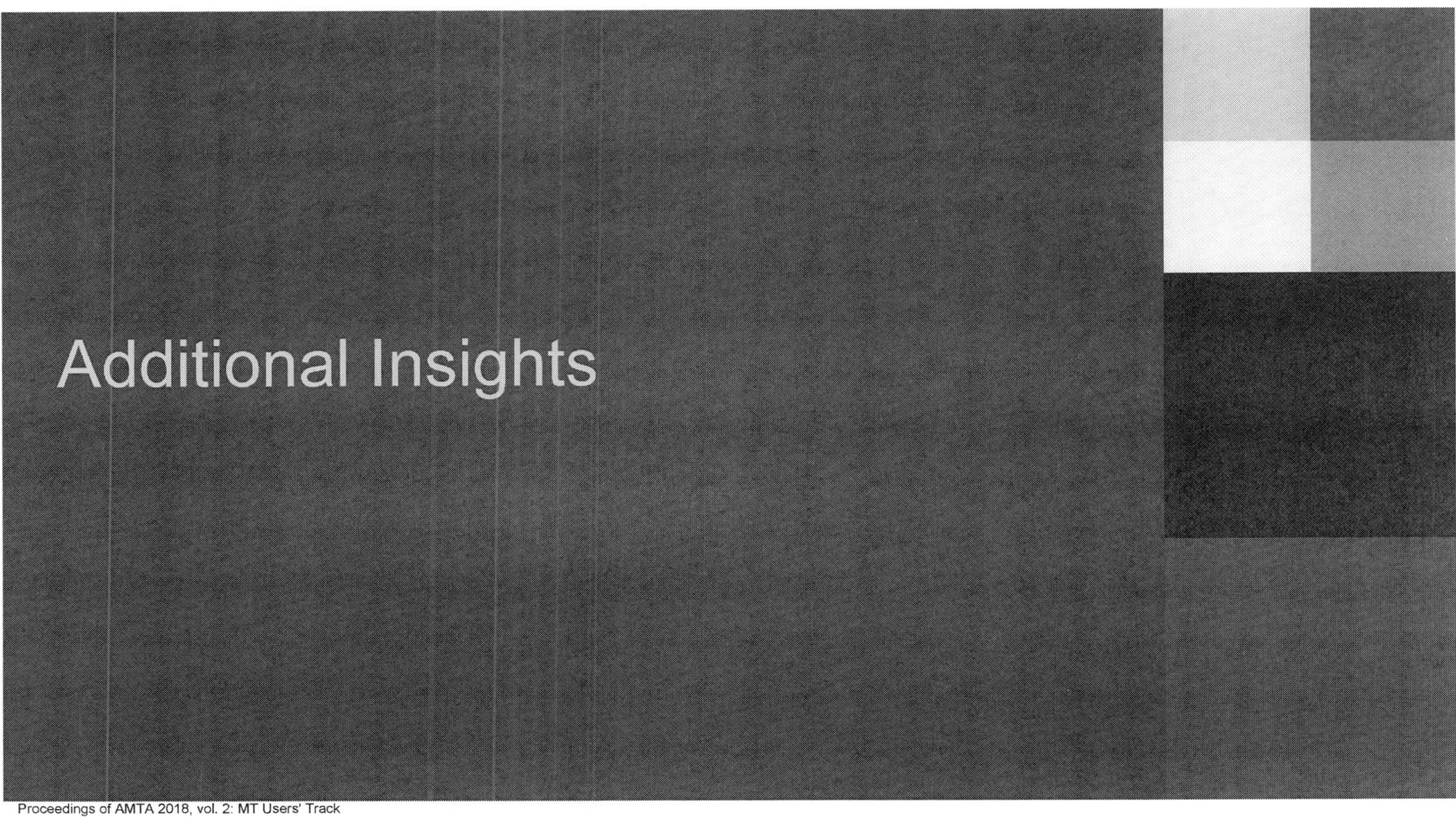
Additional Insights

Correlation 1: Outliers in Quality – Edit Distance – Time

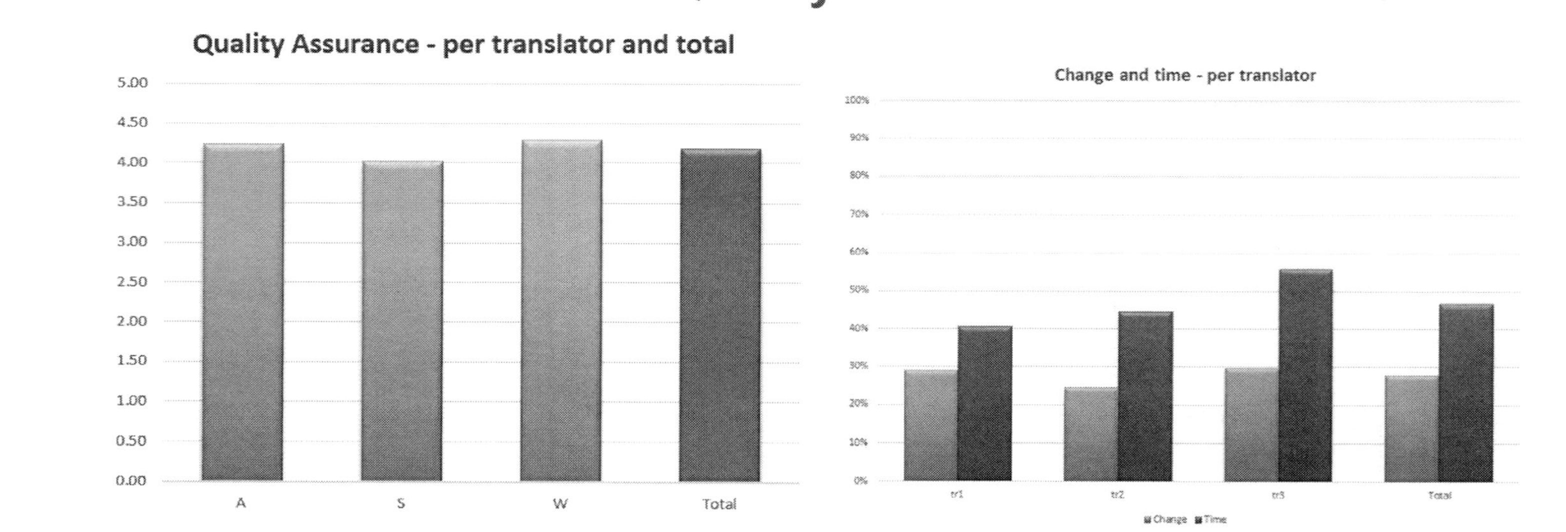

Similar quality, similar edit distance, one outlier in time spent:
Further training on post-editing may be useful

Correlation 2: HE shows BLEU bias against NMT

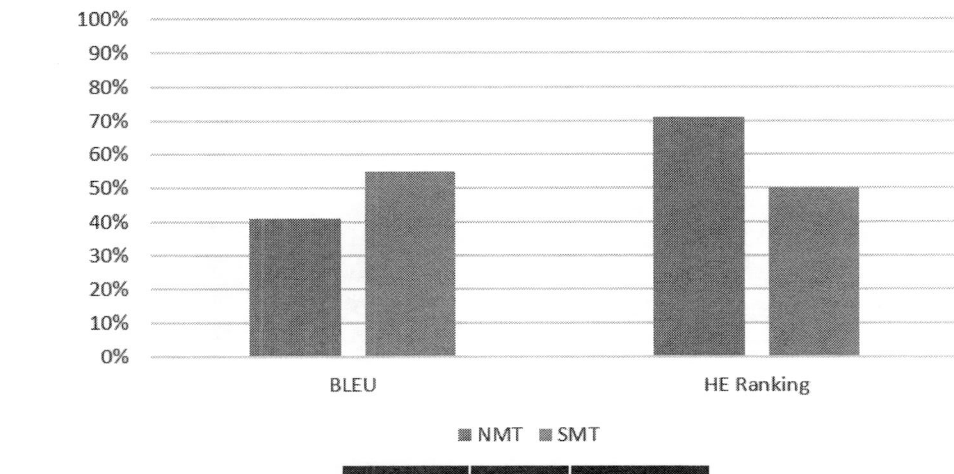

	NMT	SMT
BLEU	41%	55%
HE	71%	50%

ebay

Proceedings of AMTA 2018, vol. 2: MT Users' Track

Feedback from Participating Linguists

We surveyed all 4 linguists
involved in the pilot:

Lessons learned:

- Ensure good communication:
    - Initial presentation with high-level goals
    - For every stage, clear statement of goals and expectations
    - Clearly defined key terms (BLEU, ranking, rating, A/B test…)

- Provide sufficient context for HT/PE (no random strings, enough strings before and after)

- Minimize the number of variables: Use simple tools and basic resources (drop TM, use basic instructions)

ebay

Proceedings of AMTA 2018, vol. 2: MT Users' Track

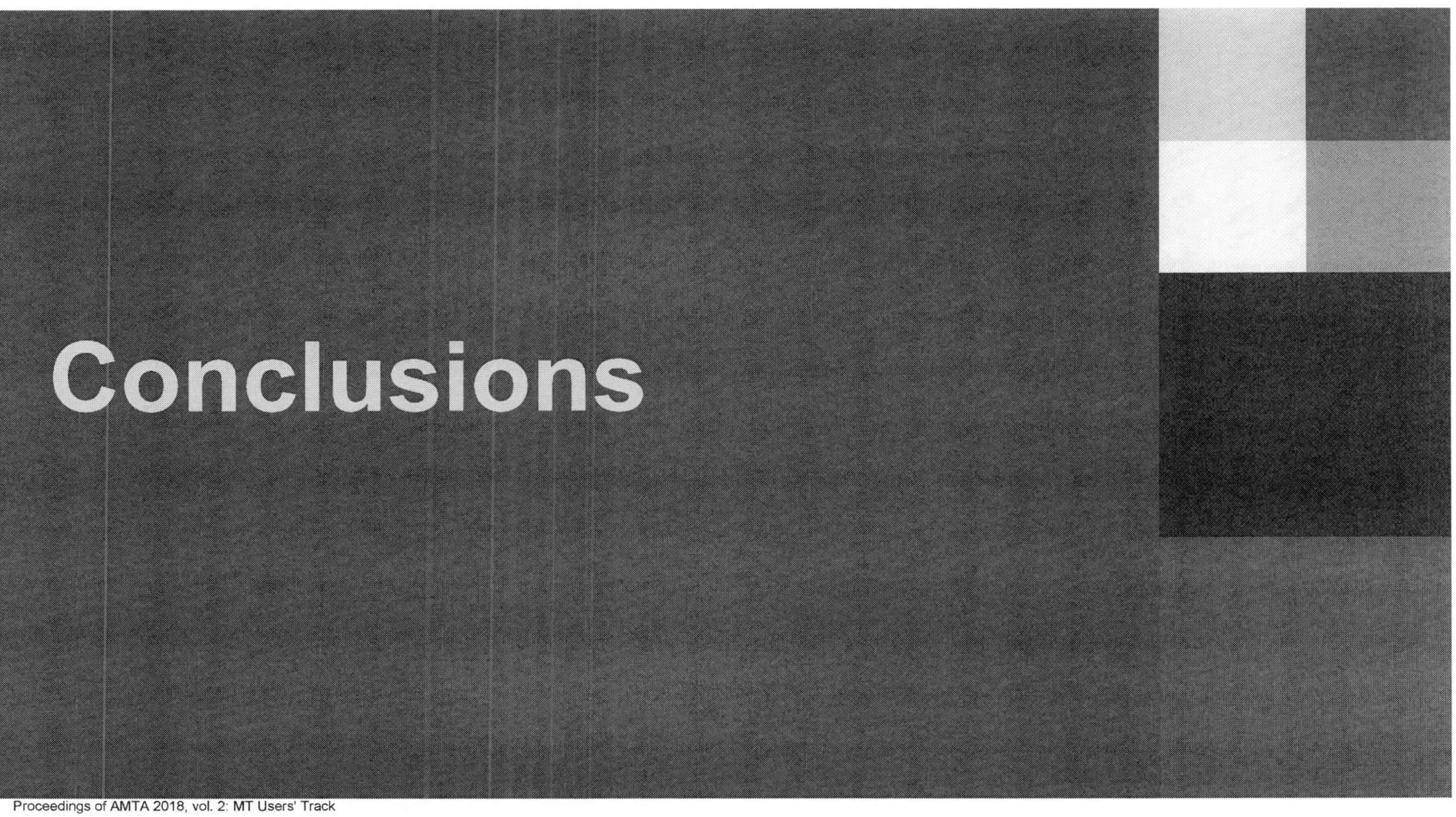

Conclusions

What We Found:

PILOT GOAL

Which is the best engine?
- For the final user: **NMT**
  For the post-editor/vendor: **NMT**

RESEARCH GOALS

- Is BLEU equally reliable for SMT and NMT? **NO**

- Is there a difference between perceived quality and PE effort? **YES**
- Segment length – HE quality:
  Does length affect adequacy/fluency **YES**
  Does NMT and SMT quality vary per segment length **YES**

ORGANIZATIONAL GOALS

- Which are the best roles for each of the stakeholders?
  - **MT Vendor**: Engine background support
  - **eBay MTLS**: engine creation, data curation, supporting/training LS for these roles
  - **eBay regular LS** (for now): quality evaluation

ebay

37

Proceedings of AMTA 2018, vol. 2: MT Users' Track

Questions?

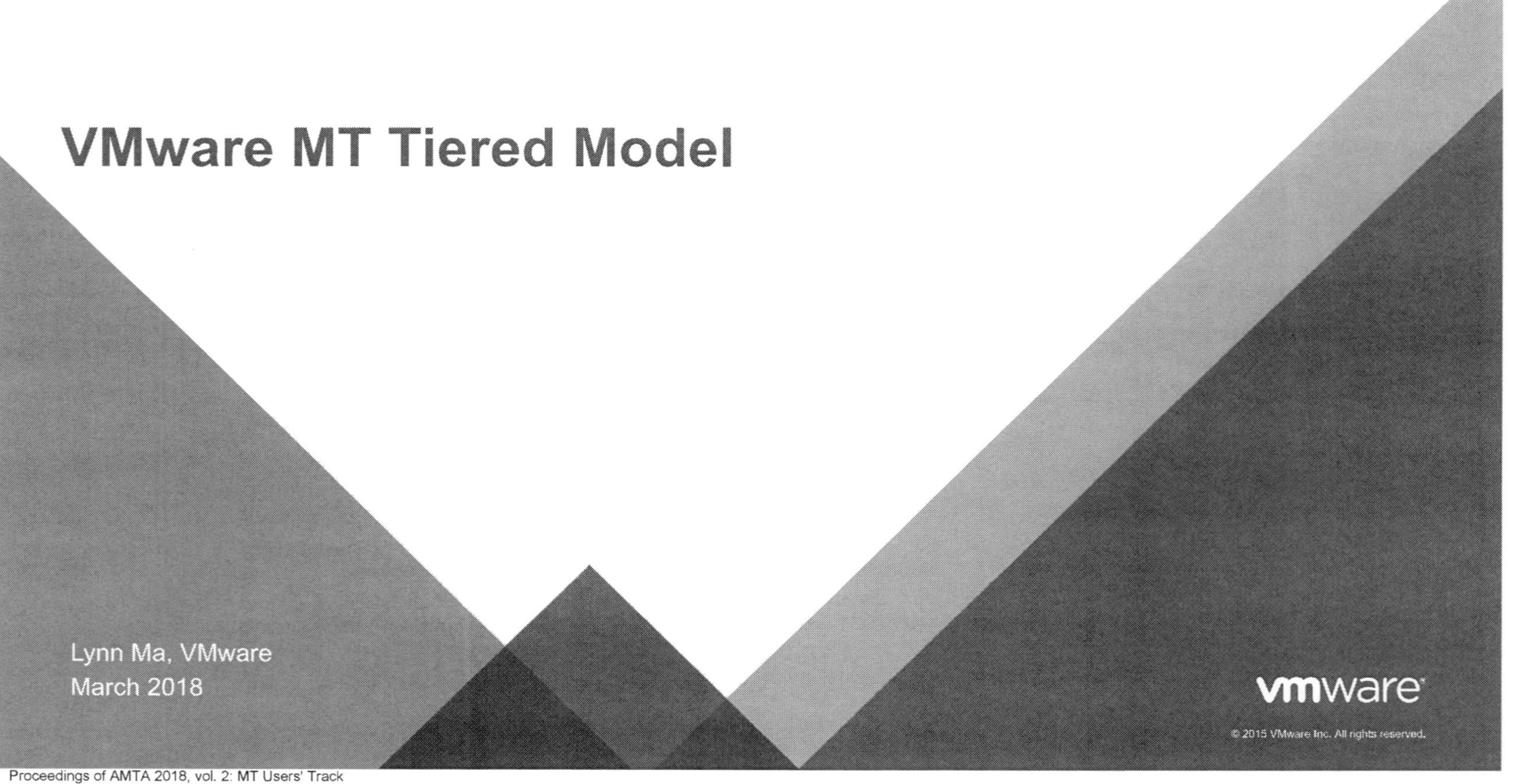

VMware MT Tiered Model
Lynn Ma, VMware
March 2018
vmware
© 2015 VMware Inc. All rights reserved.

Agenda

1   Where We Are with MT

2   MT Tiered Model Introduction

3   MT Tiered Model 1st Pilot

vmware·

2

Proceedings of AMTA 2018, vol. 2: MT Users' Track

Where We Are with MT

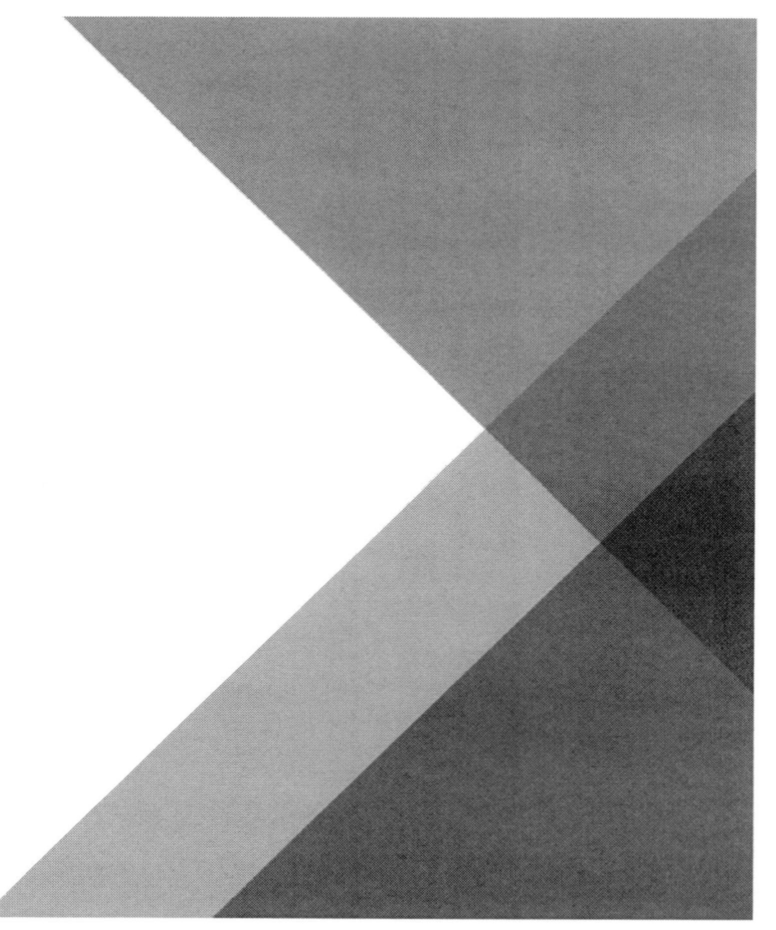

vmware®

Proceedings of AMTA 2018, vol. 2: MT Users' Track

Where We Are with MT

vmware®

CONFIDENTIAL

4

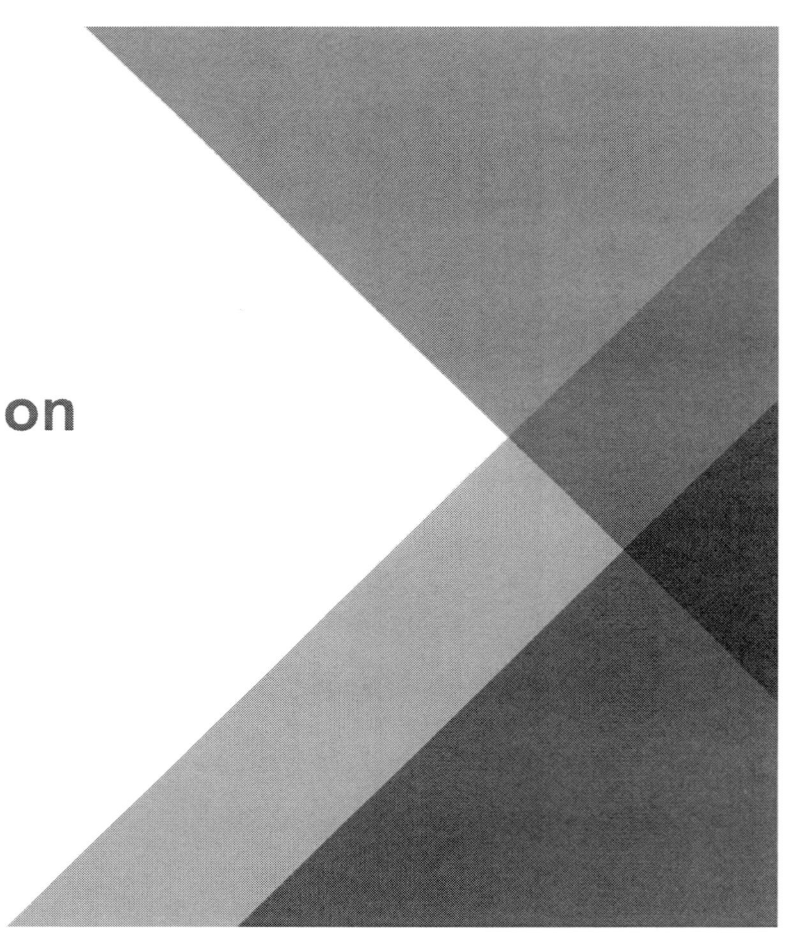

MT Tiered Model Introduction

What is MT Tiered Model

For different languages and content types, apply different Machine Translation + Post Editing strategy, to get expected quality with reasonable cost and time saving.

vmware

6

Tiered Language Structure

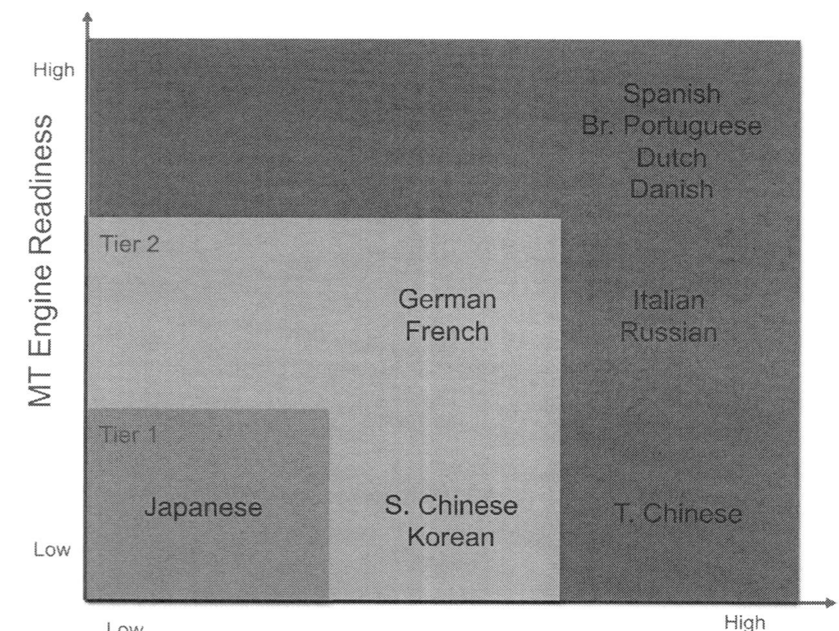

Notes:
- With trained SMT based on MS Hub
- May change after customized NMT in production

vmware

7

Language Tiers and XPE

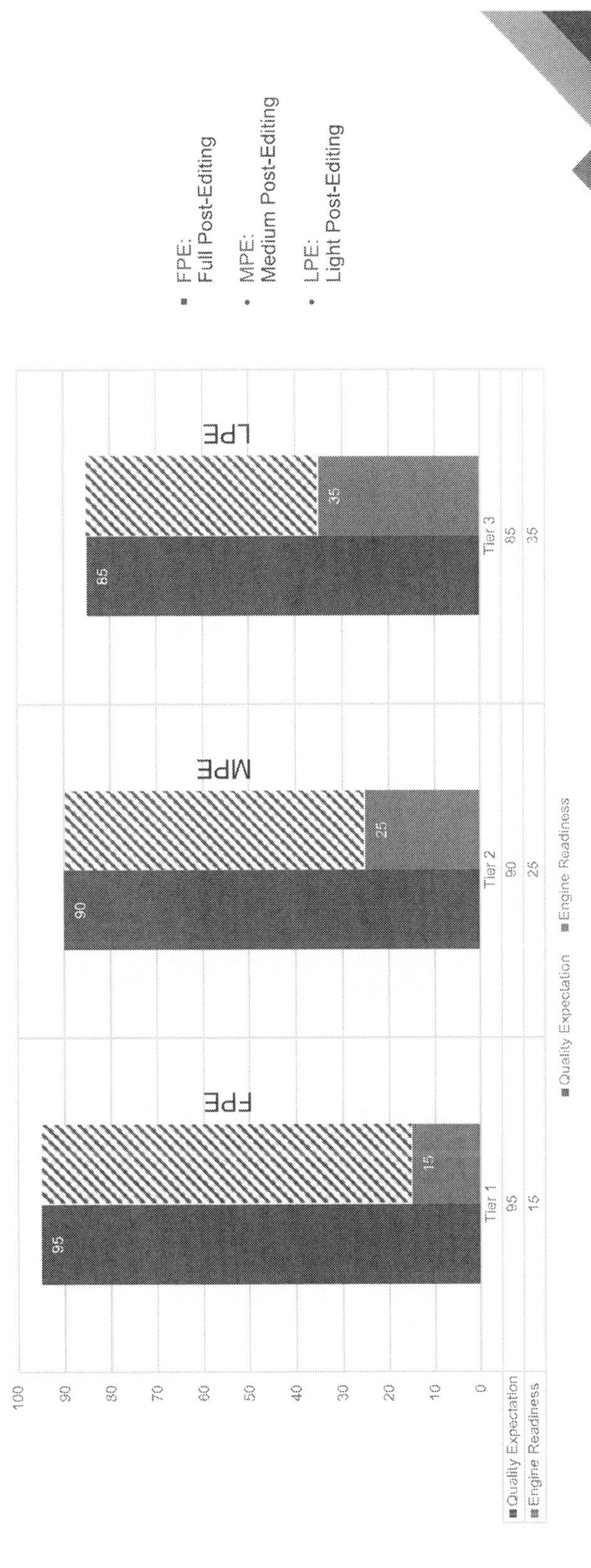

XPE Definitions

Light Post-Editing (LPE)

Accuracy –
- Semantically correct translation
- No mistranslation and ambiguous translation

Terminology –
- Correctly translate per industry practices
- Follow VMware "Do Not Translate" list
- Keep key terminology consistent

Linguistic –
- No critical grammar issues
- No critical spelling and punctuation issues

Style –
- Basic style applied to ensure the understandable meaning
- No offensive, inappropriate or culturally unacceptable content
- Keep any coding pieces correct
- Keep file format work well

Medium Post-Editing (MPE)

Accuracy –
- Accurate translation
- No mistranslation and ambiguous translation

Terminology –
- Translate key terminology per VMware product glossary
- Follow VMware "Do Not Translate" list
- Keep key terminology consistent
- UIs in documentation match with real UIs

Linguistic –
- Grammarly correct
- No critical spelling and punctuation issues

Style –
- Clean style and formatting per industry practices
- No offensive, inappropriate or culturally unacceptable content
- Keep coding pieces correct
- Keep file format work well

Full Post-Editing (FPE)

Accuracy –
- Accurate translation
- No mistranslation and ambiguous translation

Terminology –
- Translate all terminology per VMware product glossary
- Follow VMware "Do Not Translate" list
- Keep all terminology consistent
- UIs in documentation match with real UIs

Linguistic –
- Grammarly correct
- Correct spelling and punctuation

Style –
- Compliance with company style guide
- No offensive, inappropriate or culturally unacceptable content
- Keep coding pieces correct
- Keep file format work well

vmware

Proceedings of AMTA 2018, vol. 2: MT Users' Track

MT Tiered Model 1st Pilot

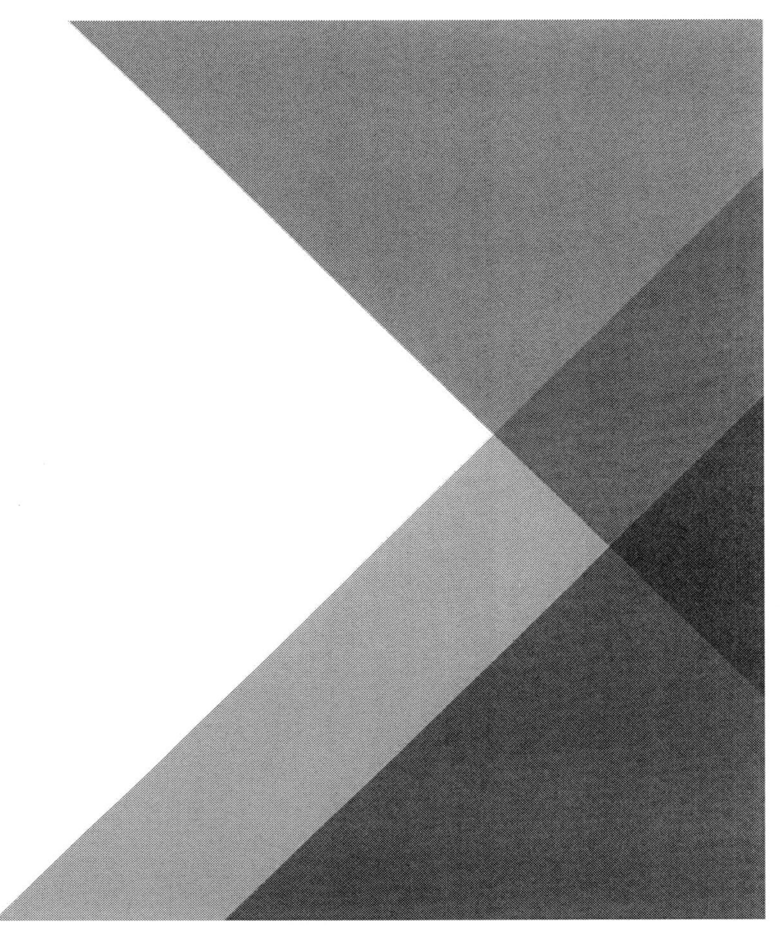

vmware

Proceedings of AMTA 2018, vol. 2: MT Users' Track

1st Pilot

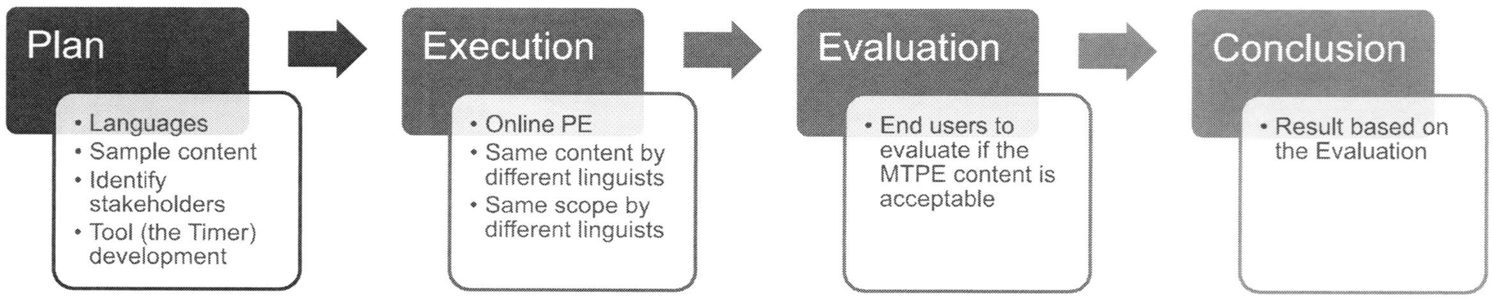
Plan
• Languages
• Sample content
• Identify stakeholders
• Tool (the Timer) development
Execution
• Online PE
• Same content by different linguists
• Same scope by different linguists
Evaluation
• End users to evaluate if the MTPE content is acceptable
Conclusion
• Result based on the Evaluation

vmware

CONFIDENTIAL 11

Tool: the Timer

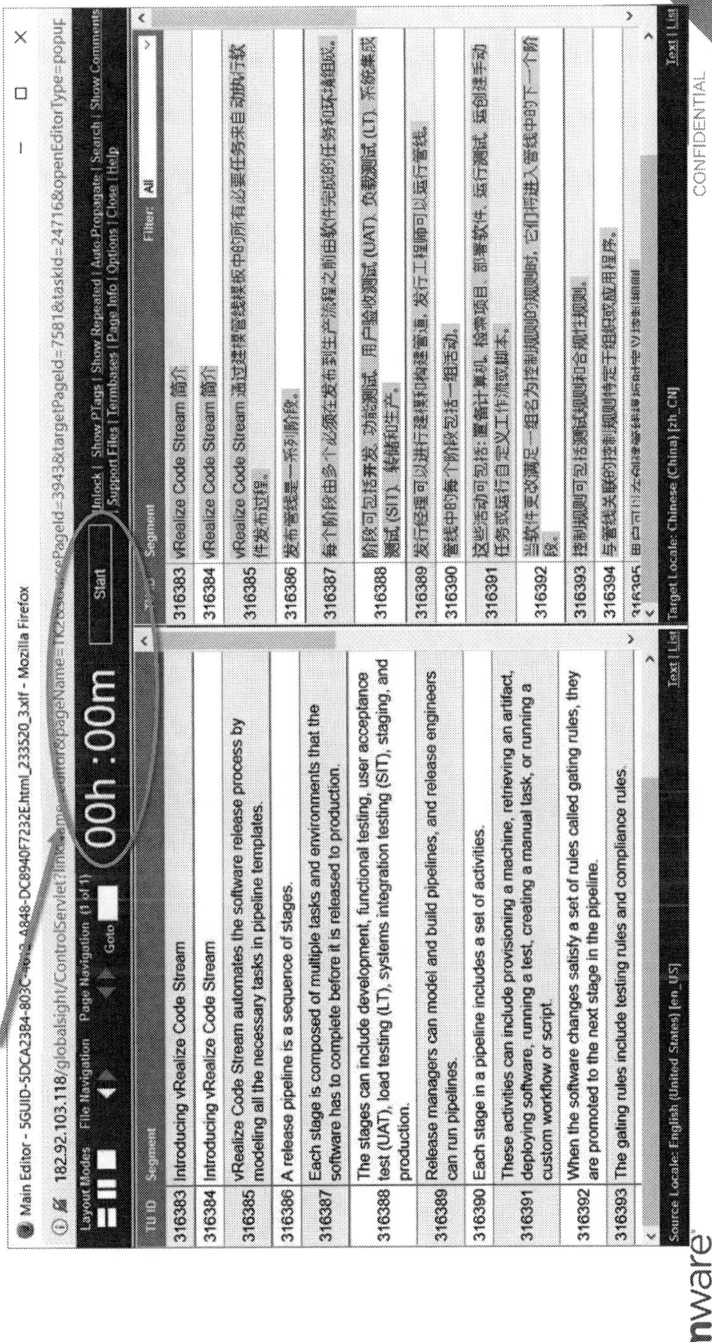

vmware

Productivity Gain Result

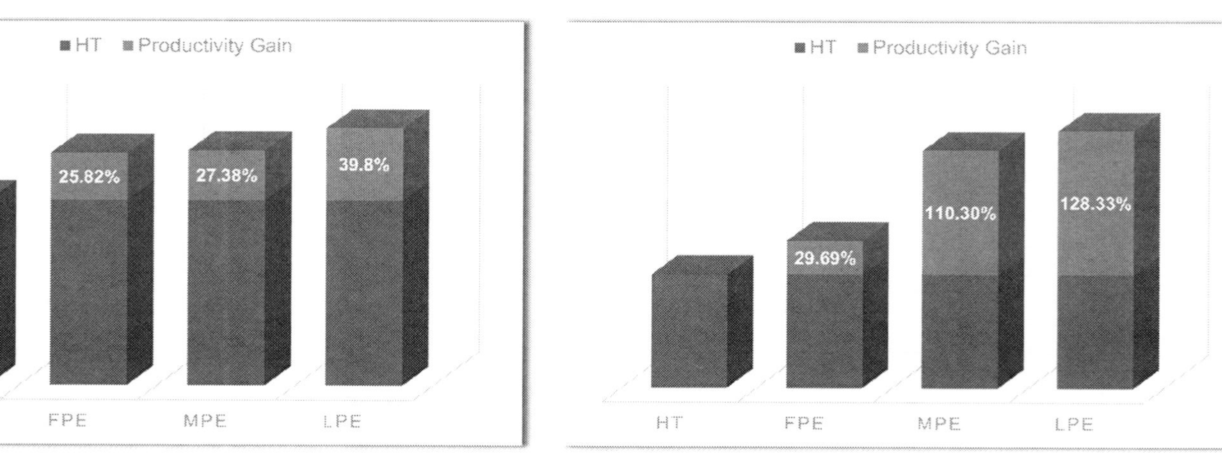

vmware

13

Evaluation Result from End Users

Simplified Chinese

Spanish

vmware

14

Next Steps

- Use MPE in Simplified Chinese – start from the lowest page-view pages.
- Re-evaluate the quality expectation and LPE guideline for Spanish.
- Evolve the XPE guidelines per language.
- Further develop the productivity tool for continuous tracking.
- NMT impact?

vmware

Q&A

vmware®

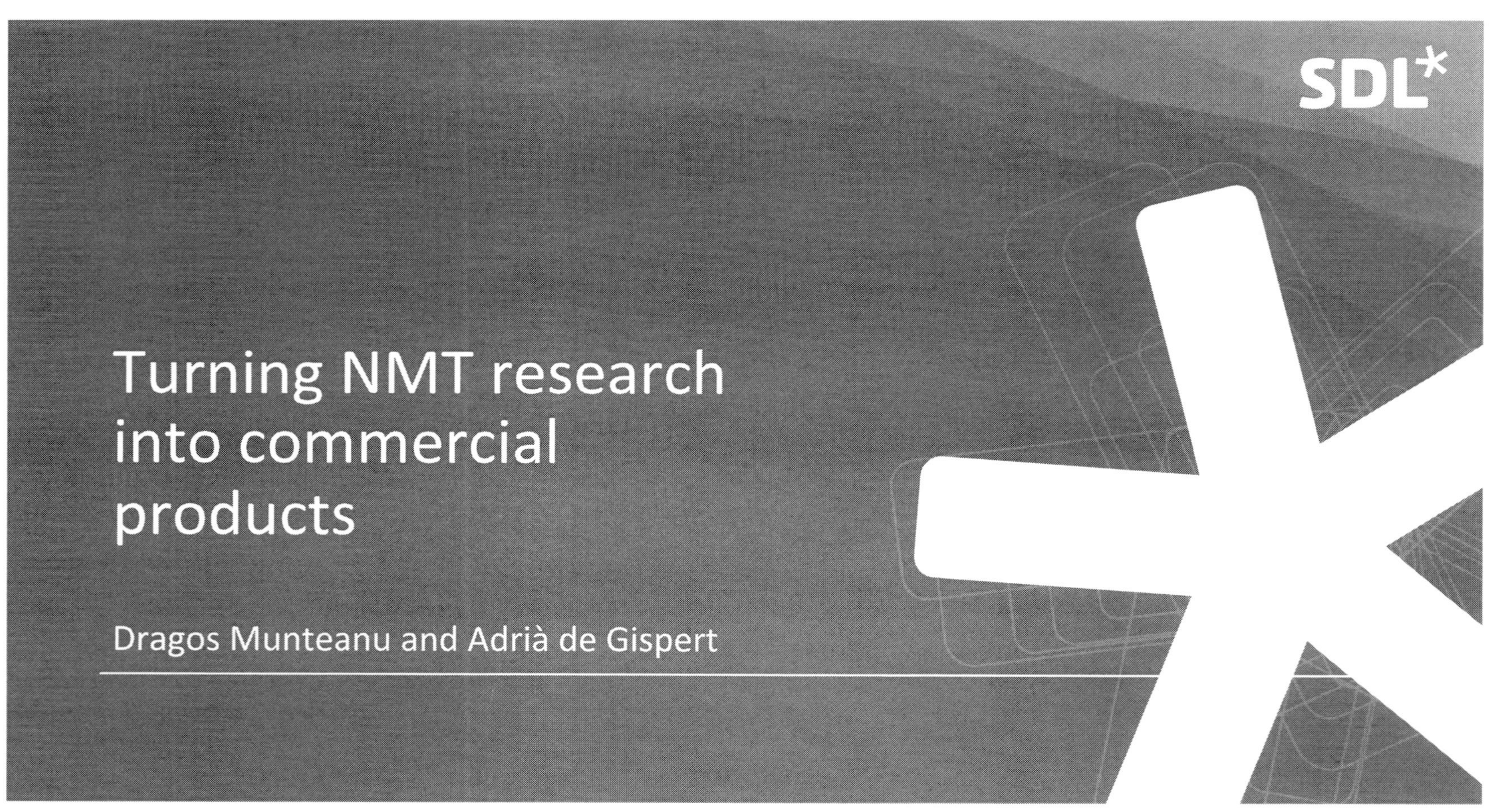

SDL*
Turning NMT research into commercial products
Dragos Munteanu and Adrià de Gispert

SDL*
helping big brands go global
Founded in 1992
3800+ Employees
56 Offices
38 Countries
400 Partners
1500 Enterprise customers
78 of the top 100 global companies work with SDL
+10 BILLION words translated monthly
marketing campaigns
eCommerce
documentation
web, social media
analytics

SDL Research – a long history in MT

- Research labs in Los Angeles (USA) and Cambridge (UK)
- Team members have published +100 on SMT and related tech
  - Bill Byrne, Abdessamad Echihabi, Dragos Munteanu, Gonzalo Iglesias, Eva Hasler, Adrià de Gispert, Steve DeNeefe, Jonathan Graehl, Wes Feely, Ling Tsou…
- Formerly Language Weaver
  - 15 years of leading expertise in SMT
  - major contributions (papers/patents) in phrase-based and string-to-tree MT, automata-based hierarchical MT, quality estimation, tuning, evaluation…
- Strong links with academia (University of Cambridge)
- Summer internships, industrial post-docs

Our mission: Bring MT research results to products

○ We strive to provide our customers:

SDL Secure Enterprise Translation Server

Data Security
- On premises/private cloud
- Used by gov't for 15 years

Quality / Customization
- Neural MT
- Custom MT out-of-the-box

Cost-effective scalability
- Elastic, optimized footprint
- Commodity hardware

Ease of Use / Integration
- deploys In hours
- MS plug-in & REST API

✓ 45 NMT engines currently available

SDL*

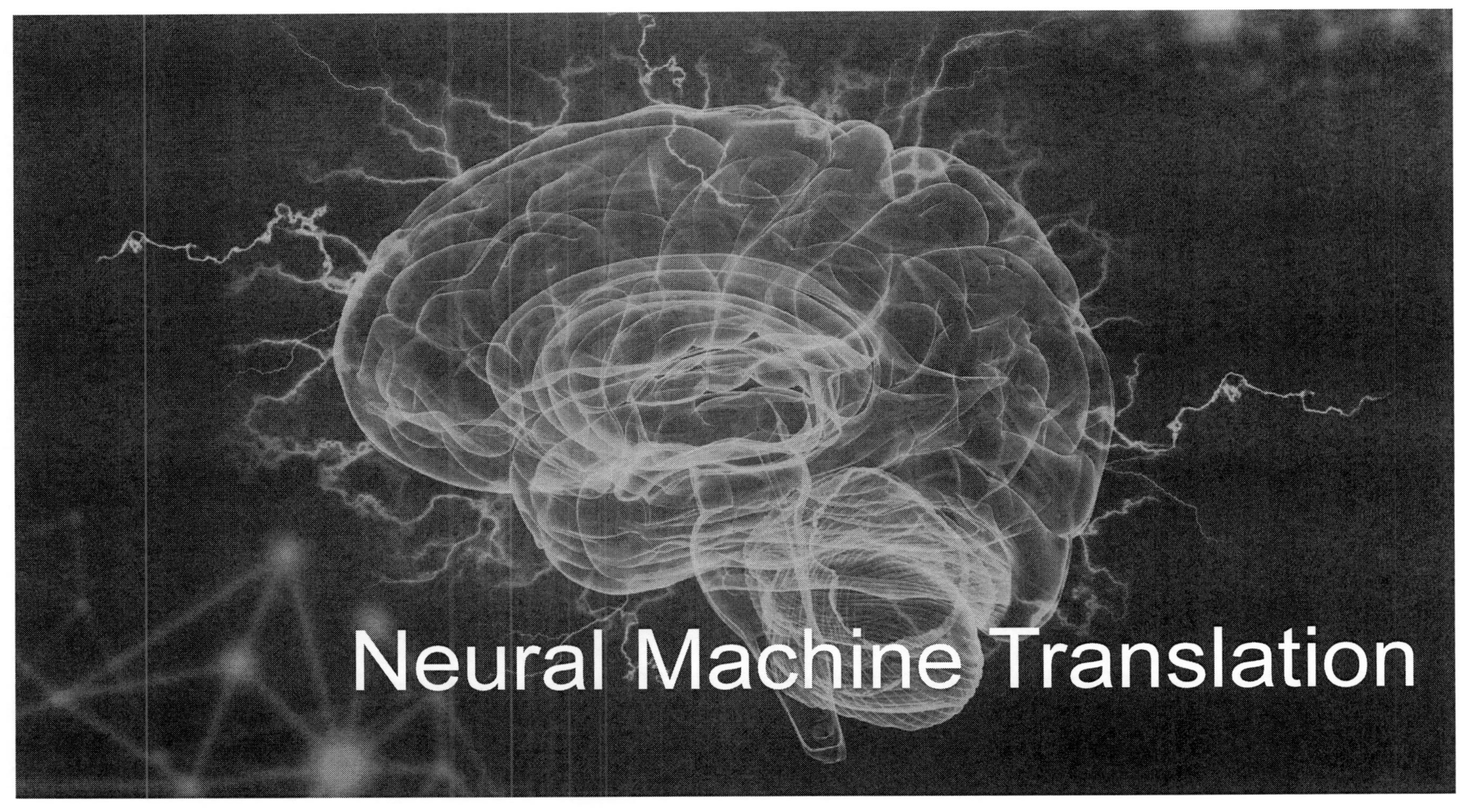
Neural Machine Translation

A paradigm shift

SMT

- Symbolic models
- Independence assumption (separate sub-problems)
- Maximum-likelihood estimation
- CPU-oriented training
- Source-side-guided decoding
- Large databases

Neural MT

- Continuous-space models
- Single end-to-end model
- Discriminative training
- Reliance on GPUs
- Target-side-guided decoding
- Smaller compact models

Better translation models

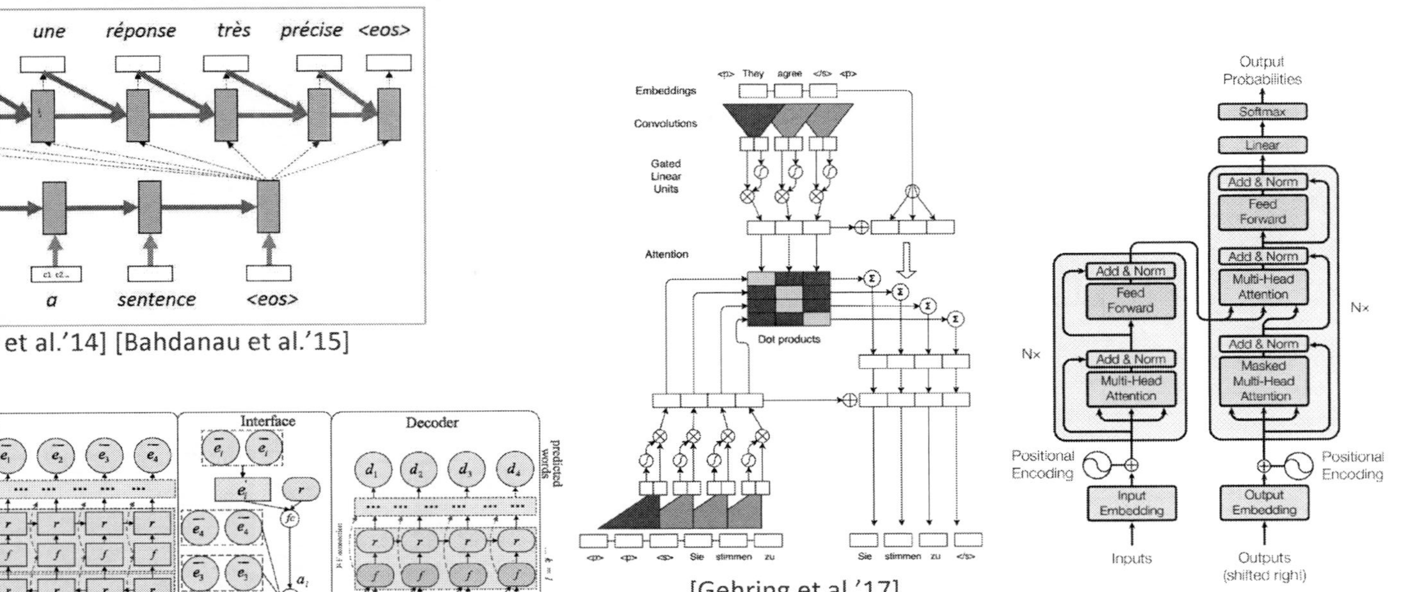

Better BLEU scores

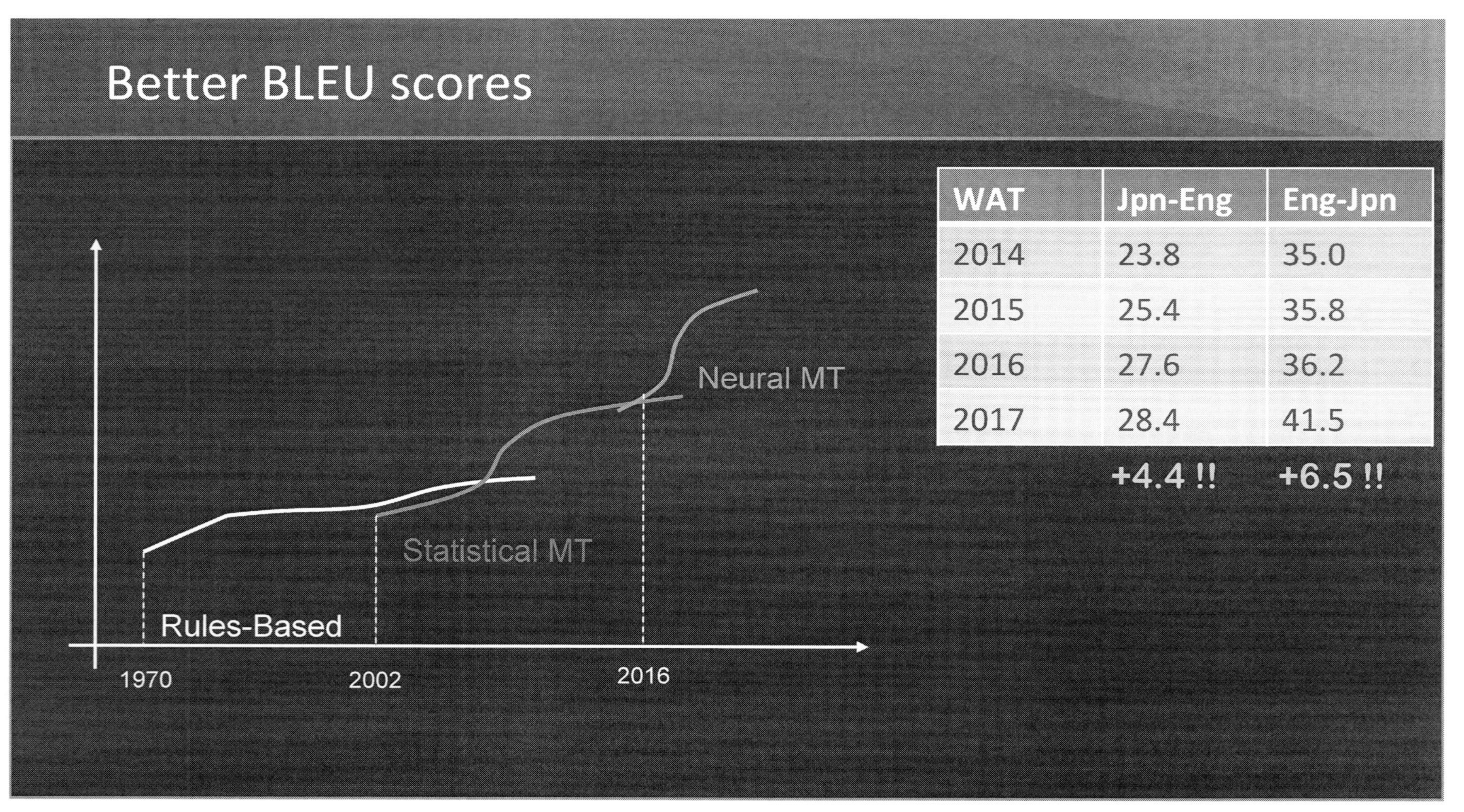

WAT	Jpn-Eng	Eng-Jpn
2014	23.8	35.0
2015	25.4	35.8
2016	27.6	36.2
2017	28.4	41.5
	+4.4 !!	+6.5 !!

COMPARING OUTPUTS
Japanese (auto-detected)
English
Dictionary
None
Settings
Translate
国連難民高等弁務官事務所（UNHCR）は、内戦状態にあるシリアから逃れた難民の数が5百万人を超えたと発表した。
The United Nations High Commissioner for Refugees (UNHCR), the office of civil war to the number of refugees escape from the Syria is exceeded 5 million people and.
Copy as Text
Download as HTML
SMT
Japanese (auto-detected)
English
Dictionary
None
Settings
Translate
国連難民高等弁務官事務所（UNHCR）は、内戦状態にあるシリアから逃れた難民の数が5百万人を超えたと発表した。
The United Nations High Commissioner for Refugees (UNHCR) announced that the number of refugees escaped from Syria in the civil war was over five million people.
Copy as Text
Download as HTML
NMT
© 2017 SDL Plc
SDL

Observable quality improvement

国連難民高等弁務官事務所（UNHCR）は、内戦状態にあるシリアから逃れた難民の数が5百万人を超えたと発表した。

Office of the United Nations High Commissioner for Refugees (UNHCR) is in a state of civil war when the number of refugees who have escaped from Syria have exceeded 5 million people.

The United Nations High Commissioner for Refugees (UNHCR) announced that the number of refugees escaped from Syria in the civil war was over five million people.

✓ 30% improvement over SMT across all our productized engines

But... is it **ALL** that good?

There are situations in which NMT fails

- When it fails, it fails **spectacularly**
  - unrelated fluent text
  - repetitions, neurobabble…
- MT user/customer expectations
  - "MT is not supposed to do this" !!!?!
  - "Can it support the features I need" ???

SDL*

Over-generation and 'neurobabble'

There was no clear correlation between the measured mass density and the measured mass density, and neither experiment A or B.

The company will pay approximately EUR 600 million in fines, and the U.S. Department of Justice (SEC) to pay for approximately EUR 600 million, and the U.S. Department of Justice and the Justice Department of Justice (SEC) to reduce the amount of internal control of the board of directors of the board of directors of the board of directors...

SDL*

Over-generation and 'neurobabble'

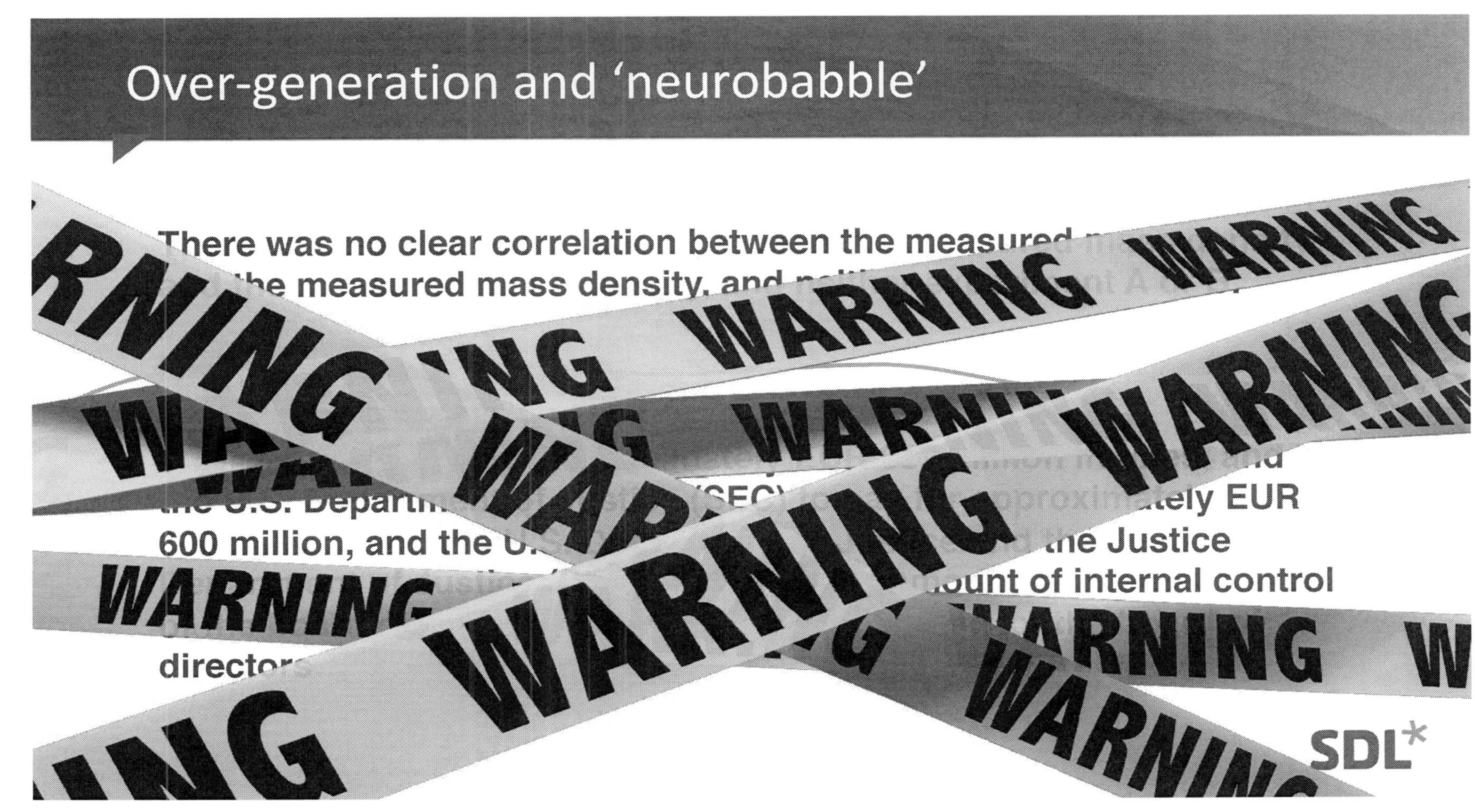

Data is EVEN MORE important

- New NMT models are better learners
  - A better fit to the training data
  - Relevant training data is key
  - Avoid babble and get huge gains!

- Domain adaptation/data selection

[Freitag and Al-Onaizan'16] [Chen et al.'17] [Britz et al.'17]
[Farajian et al.'17] [Van der Wees et al.'17] [Wang et al.'17]
…

SDL*

Adapting neural models

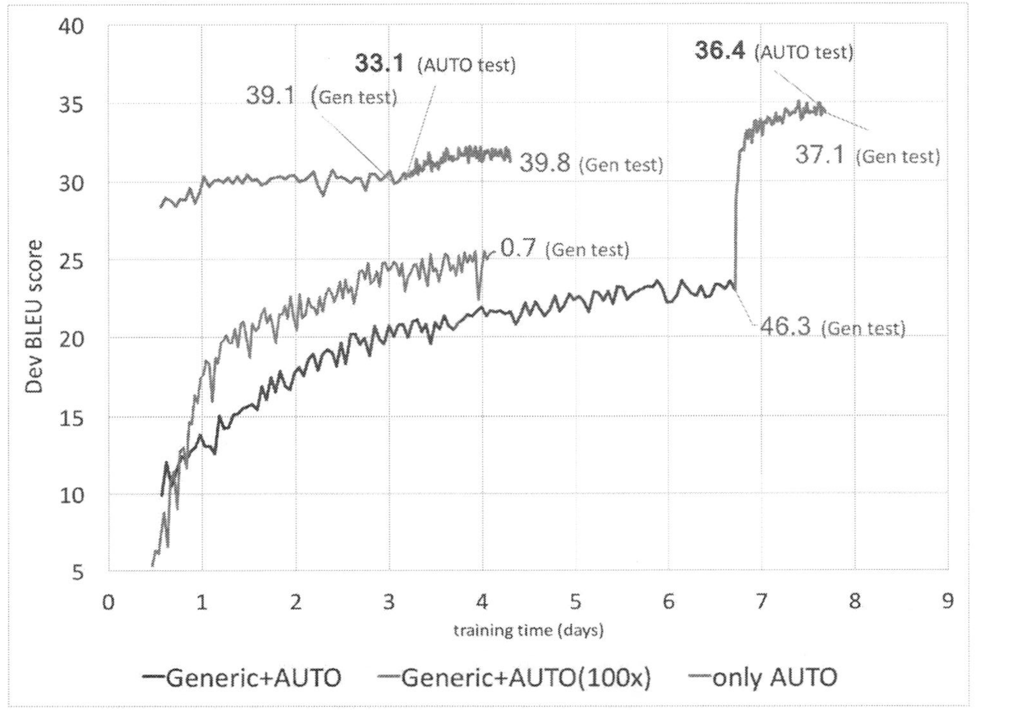

Jpn-Eng corpus	# words
Generic	> 300M
Automotive	< 1M

Major improvements!

Challenge:
- Adapt to customer domain/data with minimal re-training
- Maintain high quality across domains

Lexical selection

- NMT models have freedom to produce any target word
  - Guided by source, not constrained
- SMT engines were good at lexical selection – can we leverage?
  - T-table, n-gram and phrase probabilities, memory-augmented models/search

Input:	I come from <u>Tunisia</u>.
Reference:	チュニジア の 出身です。
	<u>Chunisia</u> no shusshindesu.
	(I'm from Tunisia.)
System:	ノルウェー の 出身です。
	<u>Noruue-</u> no shusshindesu.
	(I'm from Norway.)

[Arthur et al. EMNLP'16]

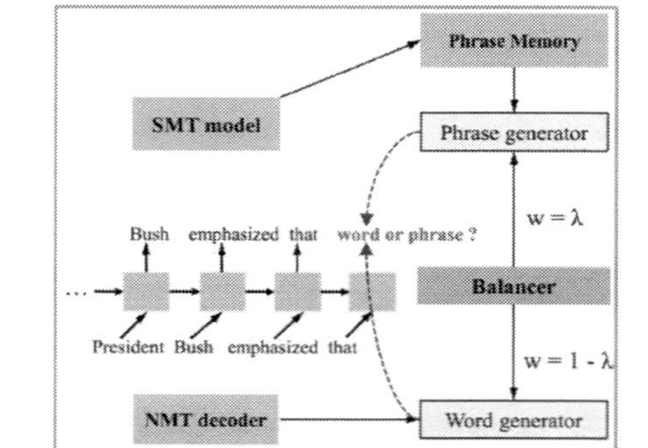

[Wang et al. EMNLP'17]

SDL*

[Arthur et al. EMNLP'16] [Stahlberg et al. EACL'17] [Wang et al.; Dahlmann et al.; Feng et al. EMNLP'17] [Zhang et al. IJCNLP'17] …

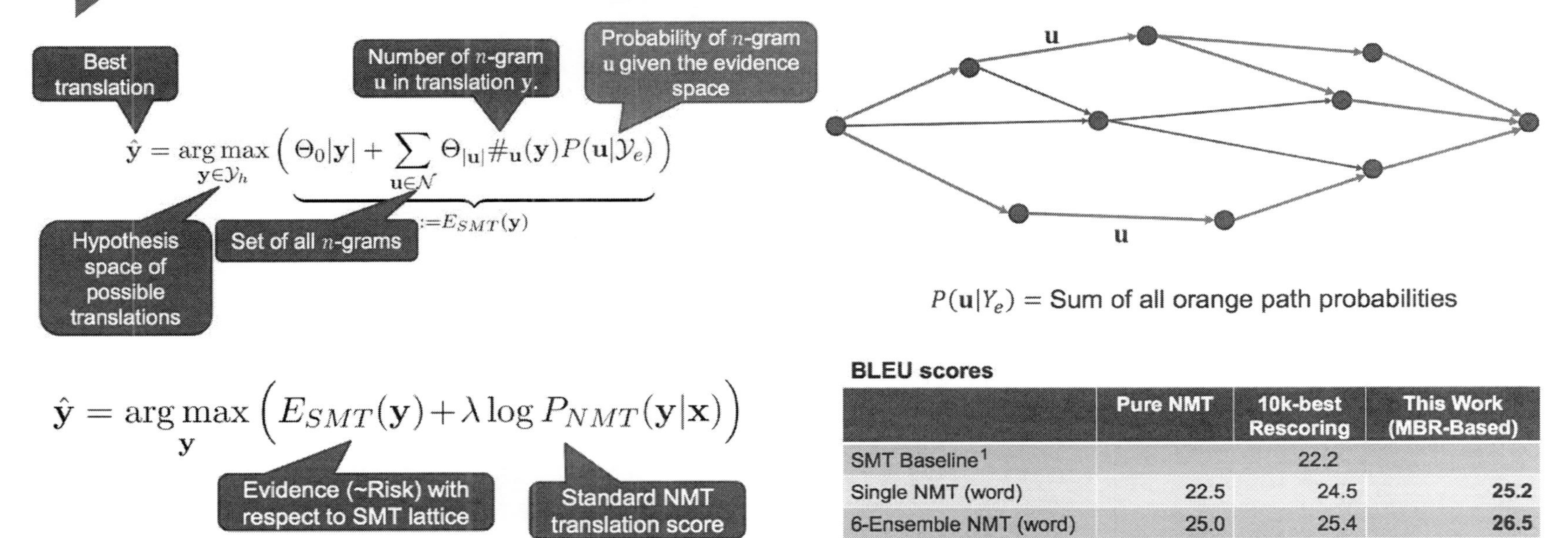

$$\hat{\mathbf{y}} = \underset{\mathbf{y} \in \mathcal{Y}_h}{\arg\max} \left(\Theta_0 |\mathbf{y}| + \sum_{\mathbf{u} \in \mathcal{N}} \Theta_{|\mathbf{u}|} \#_{\mathbf{u}}(\mathbf{y}) P(\mathbf{u}|\mathcal{Y}_e) \right)$$

$$:= E_{SMT}(\mathbf{y})$$

$$\hat{\mathbf{y}} = \underset{\mathbf{y}}{\arg\max} \left(E_{SMT}(\mathbf{y}) + \lambda \log P_{NMT}(\mathbf{y}|\mathbf{x}) \right)$$

$$P(\mathbf{u}|Y_e) = \text{Sum of all orange path probabilities}$$

BLEU scores

	Pure NMT	10k-best Rescoring	This Work (MBR-Based)
SMT Baseline[1]		22.2	
Single NMT (word)	22.5	24.5	**25.2**
6-Ensemble NMT (word)	25.0	25.4	**26.5**
3-Ensemble NMT (BPE)	25.9	25.1	**26.7**

Stahlberg et al. (EACL'17): "Neural Machine Translation by Minimising the Bayes-risk with Respect to Syntactic Translation Lattices"

But... are there guarantees?

- Control is **a must** for commercial success
- One very bad sentence can put off a customer
  - Back-off if needed

- Customers/Users expect certain 'features'
  - Decoding speed, dictionary support, formatting constraints, Adaptive MT, …

SDL*

Dictionary support

> "**Zimra Games continues to innovate with the release next month of Coke Assault 3, which will satisfy the most demanding gamers.**"

English	German
Zimra Games	Zimra Games GmbH
Coke Assault 3	Coke Assault III
…	…

- Translation output **must** translate dictionary matches exactly – constrained search
- Easy for SMT decoders
- NMT beam decoder does not keep an alignment between source and target words

[Anderson et al. EMNLP'17]
[Hokamp & Liu ACL'17]
[Chatterjee et al. WMT'17]

Dictionary support

Constrained search

- Build a finite-state acceptor with the target-side constraints
- Keep one separate stack per each acceptor state
- Output only hypotheses from the final acceptor state

➢ Constraints can be words or phrases

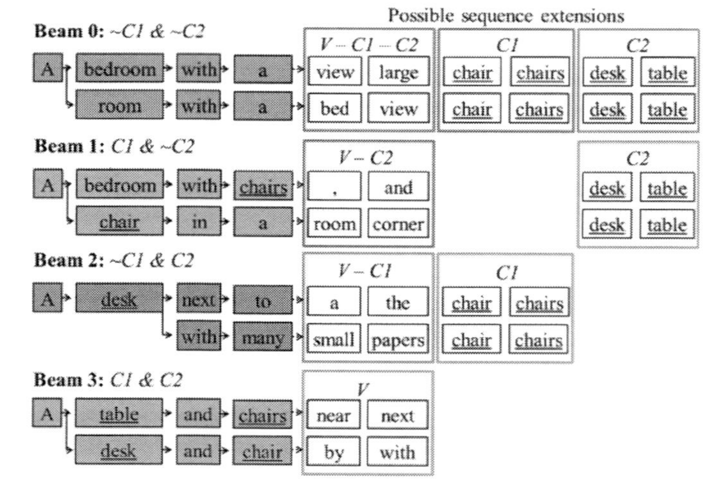

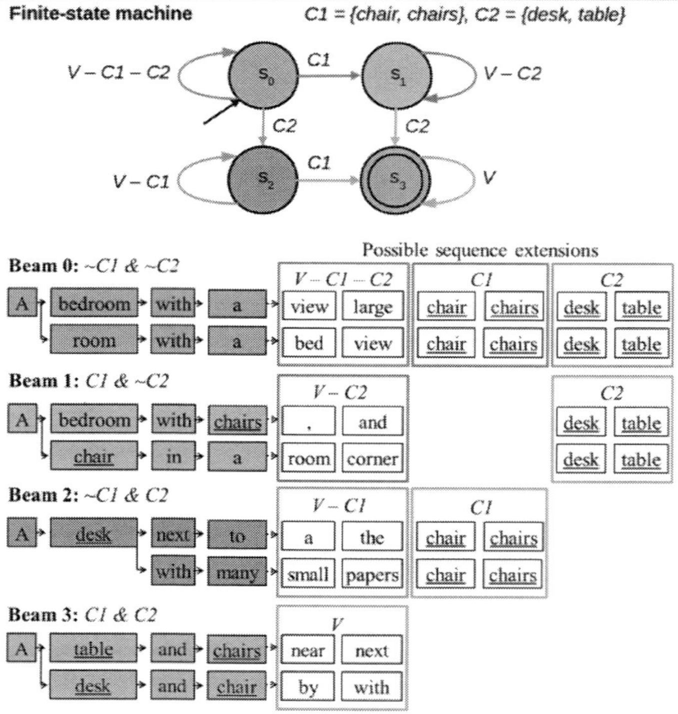

[Anderson et al. EMNLP'17]

SDL*

Dictionary support

Challenges

- Computational complexity grows exponentially with the number of constraints
  - order is unknown
- Nothing prevents repeated decoding:

> "Zimra Games GmbH setzt mit dem Veröffentlichung auf Coke Assault III im nächsten Monat der Angriff ...

SDL*

Entity constraints

"<B>Zimra Games</B> continues to innovate with the release <I>next month</I> of <B>Coke Assault <c=red>3</c></B>, which will satisfy the most demanding gamers."

- Decoder must also respect meta-tags
  - Key to support file formats used by MT users
- NMT model should not break sequential history
- Solutions require model specialization and/or decoding restrictions

Decoding speed

- **MT users are expected to certain translation speeds**
  - Target speed varies, but well above research engines
- **Goal is to provide best quality at desired speed**
  - Speed vs quality trade-off
- **NMT deployment scenarios**
  - CPU only – hand-held devices, …
  - GPU
- **NMT <u>training</u> speed also relevant**

Decoding speed vs quality trade-off (1)

- Model architecture
  - recurrent, convolutional, attentional…
  - number of parameters, layer precomputations…
  - Unfolding and shrinking ensembles

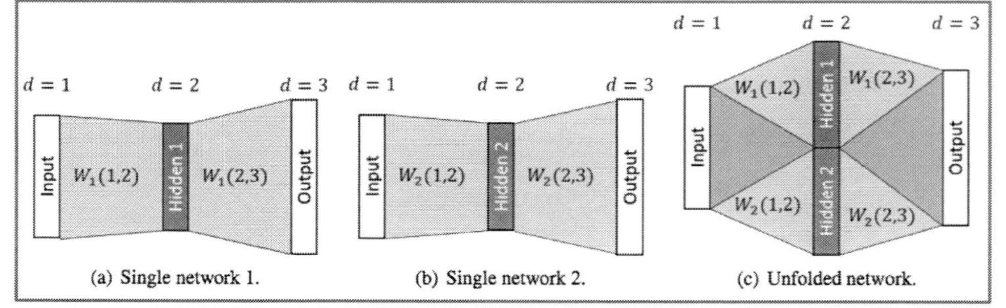

System	Words/Min.		Size	BLEU	
	CPU	GPU	Factor	dev	test
Single	323.4	2993.6	1.00	20.8	23.5
2-Ensemble	163.7	1641.1	2×1.00	22.7	25.2
2-Unfold, shrunk embed.& attention	157.2	2592.2	1.77	22.7	25.1
2-Unfold, shrunk all except maxout	308.3	2961.4	1.05	22.4	25.3

[Stahlberg and Byrne, EMNLP'17]

Stahlberg and Byrne (EMNLP'17): "Unfolding and Shrinking Neural Machine Translation Ensembles"

Decoding speed vs quality trade-off (2)

- **Hardware and Linear Algebra library**
  - Type of GPU card
  - CPU-GPU communication
  - GPU usage
- **Batching**
  - standard in training

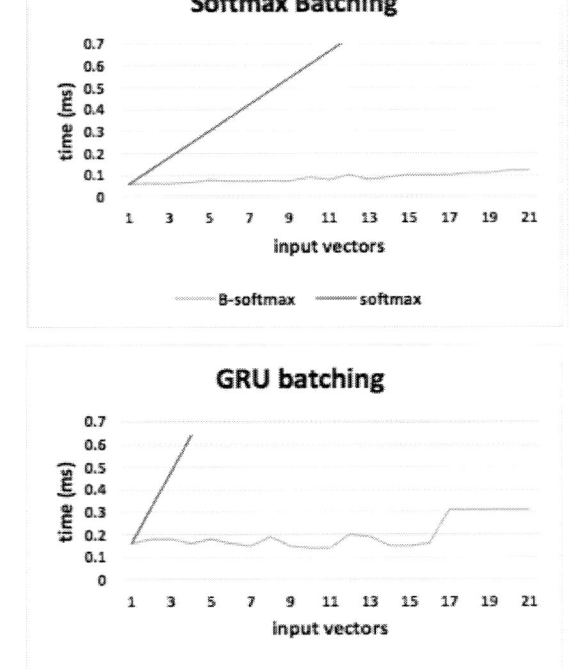

Decoding speed vs quality trade-off (3)

- **Decoding parameters**
  - beam size, early stopping…
- **Reduced vocabulary softmax** (CPU)
- **Weight clipping in training**   [Wu et al.'16] [Devlin, EMNLP'17] …
  - Low-precision inference

SDL*

Thank you for
your attention!
SDL*
Software and Services for Human Understanding
Copyright © 2008-2017 SDL plc. All rights reserved. All company names, brand names, trademarks, service marks, images and logos are the property of their respective owners.
This presentation and its content are SDL confidential unless otherwise specified, and may not be copied, used or distributed except as authorised by SDL.

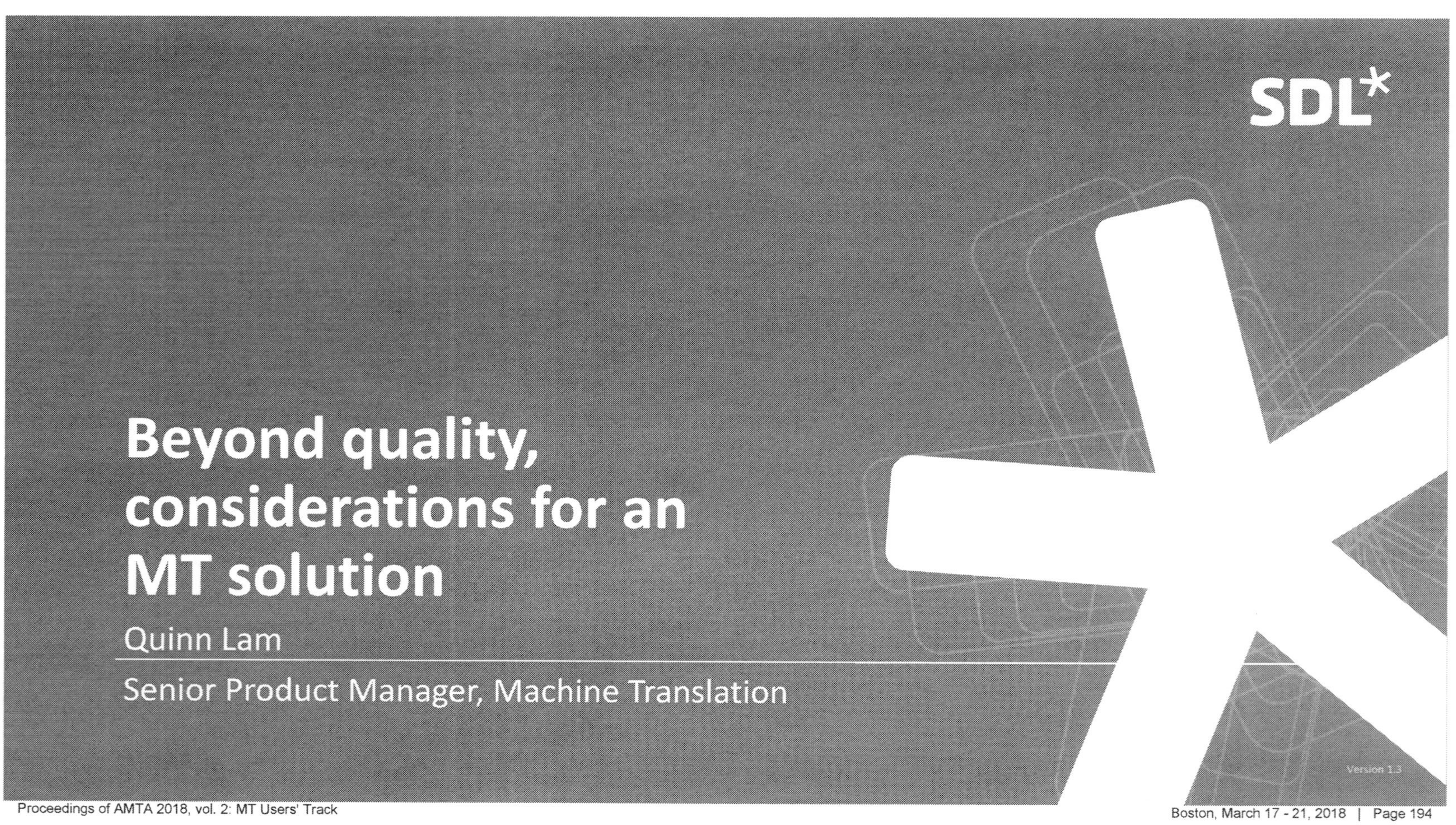
SDL*
Beyond quality,
considerations for an
MT solution
Quinn Lam
Senior Product Manager, Machine Translation
Version 1.3

Characteristics of a production ready MT solution

- **Language coverage**
  - Does it have all the language combination your enterprise need?
- **Input filetype coverage**
  - What are the file types it can take beyond plain text input? Office documents, PDFs, images, etc?
- **InfoSec approved**
  - Will your Information Security team sign-off for enterprise usage? Is your content safe from 3rd party data mining engines?
- **Comprehensive API**
  - Does it have a rich set of features in its API to opens up realms of opportunities for your enterprise applications to become integrated?

- **Out-of-the-box integrations**
  - Does it have plugins for your commonly used business applications?
- **Scalable**
  - Can it easily scale to meet your enterprise translation growth? Can it withstand million to billions of words a day?
- **Cost effective**
  - What does it cost to run the full operation? Are there associated Opex and Capex?
- **Respect user corrections**
  - Can users enforce translation changes in real-time?
- **Enterprise brand aware**
  - Can you enforce corporate terminologies on the translation?

SDL*

Proceedings of AMTA 2018, vol. 2: MT Users' Track

Content drives revenue and is critical to overall customer experience

User generated content is often more important than corporate content and messaging

An Increasing Need to Translate Enterprise Internal Content

SDL

Buy	Build
Lower cost of ownership	Control to create narrowly specialized engines
Faster roll-out to production	Develop in-house expertise
Easily add more languages	Complete assurance in training data privacy
Access to more features	
Higher quality on broad content	
More scalable and stable	
Integration ready	

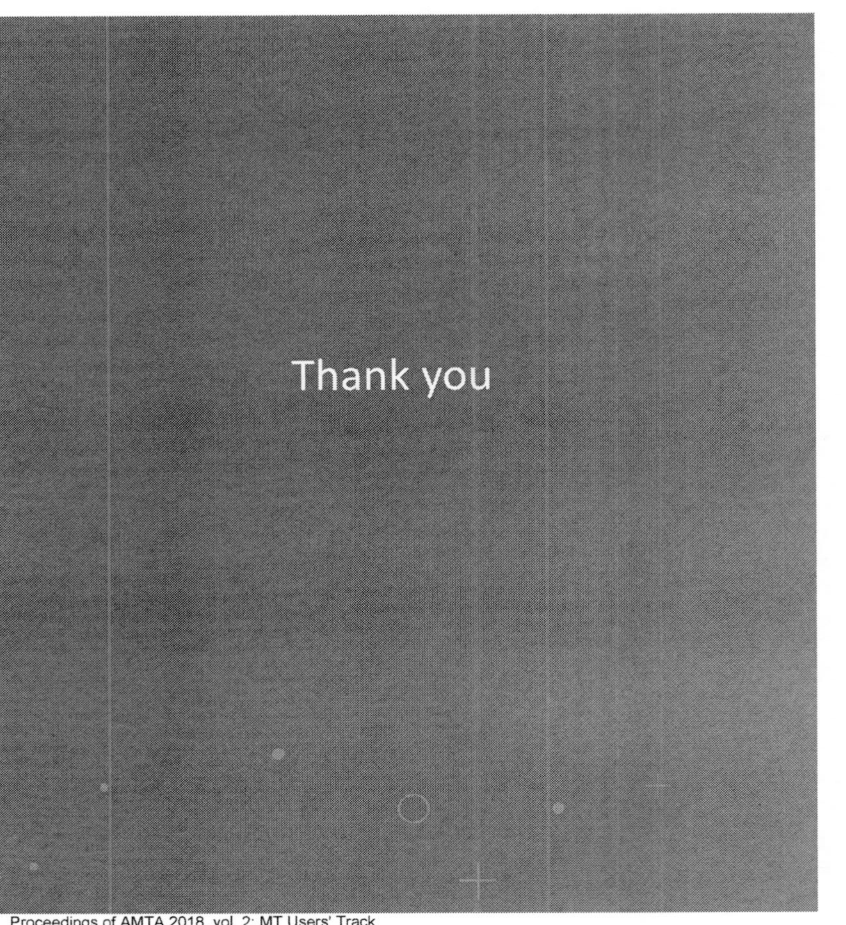

We can help with your Machine Translation Journey!

Contact us at

www.sdl.com/amta

SDL

Towards Less Post-editing

Bill Lafferty, Memsource

Memsource

- Founded in 2010
- Memsource helps global companies translate and manage translations
- Bootstrapped and profitable since 2013
- Based in Prague HQ

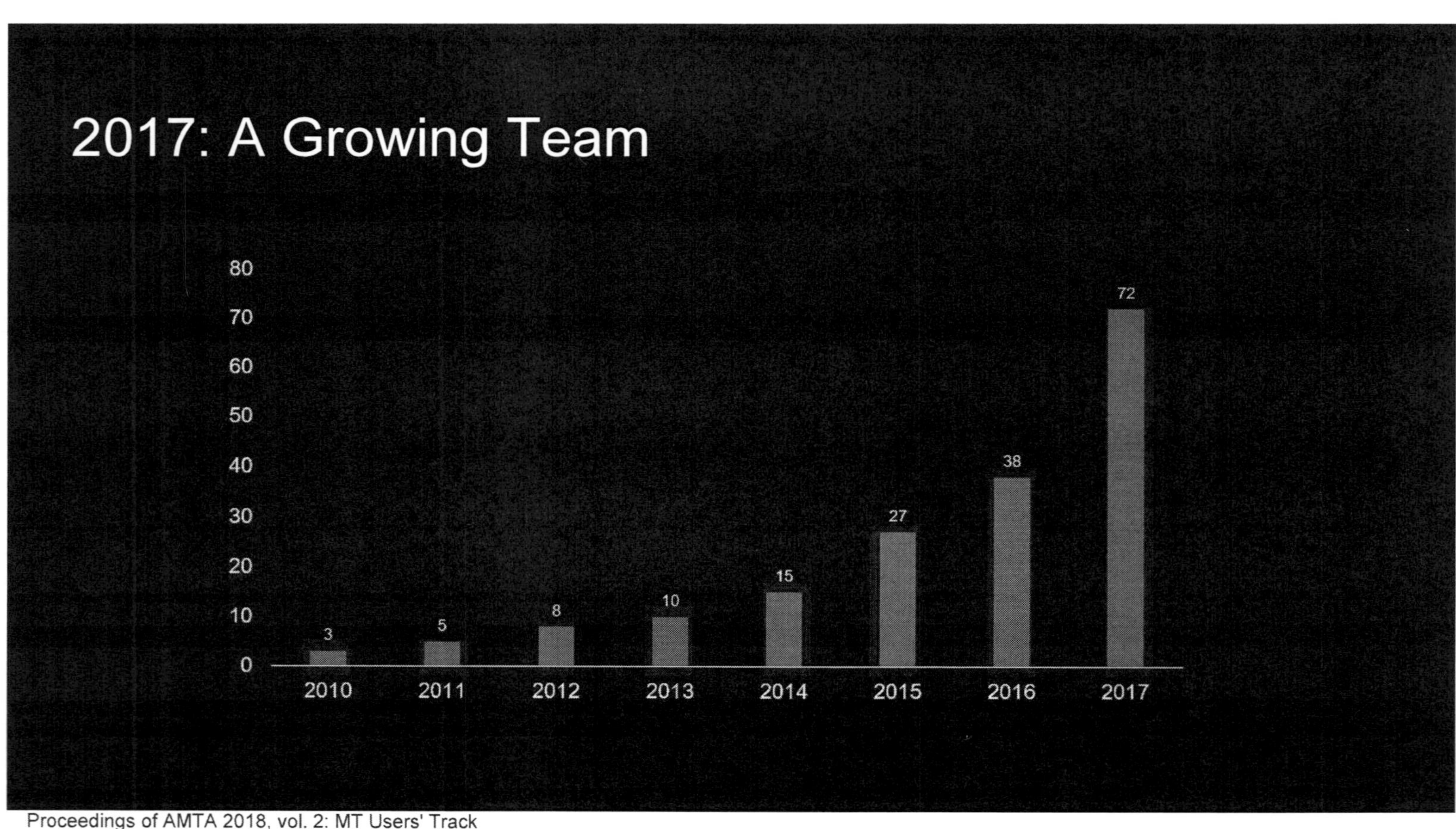

2017: A Growing Team
80
70
60
50
40
30
20
10
0
3
5
8
10
15
27
38
72
2010
2011
2012
2013
2014
2015
2016
2017

24 Billion Words in 2017

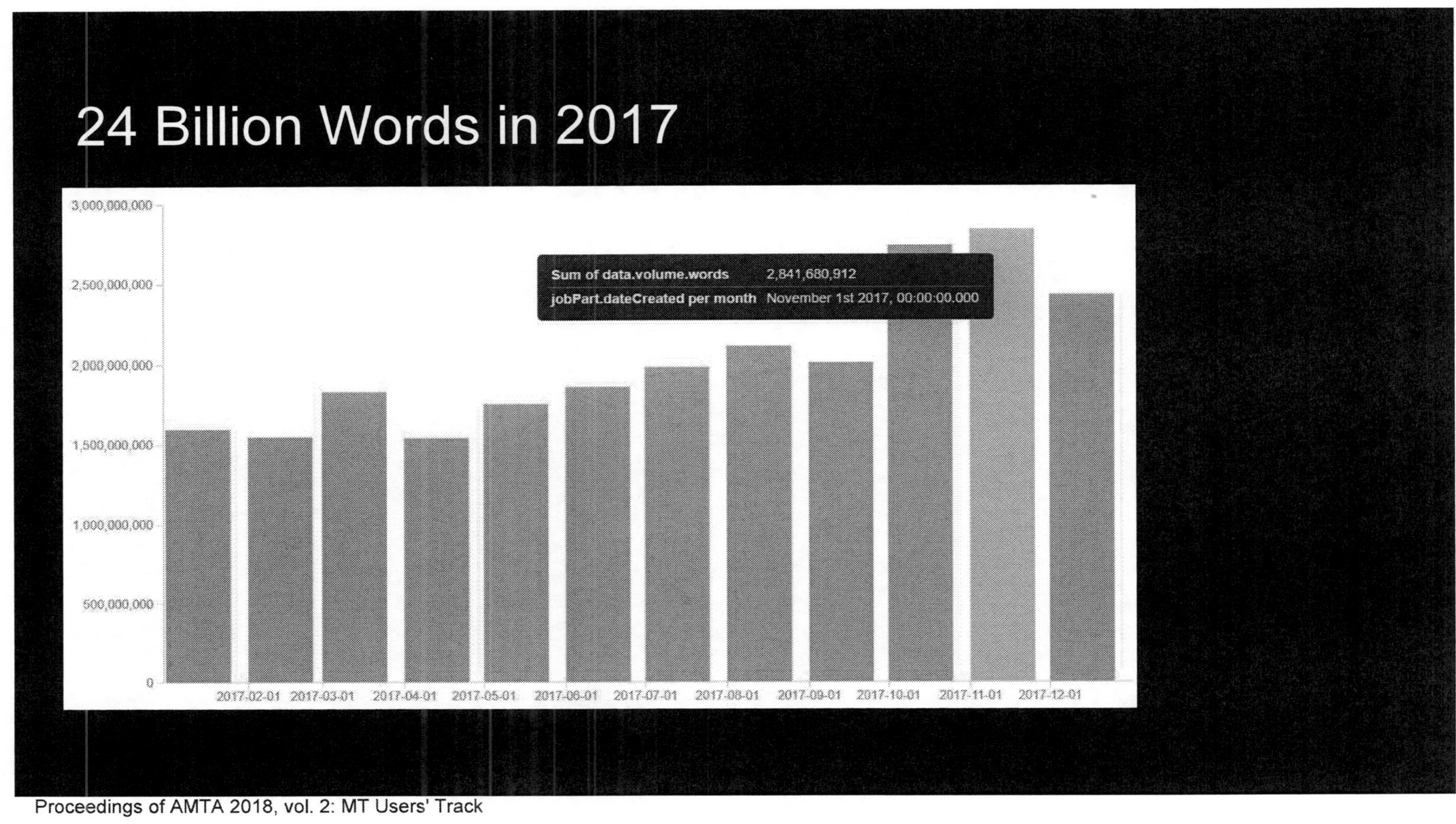

2017 - New AI Team

Back to 2012

- David Canek, Memsource CEO and founder presented at 2012 AMTA conference in San Diego
- Anyone attended? Raise hands
- At that time MT was picking up in the industry and David presented results from a survey Memsource and the GALA association ran among translation providers/LSPs

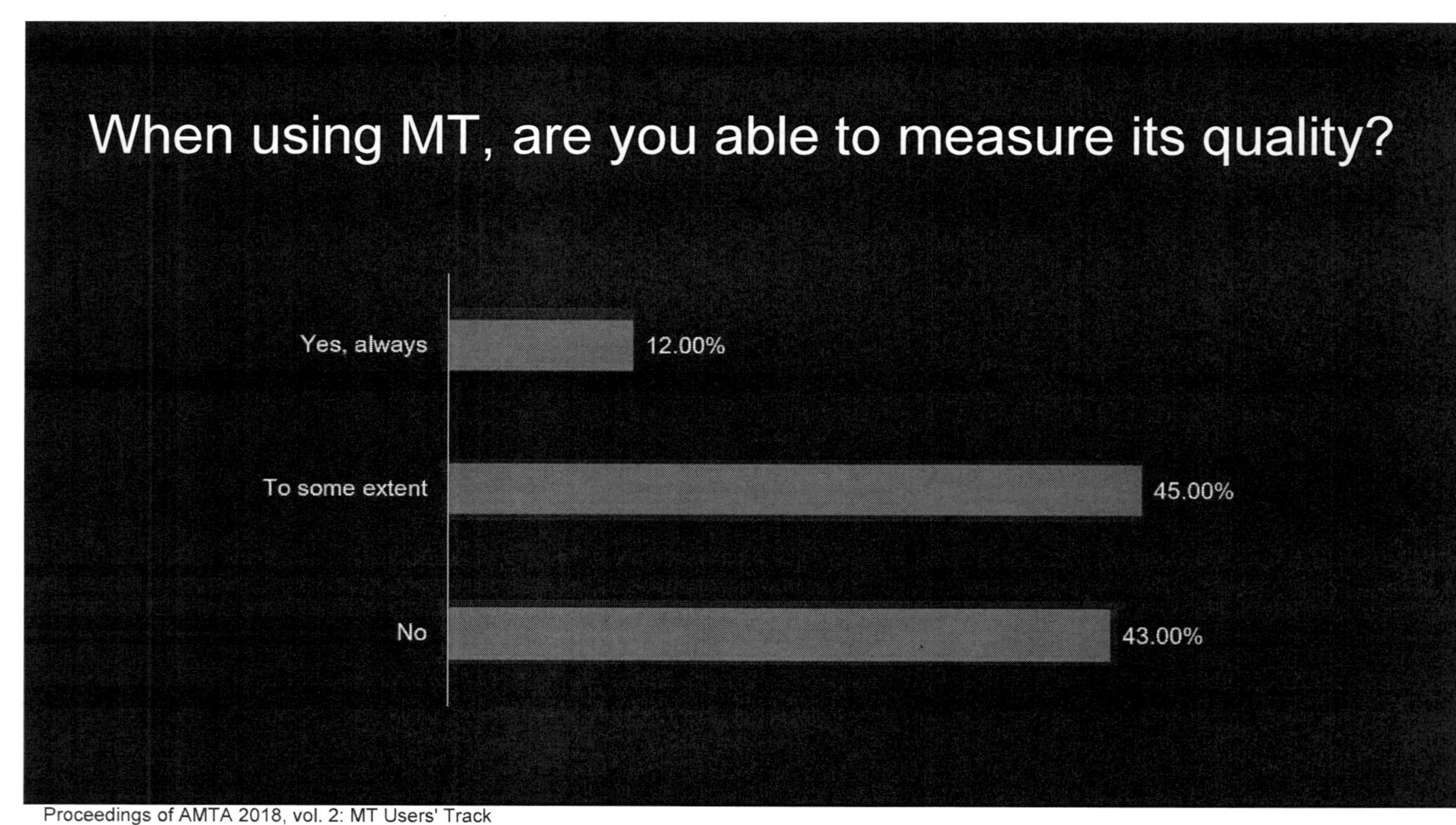

When using MT, are you able to measure its quality?
Yes, always
12.00%
To some extent
45.00%
No
43.00%

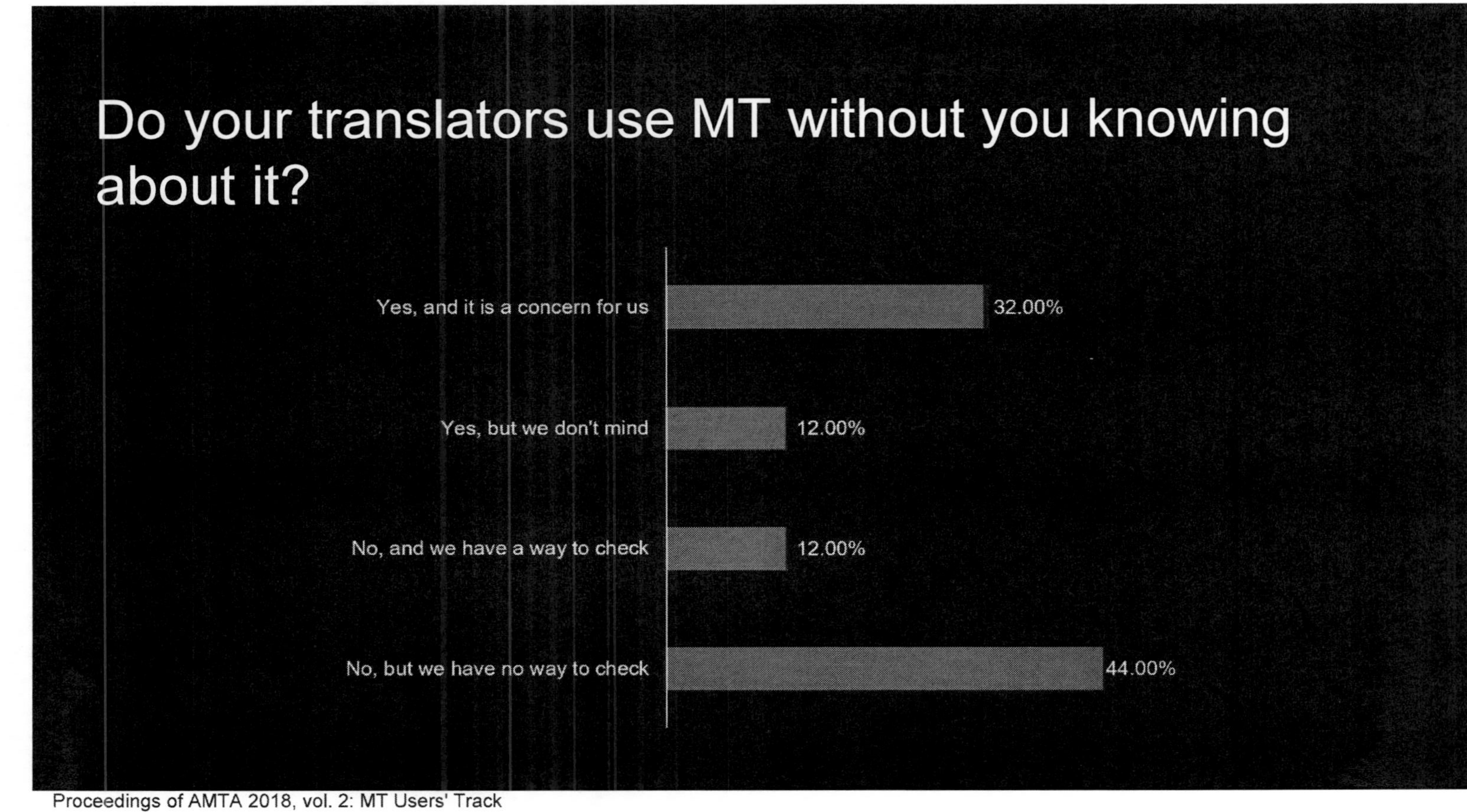

Do your translators use MT without you knowing about it?
Yes, and it is a concern for us   32.00%
Yes, but we don't mind   12.00%
No, and we have a way to check   12.00%
No, but we have no way to check   44.00%

2011: The Introduction of The Post-editing Analysis

- MT integration with CAT tools began around 2010
- Limited features supporting MT post-editing, e.g., to measure PE efficiency
- In 2011 Memsource launched the post-editing analysis

Post-editing Analysis

Introduction

The post-editing analysis in Memsource Cloud extends the traditional translation memory analysis to also include machine translation and non-translatables (NT). It analyzes the MT and NT post-editing effort for each segment and compares the MT and NT output with the final post-edited translation (edit distance). Therefore, if the MT or NT output was accepted without further editing (the linguist did not need to change it at all), it would come up as a 100% match in the analysis.

If, on the other hand, the linguist changes the MT or NT output heavily, the match rate will be close to 0%. The score counting algorithm is identical to the one that we use to calculate the score of translation memory fuzzy matches. The only difference is that the post-editing analysis is based on the target. Therefore, the post-editing analysis must be, quite naturally, launched after the post-editing job has been completed.

In This Article

1. Introduction
2. Translation Memory Analysis
3. Machine Translation Analysis
4. Non-translatables Analysis

A sample post-editing analysis:

	Segments				Pages				Words				Characters				%			
	TM	MT	NT	All	TM	MT	NT	All	TM	MT	NT	All	TM	MT	NT	All	TM	MT	NT	All
Net Rate	4	3	1	8	0.21	0.07	0.01	0.29	65	18	1	84	325	108	21	454				
All	8	9	3	20	0.38	0.23	0.04	0.64	113	60	3	176	580	356	64	1003	64.2	34.1	1.7	100
Repetitions	0	-	-	0	0	-	-	0	0	-	-	0	0	-	-	0	0	-	-	0
101%	1	-	-	1	0.02	-	-	0.02	5	-	-	5	24	-	-	24	2.5	-	-	2.8
100%	2	9	0	11	0.02	0.23	0	0.25	6	60	0	66	33	358	0	382	3.4	34.1	0	37.5
95%-99%	1	0	3	4	0.17	0	0.04	0.21	47	0	3	50	263	0	64	327	26.7	0	1.7	28.4
85%-94%	1	0	0	1	0.05	0	0	0.05	18	0	0	18	80	0	0	80	10.2	0	0	10.2
75%-84%	0	0	0	0	0	0	0	0	0	0	0	0	0	0	0	0	0	0	0	0
50%-74%	2	0	0	2	0.11	0	0	0.11	36	0	0	36	160	0	0	160	26.5	0	0	26.5
0%-49%	1	0	0	1	0.01	0	0	0.01	1	0	0	1	20	0	0	20	0.8	0	0	0.6

MT Usage Started Picking Up

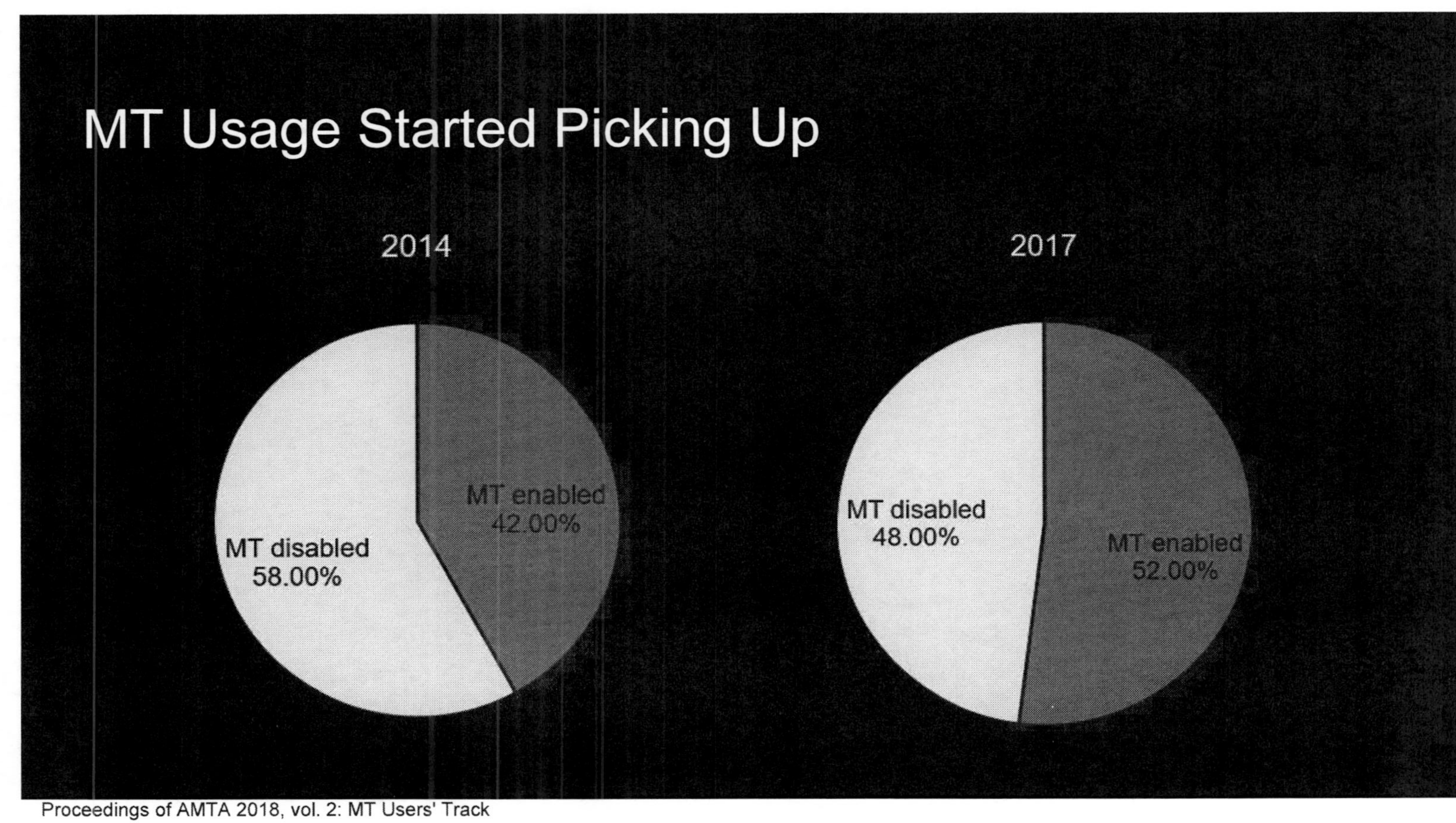

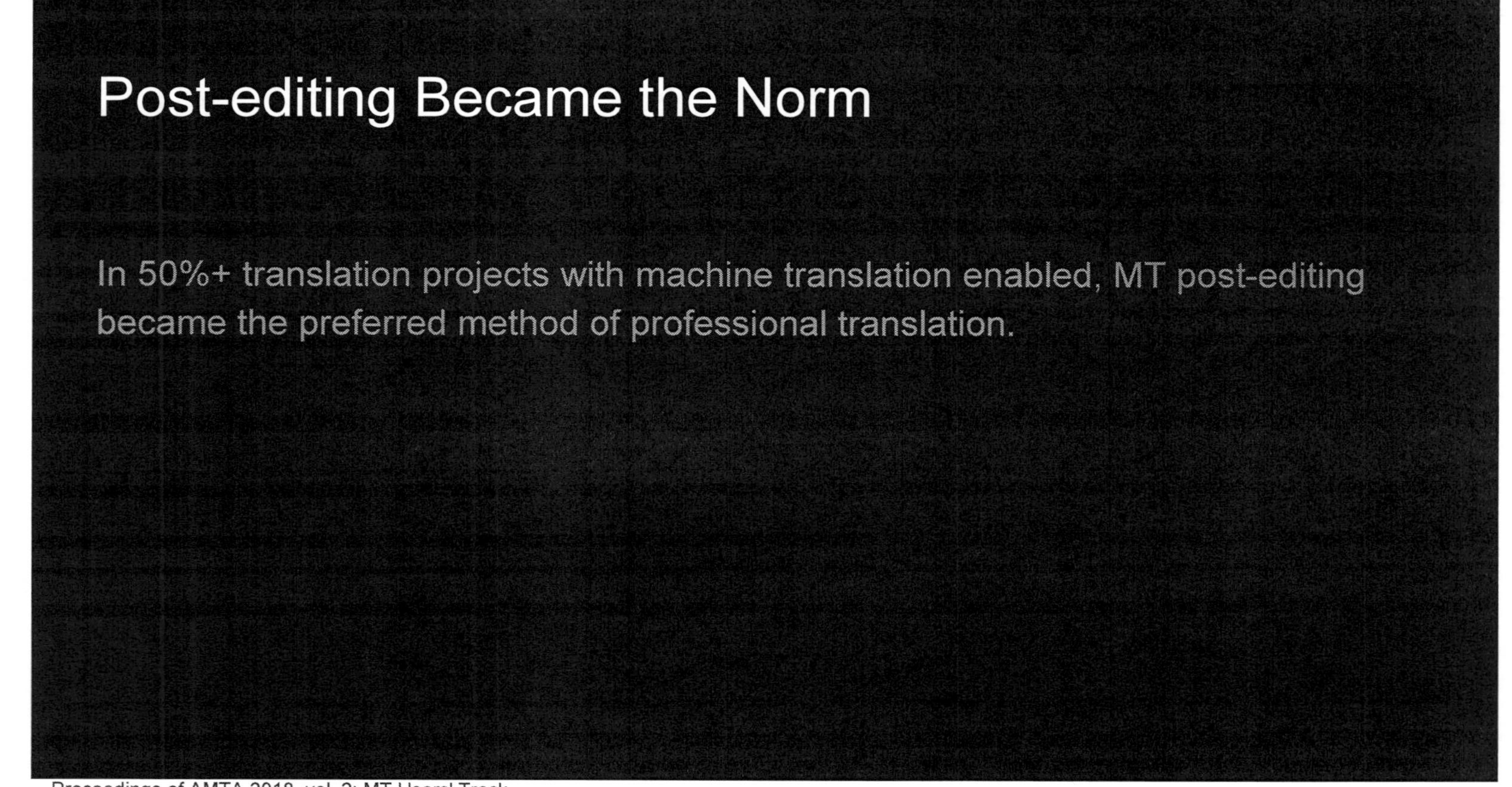

Post-editing Became the Norm

In 50%+ translation projects with machine translation enabled, MT post-editing became the preferred method of professional translation.

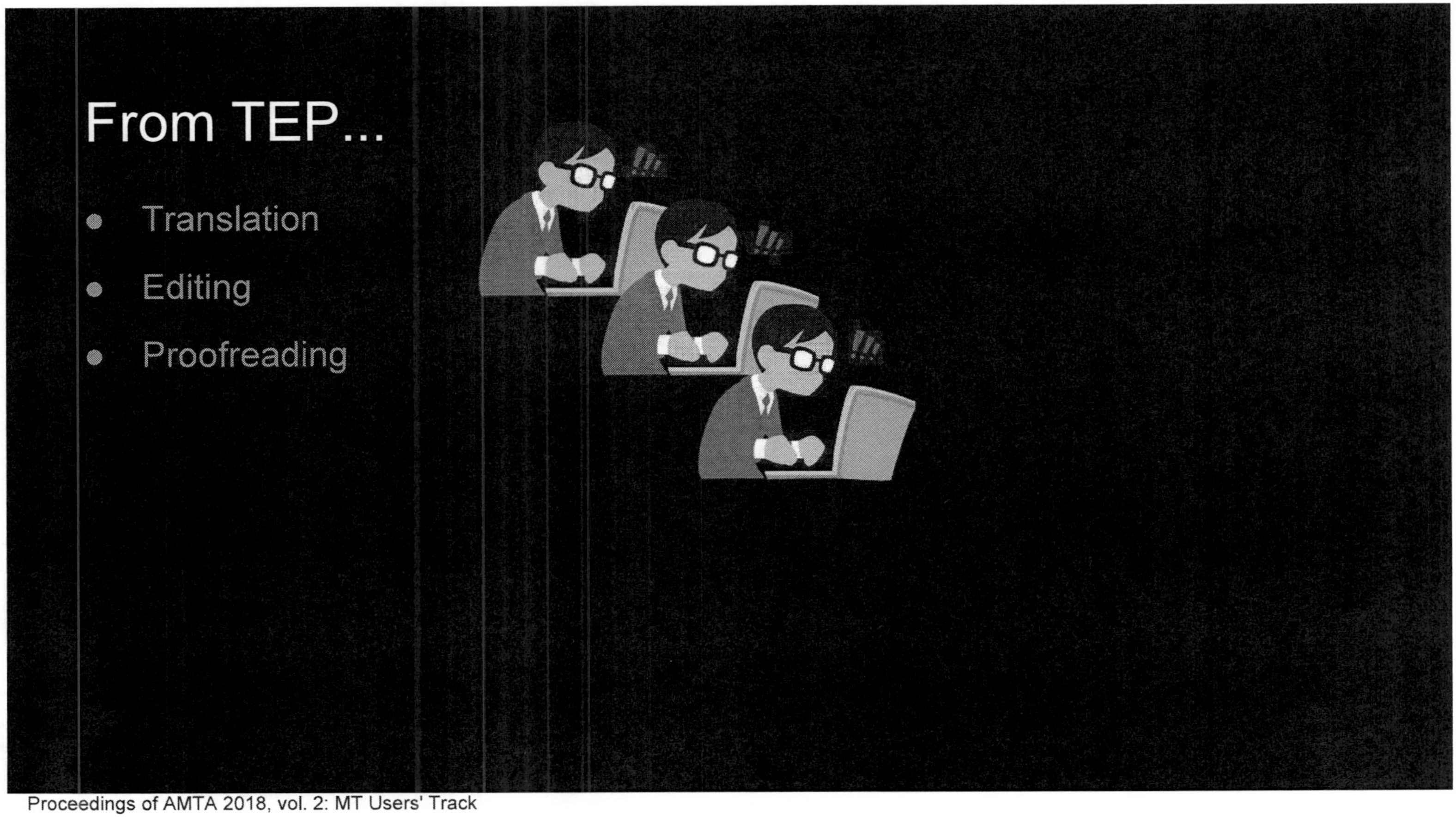

From TEP...
Translation
Editing
Proofreading

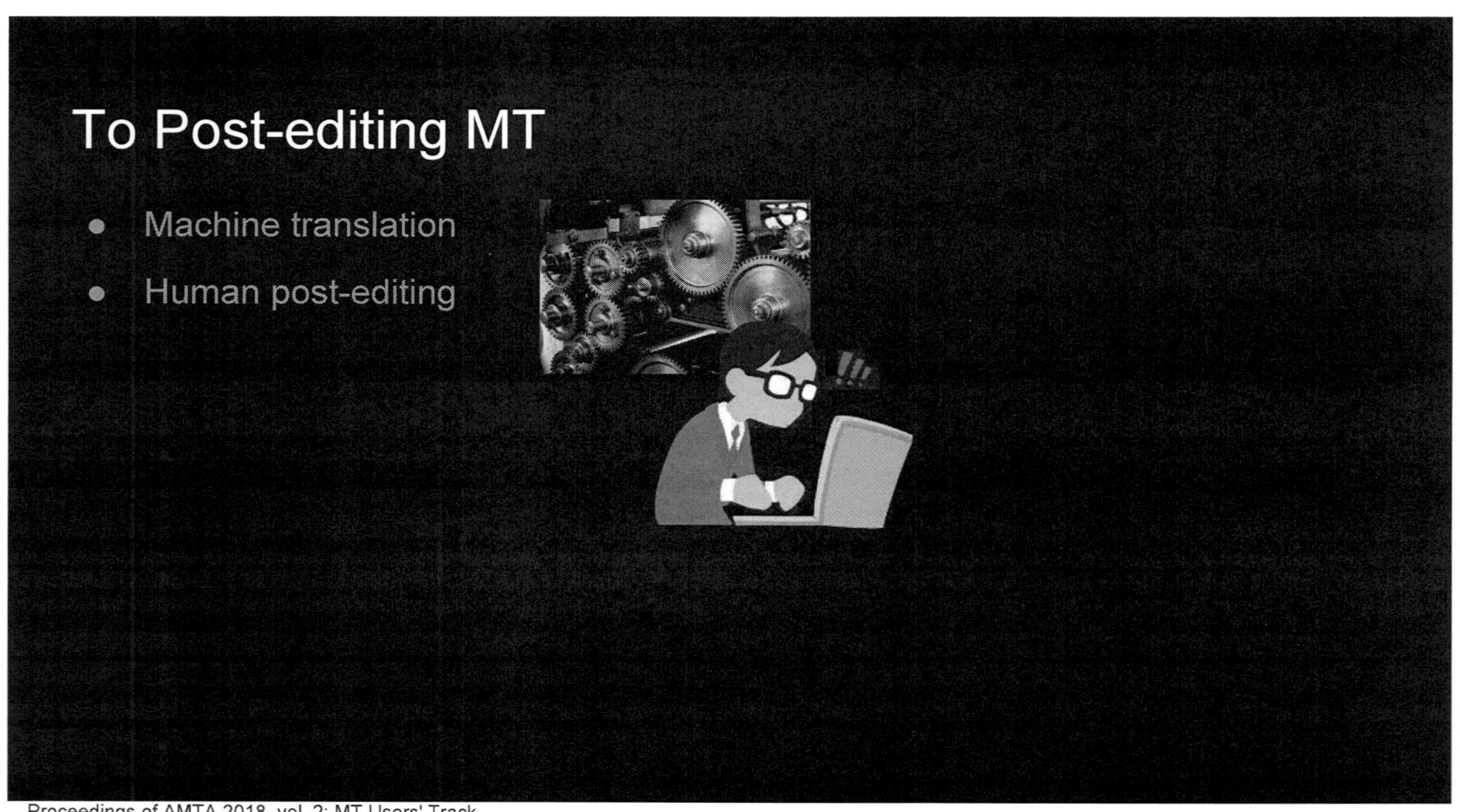

To Post-editing MT
Machine translation
Human post-editing

Translator Post-editing MT

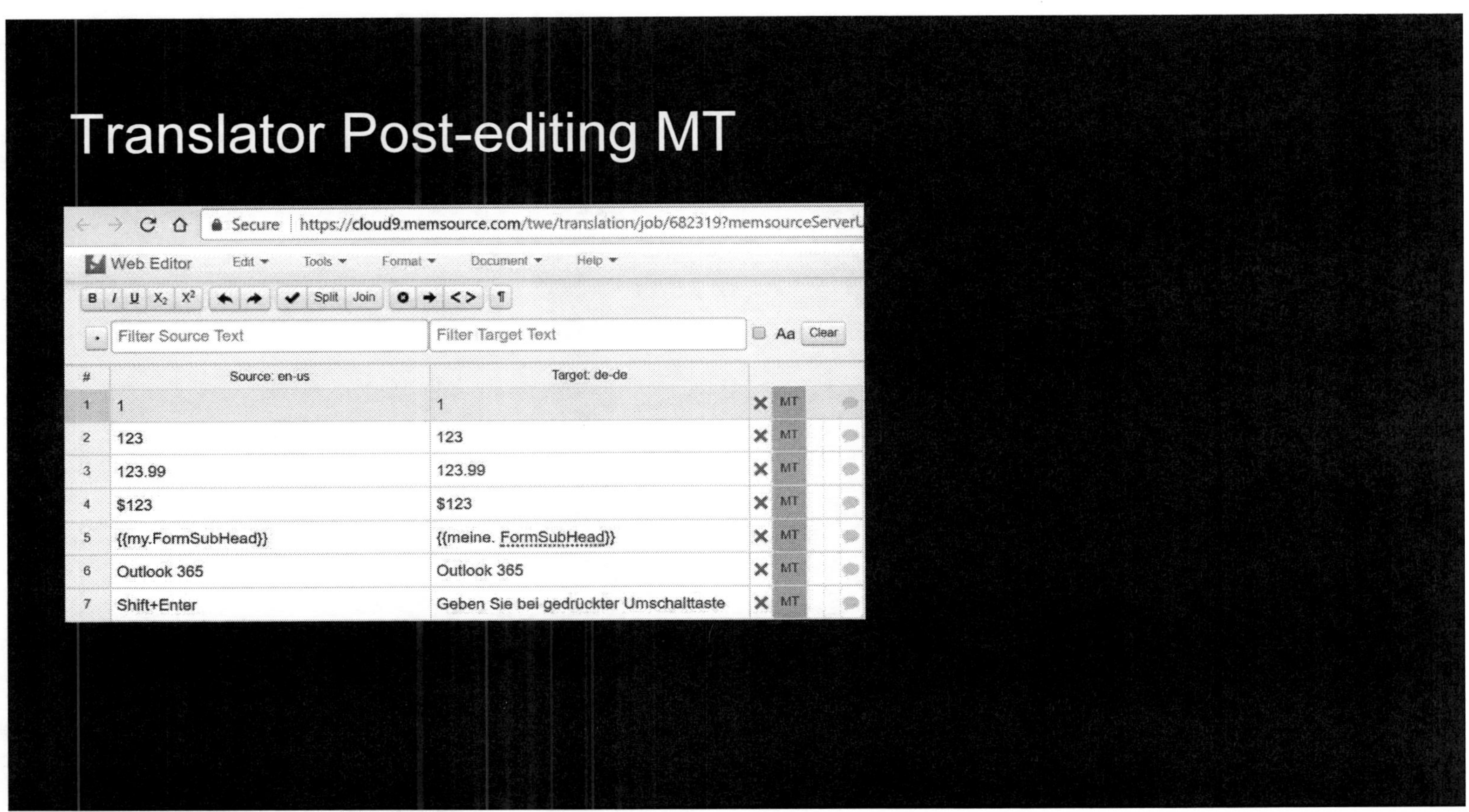

Less Post-editing

- Machine translation
- Automated quality estimation
- Human post-editing

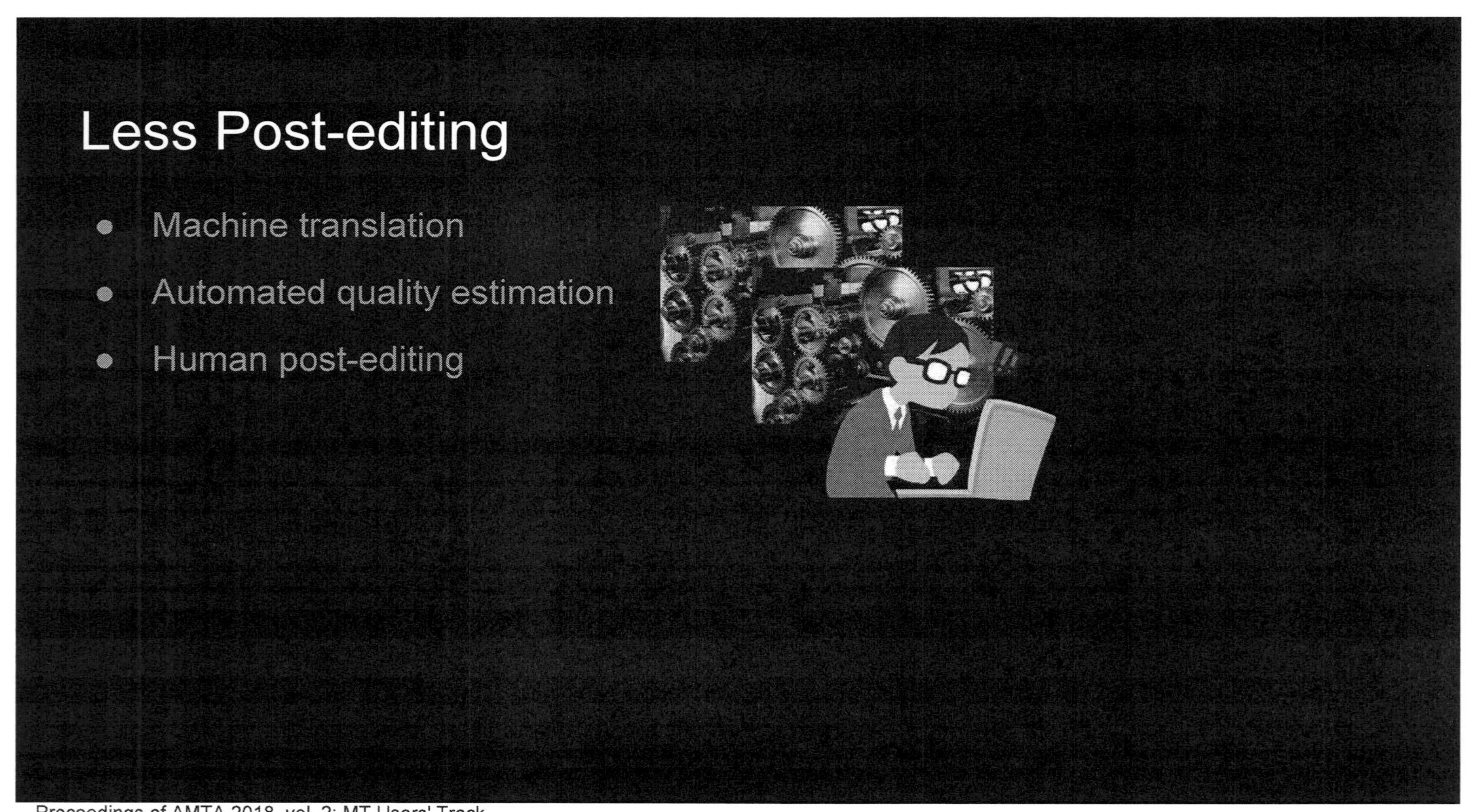

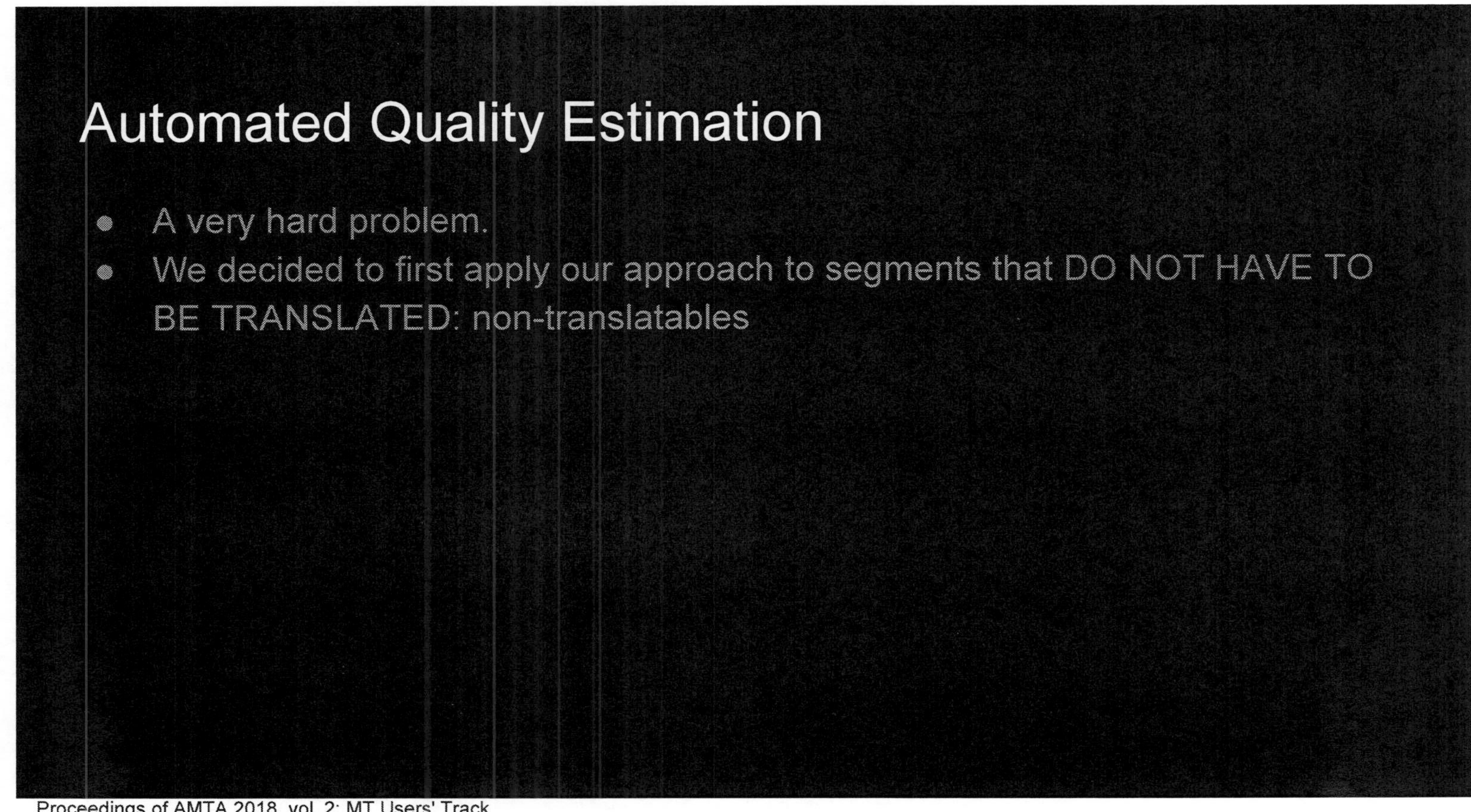

Automated Quality Estimation
A very hard problem.
We decided to first apply our approach to segments that DO NOT HAVE TO BE TRANSLATED: non-translatables

Examples of Non-translatables

- A segment that is simply copied from source to target.
- Some Examples:
  - *123*
  - *Labs.Core.Actions.IGetValueOptions*
  - *Memsource*
  - *Eva Smith*
  - *51 x 55 mm*

14% of Segments Are Non-translatable

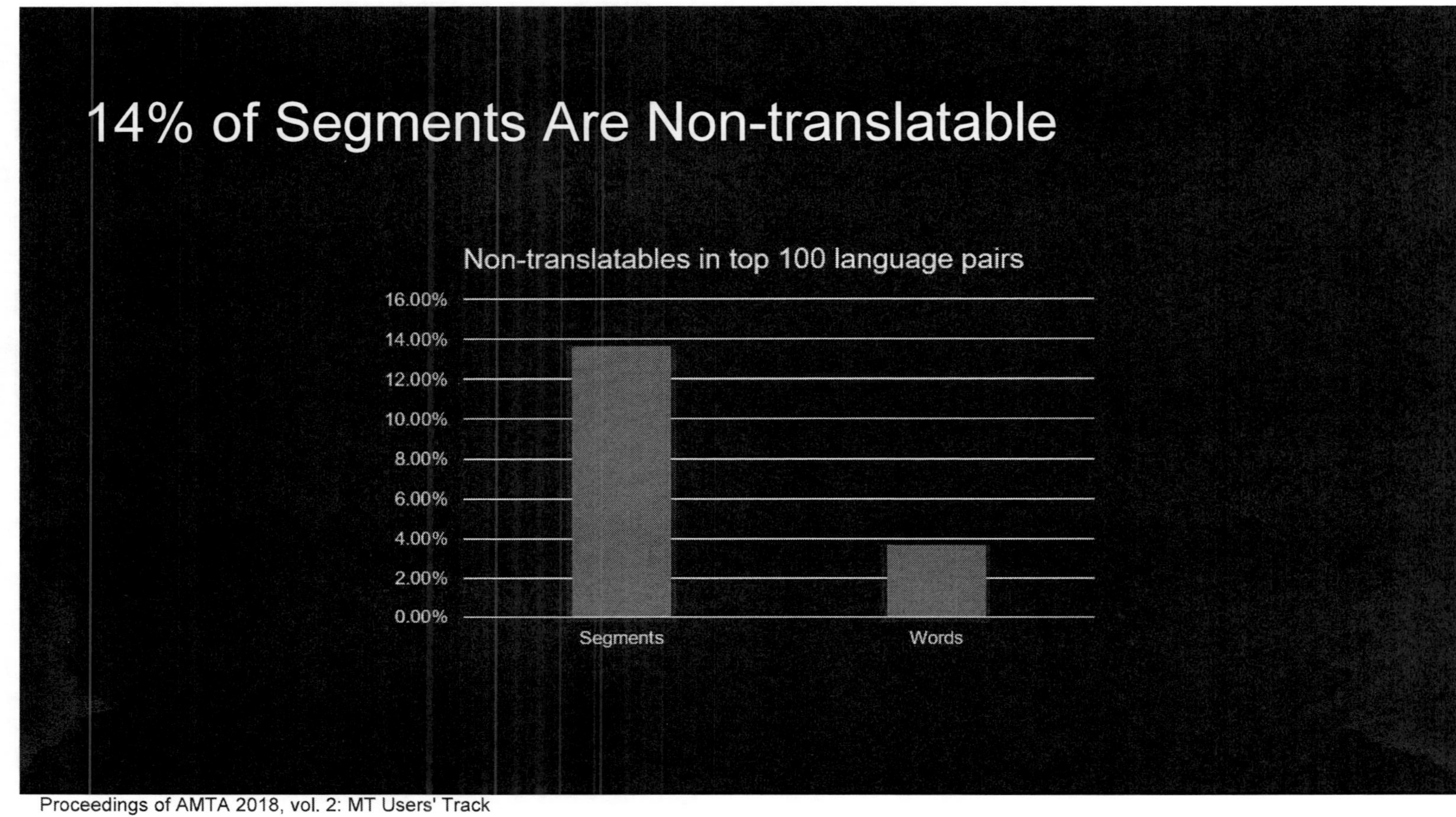

Differences between Language Pairs

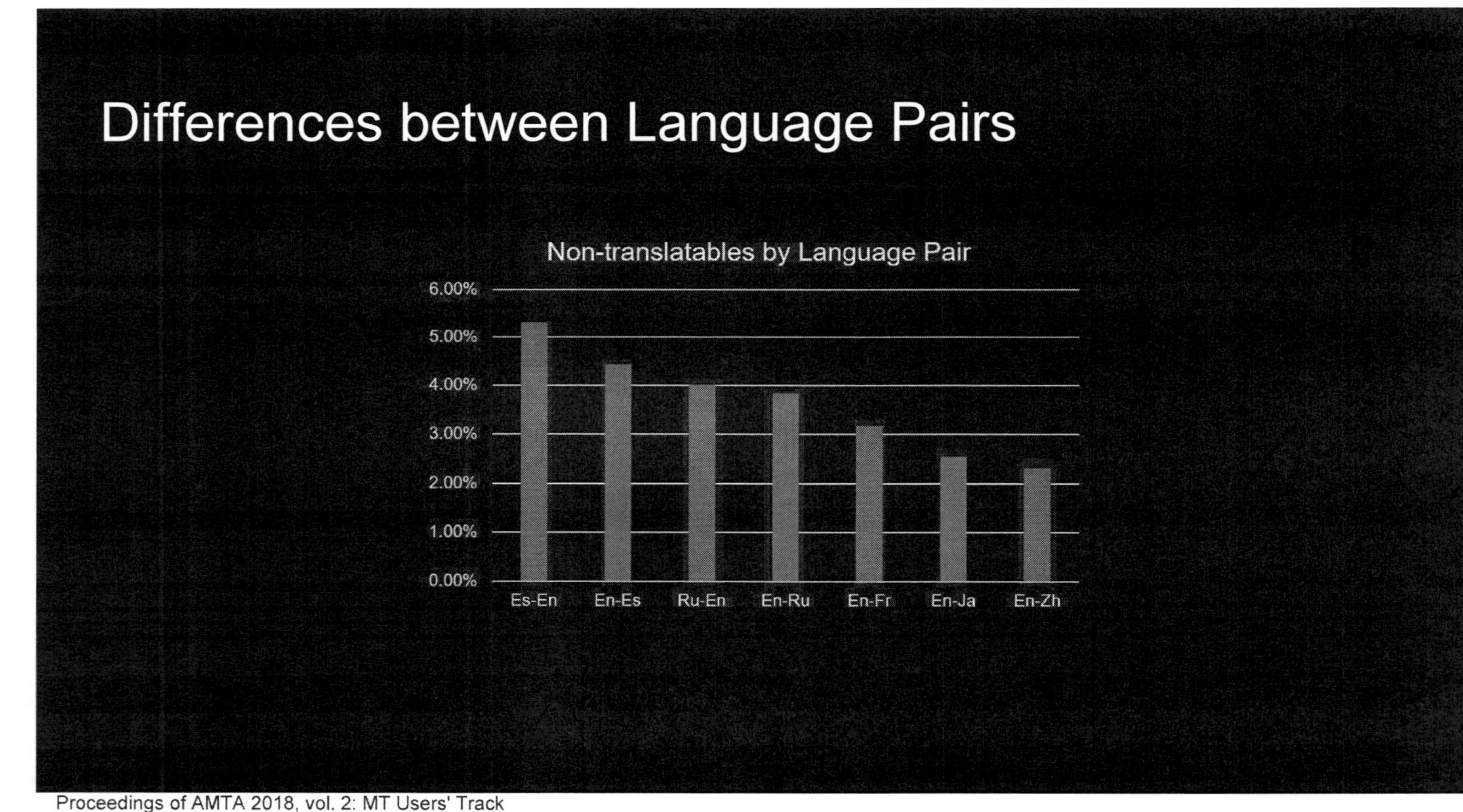

Proceedings of AMTA 2018, vol. 2: MT Users' Track

Traditional MT Post-editing

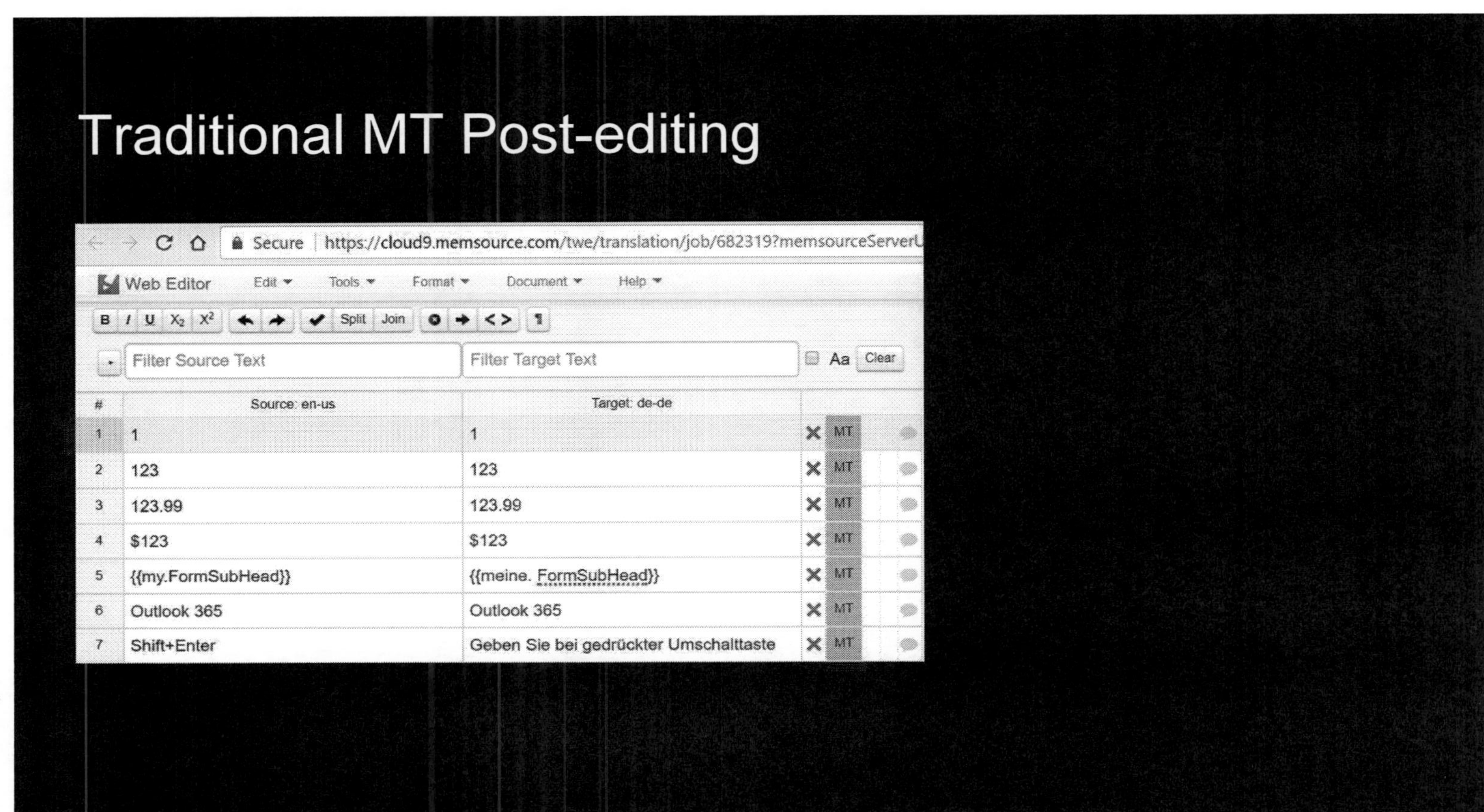

AI-powered MT Post-editing

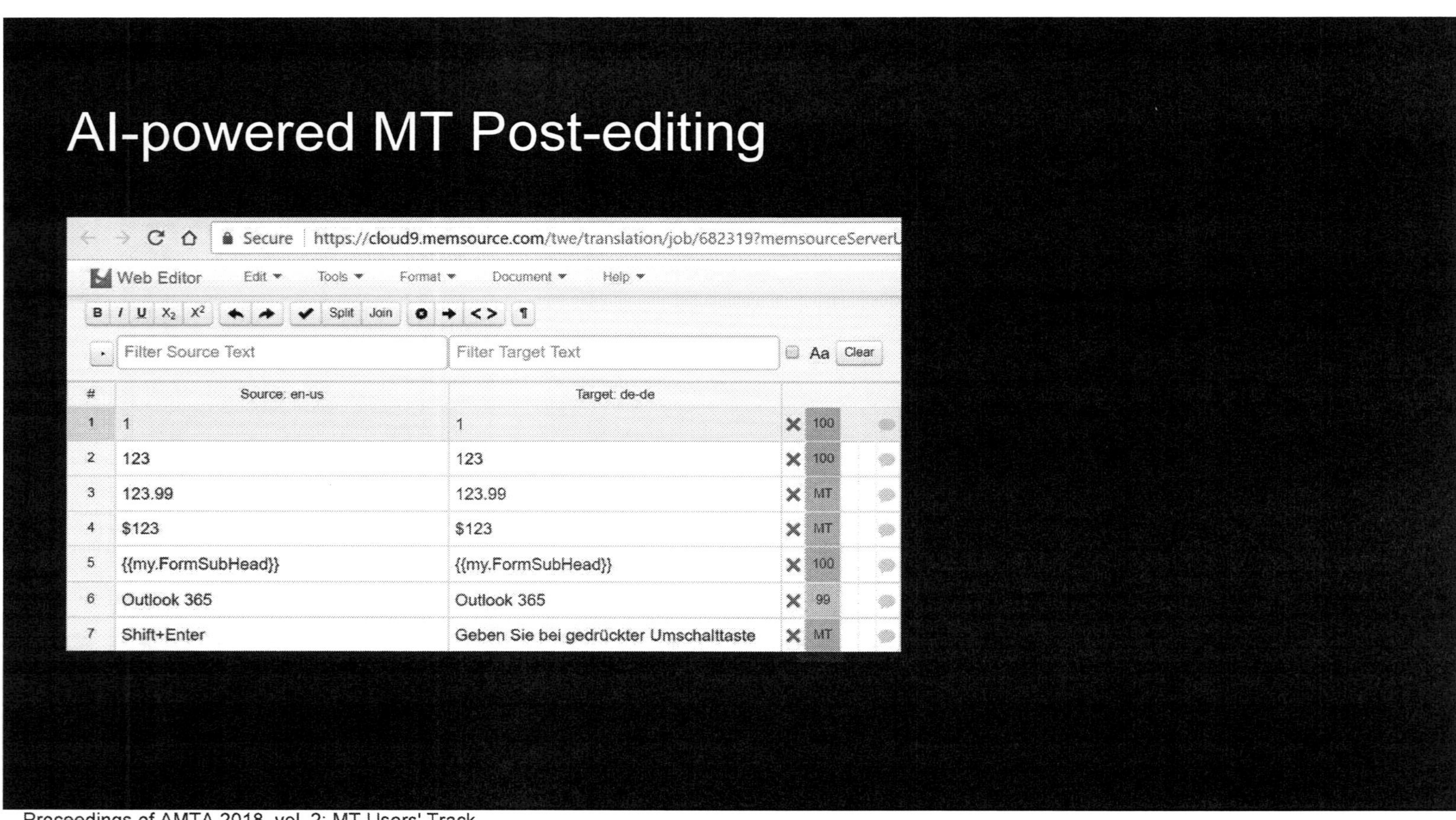

Score Distribution

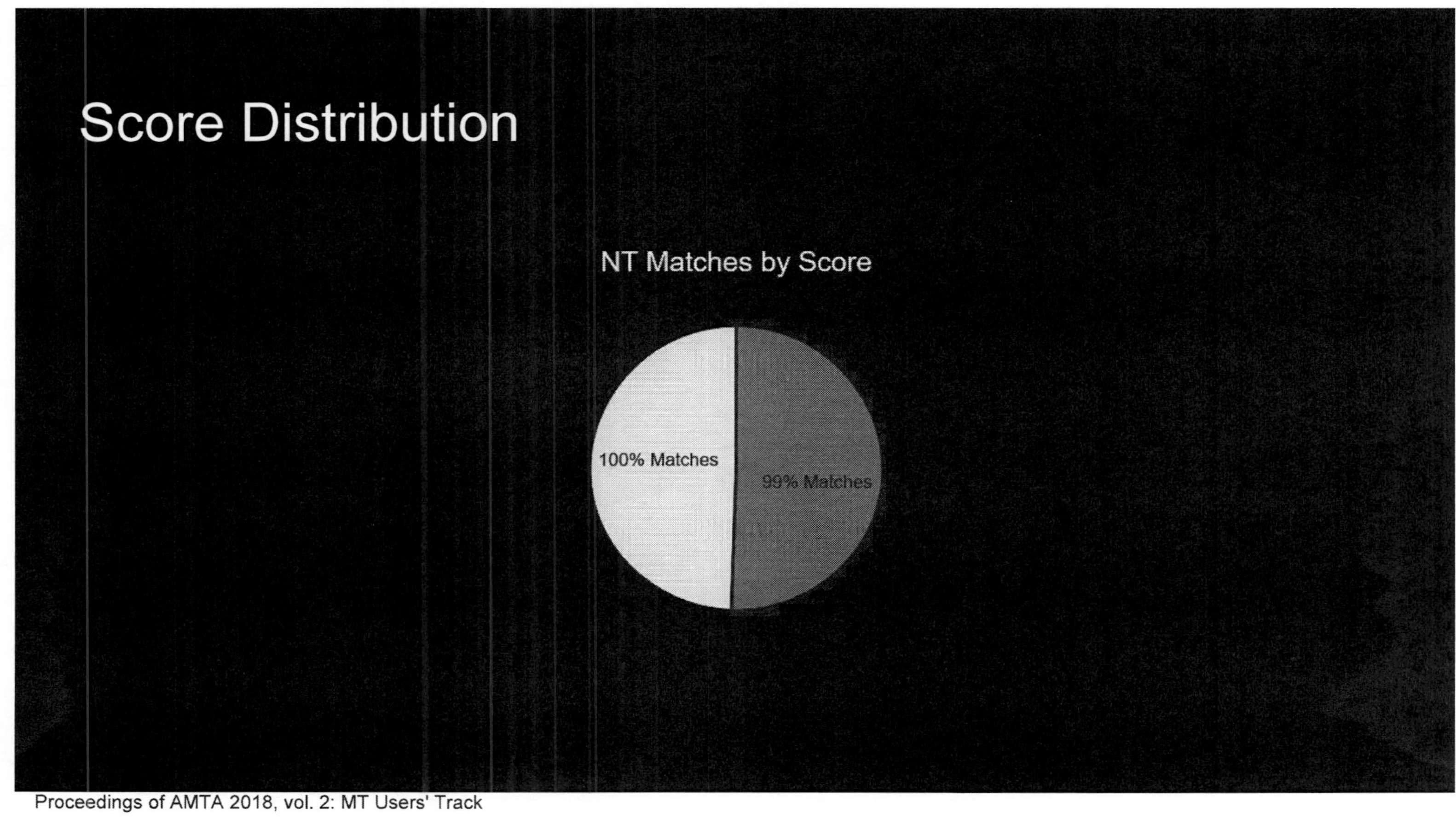

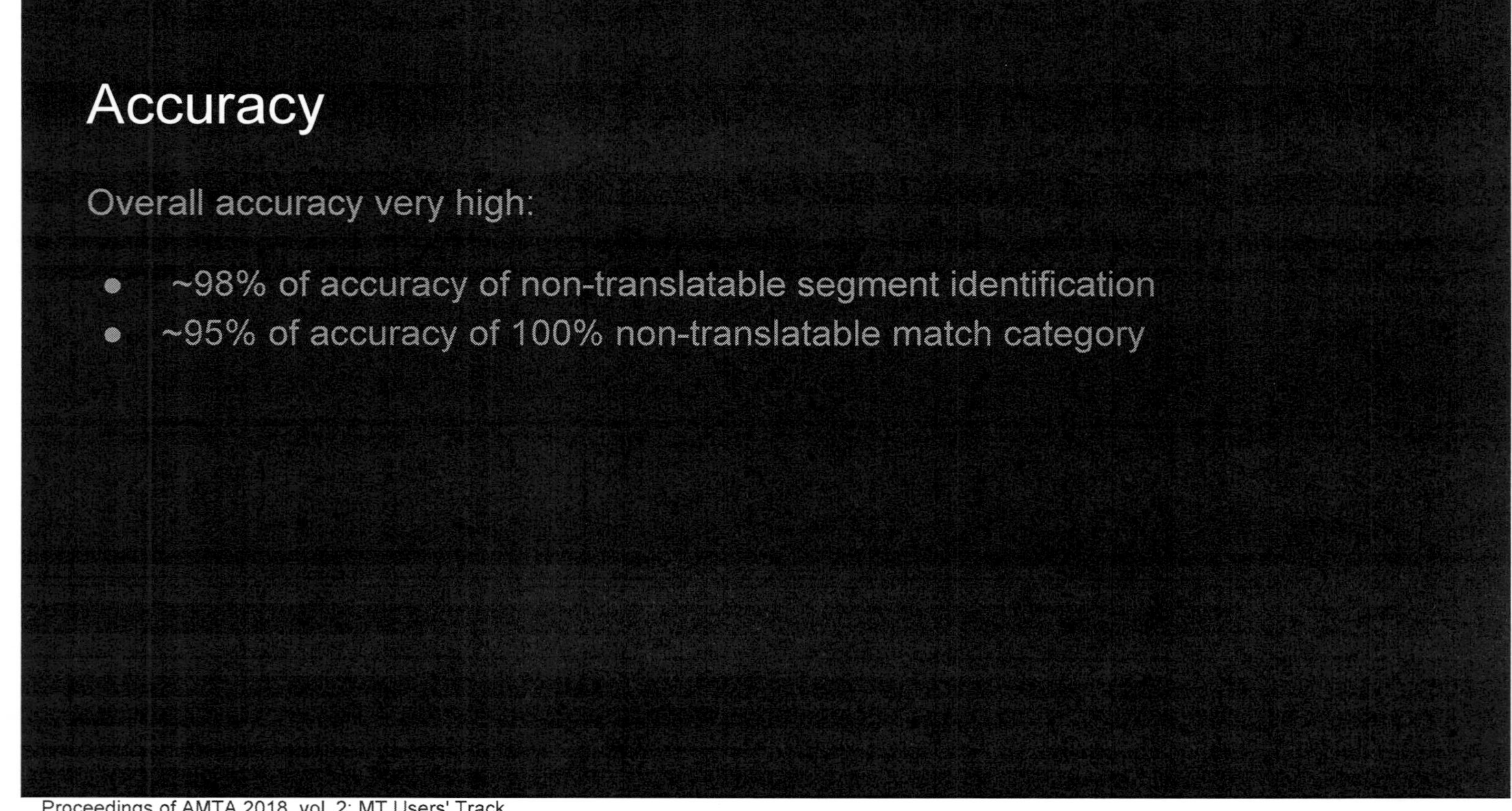

Accuracy

Overall accuracy very high:

~98% of accuracy of non-translatable segment identification
~95% of accuracy of 100% non-translatable match category

Leveraging Data Resources
for Cross-Linguistic Information Retrieval
Using Statistical Machine Translation

Steve Sloto   ssloto@amazon.com
Ann Clifton   acclift@amazon.com
Greg Hanneman   ghannema@amazon.com
Patrick Porter   pwporter@amazon.com
Donna Gates   dmg@amazon.com
Almut Silja Hildebrand   silja@amazon.com
Anish Kumar   anskum@amazon.com

Abstract

Retail websites may provide customers with a localized user experience by allowing them to use a secondary language of preference. Automatic translation of user search queries is a crucial component of this experience. Several domain-adapted SMT systems for search query translation were trained, including language pairs for which smaller-than desired parallel resources were available, such as Polish-German and Chinese-Japanese. We explored several techniques that could be used to optimize MT systems for this use-case. These included specialized forms of pre-processing, such as diacritic normalization and a weak form of language filtering, using byte-pair encoding (BPE) for automatic word segmentation, sampling monolingual query data for use as an LM, and pivoting.

To help measure the impact of these techniques, we also introduced normalized distributed cumulative gain for machine translation (NDCG-MT) as a means to measure the success of our MT system at the downstream information retrieval task. In addition to examining how close our translation is to a human-generated one, we measured the similarity in search results between reference and machine-translated queries.

One additional challenge was the difficulty in choosing a representative sample of user search queries to use as tuning and test data. The most popular search queries may occur significantly more frequently and could include vocabulary likely to be well-covered by the rest of the training data. Consequently, we will also discuss techniques that can be used to optimize selection of tune/test data. In general, we suggest assessing MT performance on both "head queries," those that occur most frequently, and "tail queries," less frequent queries that could be used to evaluate performance on difficult inputs.

1 Introduction

Cross-linguistic information retrieval is an important area for internet content providers in our current multilingual environment. Content providers make information accessible to speakers of other languages through methods such as translating content on individual webpages. Information retrieval systems may also be a part of websites, but these are much more challenging to localize. Translating an entire database, or modifying an IR system for each desired locality would be costly and would be unlikely to scale well. Another approach is to translate the user queries which are sent to the IR system. High-level descriptions of such systems can be found in many papers, including Nikoulina et al. (2012) who experimentally demonstrated using machine translation to retrieve information on a shared task for cross-lingual search in a library catalog setting, Martin (2016) who experimented with using MT for cross-linguistic information for user support forums, and Guha and Heger (2014) who use machine translation of product searches as part of a wider localization project for a global retail website.

Like numerous other internet content providers, Amazon uses cross-linguistic information retrieval as a component of a secondary language experience that we offer to customers globally. For example, users on marketplace websites such as Amazon.de have the option to browse the retail site in languages such as Czech, Dutch, English, Polish, and Turkish. Search queries from any of these languages can be translated into German and used to query the German product database. This paper focuses specifically on possible ways to optimize statistical machine translation systems for search query translation.

Numerous challenges may be encountered while training these systems. For example, adapting a system for the domain of search query translation may be challenging when significant parallel-data resources are limited. Another potential constraint is a need to optimize MT system performance, such that secondary-language users would experience limited latency. Furthermore, evaluation of these MT systems on their translation quality and performance on down-stream tasks can be important. To this end, an adapted version of the Normalized Discriminative Cumulative Gain Metric may be used to measure MT quality on the downstream information retrieval task. To leverage existing data resources, various techniques were tried, including pivoting, sub-word segmentation (using Byte-Pair Encoding), and different types of pre-processing.

2 Data and Training Setup

2.1 Search Query Data

Search query data has a few unique properties that can make it challenging to use for training MT systems. User search queries are not commonly translated. If one wishes to train an MT system for this domain, one may need to manually sample selections of queries for translation. It may also be desirable to leverage monolingual query data as a system component. Queries are short and can contain numerous untranslatable items and brandnames, which suggest different pre-processing techniques and hyper-parameter settings.

On a randomly chosen day of search traffic, search query data could contain millions of singletons, as well as hundreds of thousands of searches for the most popular queries. Over multiple days of data collection, certain popular queries could dwarf unique user traffic. We will refer to queries that may occur exponentially more frequently as "head queries." We will refer to queries such as these singletons that may occur less often as "tail queries."

If one wishes to use MT as a cross-linguistic IR system component, head queries are paradoxically the most and least important. Knowingly translating the same query hundreds of thousands of time in a day is an inefficient use of computational resources, so popular queries could be handled with a cache instead of being directly translated. Also, vocabulary pertaining to popular queries may be more likely to occur in general purpose training data. In contrast, tail queries may contain typos or fail to retrieve results, but would allow us to examine how a search-query MT system will perform in a "worst case scenario." For the purposes of these experiments, we sought primarily to optimize translations for tail queries, without having a large negative impact on performance on head queries.

For each MT system discussed in this paper, we were able to sample a selection of search query data to be translated by humans and used as tuning and test sets. We sampled tune sets of 2,400 queries, and up to two test sets of 1,000 queries each.

2.2 Other Training Data

In addition to the small amount of human-translated query data, parallel data from a variety of domains was used to train the systems discussed in this paper. Translated catalog data was used, in addition to parallel-data resources drawn from a variety of other domains less related to the query translation task. The distribution of data from these domains varied between language pairs. Systems described in this paper used between 25 and 3 million parallel segments for system training.

2.3 Training SMT Systems

We trained Phrase-Based Statistical Machine Translation systems for search query translation, experimenting with different methods of transforming and filtering the input data. We train various model components for a multi-domain system, such as alignment models, target-side language models, re-ordering models, and translation models.

When an MT system translates a segment, each of these models score possible translations as they are constructed from left to right, using beam search. The models' scores are combined using weights that are automatically learned by tuning to a held-out tune set of human-translated queries. The weighted combination of scores is used to select the best translation.

3 An IR Metric for MT

While conventional automatic evaluation metrics attempt to replicate human judgements of translation quality, these translation systems have a different use case than to have a human read and understand. Consequently, it is advantageous to use an automatic evaluation metric that reflects performance on our downstream task: search. Things that are important to a human about what makes a good translation may differ significantly from what makes a successful search query. Nuances that may be very important to a human in judging quality such as using function words (e.g., making sure to include the article before a noun) or preserving word order (e.g., "phone grey" vs "grey phone") may be irrelevant to returning the most relevant result to a query. Conversely, translation differences that a human may not mind may change the results returned from a query (e.g., "rose" may be a human-admissible synonym for "pink", but may not return the same search results).

The metrics currently used to evaluate MT systems are generally based on measuring the degree of overlap of n-grams between an MT translation and a human-generated reference translation as a way of measuring translation quality. In the case of evaluating MT for search, we want to directly evaluate based on performance on the task we care about, rather than how close our translation is to a human-generated one. We would like to be able to quantify the goodness of an MT translation by comparing the set of results returned by a query translated by our MT system to the results returned by a reference translation query.

In order to do this, for each translation, we make a call to the search index twice: once to retrieve the results for the translated output, and once for the results from the reference translation. We take the top-K results returned for the translated output and evaluate it against the top-K results returned for the reference using a common IR metric, normalized discounted cumulative gain (NDCG), which we have adapted for the MT task.

3.1 NDCG-MT

The basic idea of NDCG is that we want to evaluate the goodness of the results returned from a query based on the relevance score of each query, in proportion to its rank in the list of results returned, since we know that the first result is more important than the tenth, etc.

NDCG was designed to use relevance scores from some gold-standard measure such as human judgments. However, we don't currently have access to this type relevance evaluation for any arbitrary query/result pairs we with to test. So, we adapt it for our purposes as follows to compute NDCG-MT: instead of human-judgment relevance scores over query results, we take the results returned from the reference translation of a query to be the gold standard. Note that in this approach, we are assuming that whatever results are returned by the reference translation are the gold standard; we do not attempt to measure the actual relevance of the reference query results, or to directly learn a mapping between source-language query inputs and target-language results.

We take the numerical relevance score of a result to be the inverse of the rank of the result in the set of results returned from the reference translation query. So, for example, in a list of ten results returned from the reference query translation, the first result would have a relevance score of 10, and the last would have a score of 1. We can then evaluate the MT system output queries against this scoring. Thus, rather than taking the best possible score as the ideal ordering of the MT output results, we take this from the reference results ranking, so as not to artificially inflate the scoring of the MT results. The full formulation is as follows:

$$\text{NDCG-MT} = \frac{\text{DCG-MT}}{\text{IDCG-MT}},$$

where

$$\text{DCG-MT} = \sum i \in \text{MT-RESULTS} \frac{2^{rel_i} - 1}{\log_2(i + 1)}$$

and

$$\text{IDCG-MT} = \sum i \in \text{REF-RESULTS} \frac{2^{rel_i} - 1}{\log_2(i + 1)},$$

where rel_i denotes the relevance score of result "i".

In addition, we modify the original formulation of NDCG: we base the DCG (discounted cumulative gain) on the MT output results, and the IDCG (ideal cumulative gain) on the reference results ranking, where the original NDCG computes both DCG and IDCG over the same set of results. This is because in the IR tasks for which this metric was originally developed, it was presupposed that there was a fixed set of results, and the DCG and IDCG only differ in how they rank these results. In our case however, we can't assume that the MT output query will return the same set of results as the reference query. In cases where the output translation retrieves no results, it gets a score of 0. When the reference translation doesn't return any results from the index, we disregard the example and it does not contribute to the test set score.

This gives us a tunable metric that can function as a drop-in replacement for BLEU or METEOR, introduced in Papineni et al. (2002) and Banerjee and Lavie (2005) respectively.

4   Pre-Processing Techniques Used To Leverage Data Resources

Since search query translation is vastly different from general purpose machine translation, it may be desirable to preprocess the data to remove differences that might matter to a human, but not to an information retrieval system, such as lowercasing the data and removing diacritics.

By using the NDCG-MT metric, one can directly measure how procedural differences affect the quality of downstream search results.

4.1   Normalization

We tokenized and lowercased the training data for all systems discussed in this paper.

4.1.1 Diacritic Normalization

Many alphabets contain characters with particular diacritic markers added to them to distinguish between sounds. These characters are not always used by speakers of those languages in casual scenarios, such as when typing search queries.

Normalizing diacritic makers for system input could maximize the likelihood of providing a correct translation for these queries. However, it is also possible that words with very different meanings could be normalized to the same form. This potential side-effect could increase ambiguity in the MT system.

If performed, it is optimal to normalize diacritics in a language-specific manner. For example, it is common for German speakers to use 'oe' to represent 'ö'. However, this may not be the case for users with different first languages, such as Turkish or Czech, where 'ö' was more commonly normalized as 'o'. Experimentally normalizing 'ö' to 'oe' for Turkish or other input languages into German, caused a decline in MT performance compared to not normalizing at all.

Table 1 shows the results from experimenting with different normalization heuristics for the Czech-language input for the Czech-German MT system. We built MT systems with the identical hyper-parameter settings and only varied whether diacritic normalization was included as a part of tokenizing system input. The system with the baseline setting did not include any diacritic normalization. The system built with 'strong normalization' normalized all Czech letters with diacritics to the most similar single-letter that did not feature a diacritic. The German-style system did not normalize these characters, and normalized 'ö' to 'oe'. In this case, instead of better leveraging our training data by combining similar representations of words together, we arbitrarily separated these words into distinct forms with no real motivation, with a corresponding performance loss on the test sets.

On our test set of head queries, our normalization-free baseline outperforms all normalization heuristics. For the tail queries, diacritic normalization moderately improves our success on information retrieval and translation, but not to a significant degree. This result suggests that diacritic normalization is most useful for tail-query translation. It also suggests that normalization may be a particularly challenging area for experimentation, since it normalization may substantially hurt general-case performance with marginal worst-case improvement.

Test Set	Normalization	BLEU	NDCG-MT	METEOR	TER	Length
Head	Baseline	55.2	59.6	64.0	36.6	102.9
Head	Strong Normalization	54.0	57.5	62.9	37.7	102.7
Head	German-Style	54.8	59.4	63.1	37.6	103.0
Tail	Baseline	43.3	70.2	62.7	41.4	102.7
Tail	Strong Normalization	43.6	70.9	63.0	41.4	103.0
Tail	German-Style	41.5	70.6	62.0	42.8	103.8

Table 1: Comparison of Different Normalization Heuristics on Test Sets for the Czech-German System

4.2 Language Filtering

Many parallel corpora are noisy, and contain data that is in the incorrect language. For general-purpose MT systems, it may be advisable to filter incorrect language segments out of the training data. User search data can complicate thsi process. As mentioned in Section 2.1, queries are generally short, so a character-based language detection model may have lower accuracy. Search queries also commonly include brand names, which may be in languages other than those that we are targeting for translation. If "Pomme De Terre" was a French brand name, we may want to include it in non-French training data.

To measure the effect of language filtering on a finished system's MT output quality, Polish-German data was filtered four ways using a character-based language detection library. We tested allowing Polish, German, and English on both sides of the training data, allowing the desired language and English on either side of the training data, allowing only Polish and German on both sides, or allowing only the desired language on either side. Changing the filtering setting had a marginal effect on our overall data size. No more than 1% of the data was discarded compared to our 'weak' baseline. System variants were otherwise identical with respect to hyper-parameter settings, including Byte-Pair encoding. We scored the system against a test set of 1,000 Polish-language queries with corresponding German translations. These queries had been specifically hand-picked to be in the Polish language. Despite the marginal change in training data size, a noticeable effect could be seen in our metrics scores, shown in Table 2.

The more permissive language-detection setting performed best on the downstream information retrieval task, as measured by the NDCG-MT score. Despite the fact that our queries were almost exclusively in the Polish language, retaining a marginally larger variety of untranslatable items in our training data improved our performance.

Allowed Languages	BLEU	NDCG-MT	METEOR	TER	Length	% of Data Used
pl,en,de $\rightarrow$ de,en,pl	44.1	66.1	57.1	43.6	95.3	100.000%
pl,en $\rightarrow$ de,en	45.0	65.3	57.0	43.5	95.7	99.929%
pl,de $\rightarrow$ de,pl	45.2	65.5	56.8	42.9	95.1	99.788%
pl $\rightarrow$ de	43.7	64.9	56.0	43.5	94.0	99.775%

Table 2: Comparison of Language Filtering Settings on Polish-German System

5 Byte-Pair Encoding

5.1 Motivation & Previous Work

There are many scenarios where we may be interested in examining features below the word level for training MT systems. Some languages, such as Turkish, are morphologically complex, such that a word may contain many affixes. Breaking apart these words into constituent components may enhance translation quality. When translating between related languages, such as Dutch and German, one could be interested in looking at sub-word features to improve performance on transliteration, or other situations in which common changes apply to the input. Lastly, segmentation may also be useful for languages written in characters, such as Mandarin Chinese and Japanese, where discrete spaces between word units may not already exist.

Sennrich et al. (2015) popularized Byte-Pair encoding as an algorithm for unsupervised sub-word segmentation. Intuitively, Byte-Pair Encoding works by breaking apart words into characters, and joining characters into sub-word units based on their most frequently occurring neighbors. This technique does not make use of intuitive phonetic or morphological boundaries, and its output does not look particularly intelligent to human eyes. BPE has been commonly adopted for use in Neural Machine Translations systems, where it reduces vocabulary size and improves performance.

Although Byte-Pair Encoding is commonly used for training NMT systems, it has rarely been used for training statistical models. Kunchukuttan and Bhattacharyya (2016) experimented with using BPE to subsegment data for SMT systems translating between related languages. They built systems for sixteen language pairs in ten different writing systems. They found that BPE works well as a paradigm for segmentation regardless of data size. Byte-Pair encoding out-performed other forms of sub-word segmentation, as well as baseline systems trained without segmentation, and led to an increase in BLEU score in all but one case. They also experimented with different numbers of merge operations for BPE, but tended towards extremely small settings, experimenting between 1k and 4k.

Östling et al. (2017) experimented with using BPE for sub-word segmentation in SMT systems baseline systems trained as part of the University of Helsinki entry into the WMT Shared Translation task in 2017. Their results showed that BPE was not particularly helpful in training SMT models. They attributed this failing to the small number of operations chosen for NMT and not optimized for SMT specifically. Their vocabulary size was around 20,000.

5.2 Our Setup

We used BPE to subsegment our data after it was already tokenized, lower-cased, and pre-processed in any other manner. Our experimental usage of BPE differed from that described by Kunchukuttan and Bhattacharyya (2016) in two ways. First, like Östling et al. (2017), we found that too low of a number of operations led to the possibility of degraded performance. In particular, we found that too low of a setting led to an increased number of garbled translations, in which not all of the BPE-segments in a word were translated. Second, we usually trained BPE using a joint model that learned sub-words from both source and target language training data, instead of using separate models for source and target. Search queries and product names often include non-translatable items that occur in both versions of a parallel segment. Consequently, better performance could be achieved by splitting source and target representations of non-translatable items into the same sub-word units on both halves of our training corpora. For Turkish-German MT, we experimented with training source and target separately, and found that we experienced a loss of 2 BLEU points compared to a joint model. We also experimented with using only a source-side BPE model, and no sub-word segmentation on the target, and experienced a loss of 11.8 BLEU.

After settling on the general experimental setup of training a joint BPE-model as an MT system component, we varied the number of BPE operations. Table 3 shows the result of choosing different numbers of BPE Operations on the quality of MT output measured in BLEU, and Table 4 shows results for the same systems and test sets scored with the NDCG-MT metric. "None" denotes a system without sub-word segmentation, and "0" denotes a system that was built at the character level rather than the word level. For the purposes of this comparison, all systems were built with a re-ordering window of four. All data and hyper-parameter settings are consistent across different versions of a given system.

	0	50,000	100,000	200,00	None
NLNL-DEDE	58.9	63.7	62.5	62.2	61.7
PLPL-DEDE	36.8	43.4	45.1	45.5	42.5
ZHCN-JAJP (Head)	41.5	40.3	40.9	42.2	34.5
ZHCN-JAJP (Tail)	29.6	29.2	28.7	27.5	21.2
CSCZ-DEDE (Head)	49.4	52.8	54.0	52.5	46.1
CSCZ-DEDE (Tail)	29.3	43.0	43.2	43.4	41.7

Table 3: Effect of Different BPE Number of Operations Settings on BLEU Scores

Variants built with BPE strongly outperformed systems that were built without sub-word segmentation. These results suggest that 50,000 or 100,000 Operations may be a suitable baseline setting. 50,000 appears more suitable in cases where both more information is likely to be shared between the source target in segment. It is also worth noting that the NDCG-MT scores

	0	50,000	100,000	200,00	None
NLNL-DEDE	72.2	79.2	78.9	77.3	75.9
PLPL-DEDE	57.8	65.9	67.1	66.2	64.1
ZHCN-JAJP (Head)	57.1	58.3	56.9	56.5	52.3
ZHCN-JAJP (Tail)	45.1	47.5	45.9	45.5	39.9
CSCZ-DEDE (Head)	51.9	57.4	57.5	56.6	55.3
CSCZ-DEDE (Tail)	63.9	70.6	71.3	69.2	66.2

Table 4: Effect of Different BPE Number of Operations Settings on NDCG-MT Scores

shown in Table 4 provide a much cleaner look at the effect of sub-segmenting with different number of BPE operations.

5.3 Interactions Between BPE Model Hyper-Parameter Settings

Utilizing sub-word tokens rather than full-sized word units may affect optimal model hyper-parameter settings, such as the desired size of N-Gram language models, or re-ordering window in re-ordering models. For the specific use-case of search query translation, using BPE did not have as large of an impact on optimal hyper-parameter settings as it may have for other use-cases. For search query translation without BPE, lowering the size of the re-ordering window resulted in roughly equivalent NDCG-MT scores, as well as faster decoding speed. There are two reasons for this: search queries tend to be short, so there are fewer tokens to move around. Also, the order of segments in the MT output is less important in an information retrieval scenario.

Even when breaking up MT system output into smaller sub-word chunks, a relatively small re-ordering window remained an appropriate hyper-parameter choice. Table 5 shows the result of experimenting with the size of the re-ordering window for the Dutch-German system, and resulting systems' performance on BLEU and NDCG-MT. Systems built with BPE were built with 50,000 operations, the setting shown to have the highest performance for Dutch-German in the previous section. The NDCG scores for the system without BPE show best performance with a ROW of 4. For systems built with BPE, there is no real significant difference in IR performance as the ROW is increased, though a ROW of 6 appears to be a good compromise between speed, NDCG-MT, and BLEU.

ROW	BLEU without BPE	NDCG-MT without BPE	BLEU with BPE (50k Ops)	NDCG with BPE (50k Ops)
2	60.1	75.6	62.9	79.1
4	61.7	75.9	63.7	79.2
6	61.7	75.7	64.5	79.6
8	60.8	76.2	63.2	79.7
10	60.9	75.1	63.0	79.9
12	60.9	75.8	63.7	79.3

Table 5: Comparison of Re-Ordering Window Settings With & Without BPE on the Dutch-German System.

6 Using Non-Parallel Data Resources

6.1 Monolingual Data

Among the most common techniques for increasing SMT performance is leveraging monolingual data. For the use-case of search query MT, one can do so by building a language model based on a sample of target-side monolingual search query data. Including this model impacted system performance positively, as shown in Table 6.

System	BLEU	NDGC-MT	METEOR	TER	Length
PLPL-DEDE Including Monolingual Queries	44.1	66.1	57.1	43.6	95.3
PLPL-DEDE Without Monolingual Queries	41.7	64.8	56.3	64.7	95.7

Table 6: Effect of Including Monolingual Search Query Data as a System Component

6.2 Pivoting

Pivoting is an extremely common technique in low-resource scenarios. In general, it has been shown to be useful when there are more substantial amounts of translation data available between the desired source and target languages and a third language, than exist between the source and target languages alone. There are many possible setups for pivoting, including training MT model to translate training data between the pivot language and desired language, or tying together two MT systems in a cascade approach. We experimented with two approaches.

In the first approach, our training corpora were experimentally augmented with data pivoted through English. A simple technique was used, in which we directly pivoted between training data corpora. A desired source-language and target-language string were considered to be a translation if they had an exact string match on an intermediate language string. These segments were grouped with non-pivot segments and added to the training data. All other settings are identical between MT systems including and excluding this pivot data.

We also experimented with cascade approach for Mandarin-Japanese translation. Data was sequentially sent through non-production Mandarin-English and English-Japanese Search Query MT models in sequence. One potentially interesting qualitative side effect of doing this was an increased likelihood of English in the output. The system is forced to translate into English at an intermediate stage. Since there may be numerous Japanese product titles that contain untranslated English, more English appears in the final translation, compared to direct Mandarin-Japanese translation. This result suggests that this technique would be unsuitable for production use without further refinement.

Data	BLEU (Head)	NDCG-MT (Head)	BLEU (Tail)	NDCG-MT (Tail)
Without Pivots	40.5	54.0	28.9	46.5
With Pivots (48% larger)	42.2	56.5	27.5	45.5
Cascading	8.5	20.8	9.7	22.1

Table 7: Comparison of Three Forms of Pivoting on Two Test Sets for Mandarin-Japanese Translation

Table 7 shows a comparison of different pivoting techniques for system performance on Mandarin-Japanese query translation. No system including pivot data outperformed a system without pivot data. There are two main factors that may have contributed to this:

1. Much (though not all) of the pivot data could have come from domains that were farther away from the Search Query Translation task.

2. As was the case for other systems, weak language detection allowing English was used for the Mandarin-English and English-Japanese MT systems. When combining the two in a pivot scenario, the cascade system was considerably more likely to have English in the output. Evidently this setup was extremely harmful for both translation quality, and for downstream search accuracy.

Table 8 shows comparative results over including pivot data in the general PLPL-DEDE training data as scored on an exclusively-Polish test set of 1,000 queries. Including pivot data in the general training data led to a drop in BLEU score, but had no significant impact on the downstream information retrieval task, as measured by NDCG-MT.

Data	BLEU	NDCG-MT	METEOR	TER	Length
Without Pivots	45.2	66.2	57.2	43.2	95.1
With Pivots (15% larger)	44.1	66.1	57.1	43.6	95.3

Table 8: Results of Including Pivot Data in the General Polish-German Training Corpus

7 Conclusions

In this paper, we discussed specific modifications to standard SMT system training in order to optimize for the use-case of search query translation. Several techniques increased the quality of our output in an experimental setting. We summarize these as follows:

- Filtering training data with weak language detection moderately improved system quality compared to stricter filtering. We gained 1.2 NDCG-MT on PL-DE.

- Diacritic normalization potentially improved translation for edge cases, but substantially negatively impacted system performance on "head queries". We gained 0.7 NDCG-MT on a test set of Czech-German tail queries, counterbalanced by a loss of 2.1 NDCG-MT on head queries.

- Using a joint BPE model for sub-word segmentation substantially improved model quality We saw improvements between 1.3 and 6.6 NDCG-MT across language-pairs and test-sets. BPE also outperformed character-based models, though it is possible that those may be competitive for language-pairs such as Mandarin-Japanese and Dutch-German. 50k or 100k operations, and a re-ordering window of 6 is a good baseline for BPE.

- Including monolingual data substantially improved performance. The Polish-German system gained 1.3 NDCG-MT.

- Adding pivot data to the model had mixed results. In the best case, we gained 0.1 NDCG-MT for Polish-German translation, and 2.5 NDCG-MT on Mandarin-Japanese head queries, but lost 1.4 NDCG-MT on Mandarin-Japanese tail queries. A cascade approach to pivoting would be unsuitable without optimizing the constituent MT systems to be used in tandem for this domain.

From the above, it is clear that a combination of sub-word segmentation with BPE and use of monolingual LM data may greatly enhance model performance for this domain. Avoiding strict language filtering may also be useful. Diacritic normalization or the inclusion of pivot data in the general training corpus may be more or less desirable depending on whether one wishes to optimize a system for the translation of head or tail queries.

Lastly, the NDCG-MT metric itself was very useful for evaluating translation quality for the downstream information retrieval task. In particular, NDCG-MT was useful in cases where changes in traditional machine translation metric scores were not reflected by downstream information retrieval quality. For instance, MT metrics alone do not make a compelling case for weak language detection, compared to the NDCG-MT metric, which shows a strong preference for it in table 2. The NDCG-MT score provided much-needed visibility into downstream task performance.

References

Banerjee, S. and Lavie, A. (2005). Meteor: An automatic metric for mt evaluation with improved correlation with human judgments. In *Proceedings of the acl workshop on intrinsic and extrinsic evaluation measures for machine translation and/or summarization*, pages 65–72.

Guha, J. and Heger, C. (2014). Machine translation for global e-commerce on ebay. In *Proceedings of the AMTA*, volume 2, pages 31–37.

Kunchukuttan, A. and Bhattacharyya, P. (2016). Learning variable length units for SMT between related languages via byte pair encoding. *CoRR*, abs/1610.06510.

Martin, R. (2016). Multilingual search with machine translation in the intel communities. In *Proceedings of the AMTA*, volume 2, pages 65–71.

Nikoulina, V., Kovachev, B., Lagos, N., and Monz, C. (2012). Adaptation of statistical machine translation model for cross-lingual information retrieval in a service context. In *Proceedings of the 13th Conference of the European Chapter of the Association for Computational Linguistics*, pages 109–119. Association for Computational Linguistics.

Östling, R., Scherrer, Y., Tiedemann, J., Tang, G., and Nieminen, T. (2017). The helsinki neural machine translation system. *CoRR*, abs/1708.05942.

Papineni, K., Roukos, S., Ward, T., and Zhu, W.-J. (2002). Bleu: a method for automatic evaluation of machine translation. In *Proceedings of the 40th annual meeting on association for computational linguistics*, pages 311–318. Association for Computational Linguistics.

Sennrich, R., Haddow, B., and Birch, A. (2015). Neural machine translation of rare words with subword units. *CoRR*, abs/1508.07909.

The Impact of Advances in Neural and Statistical MT on the Translation Workforce

Association for Machine Translation in the Americas

March 18, 2018

Jennifer DeCamp
jdecamp@mitre.org

MITRE Corporation

When Will AI Exceed Human Performance?
Evidence from AI Experts　2024

- Abstract: "Researchers predict AI will outperform humans in many activities in the next ten years, such as translating languages (by 2024), writing high-school essays (by 2026), driving a truck (by 2027), working in retail (by 2031), writing a bestselling book (by 2049), and working as a surgeon (by 2053)."[1]

- 352 of the 1634 researchers publishing at two major AI conferences in 2015

- Estimate of "when AI will do this task better and cheaper than a team of human experts":

  - "Perform translation about as good as a human, who is fluent in both languages, but unskilled at translation for most types of text and for most popular languages." [2]

  - What does this mean?

  - What about about other kinds of translation (e.g., with skilled translators)?

[1]K. Grace, J. Salvatier, A. Dafoe, B. Zhang, and O. Evans (May 2017). *Will AI Exceed Human Performance? Evidence from AI Experts.* Downloaded 13 February 2018 from Cornell Library site: arXiv:1705.08807v2 [csAI} 30 May 2017.

[2]Ibid.

What is Happening to MT?

- More improvements to machine translation, computer assisted translation, optical character recognition, and speech
  - Deep learning and neural nets increasing accuracy
  - Statistical and Rule-Based MT
  - More translation memory
  - More annotated data
  - More current machine translation to use, including for pivots
  - Many small improvements, including easier customization
- Market forces
  - Drive for new markets
  - Capitalize on Artificial Intelligence (AI) hype

- Better fluency in MT
- More machine translation and computer assisted translation options, including for dialects
- Somewhat better accuracy in many tools supporting MT (e.g., OCR)
- More need for localization
  - More need for cultural input
  - More interest in single-source authoring (and more need for guidance for customers)
- More marketing
  - More need for good evaluation
  - More need to help customers understand options for tools and humans

Proceedings of AMTA 2018, vol. 2: MT Users' Track

What does the MT Look Like?

- Often more accurate, including with specialized domains
- More specialization, due to ease of creation in Statistical MT (SMT) and Neural MT (NMT)
- Significantly more fluency although not always greater accuracy
- Some high-risk in NMT, including problems with:
  - Negatives
  - New text inserted
  - Source text left out
- Sometimes higher cost for NMT due to hardware and data—thus not feasible for some languages and domains

Experiment by Sue Ellen Wright, October 2017

DeepL (Deep Learning/Linguee)

DeepL Translator - English user interface

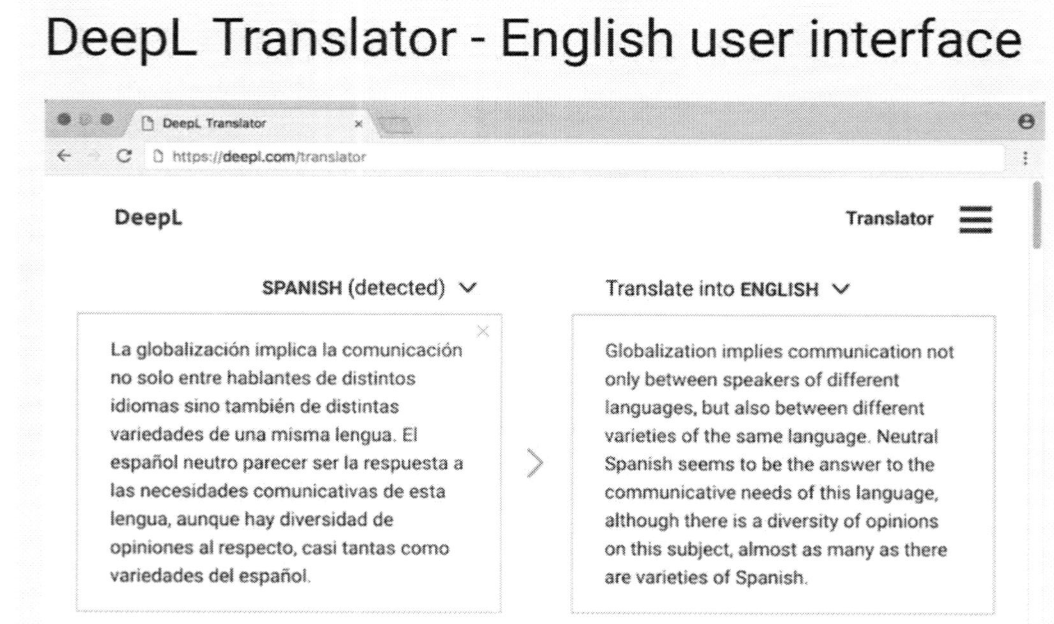

No post editing

DeepL Challenged (Sue Ellen Wright)

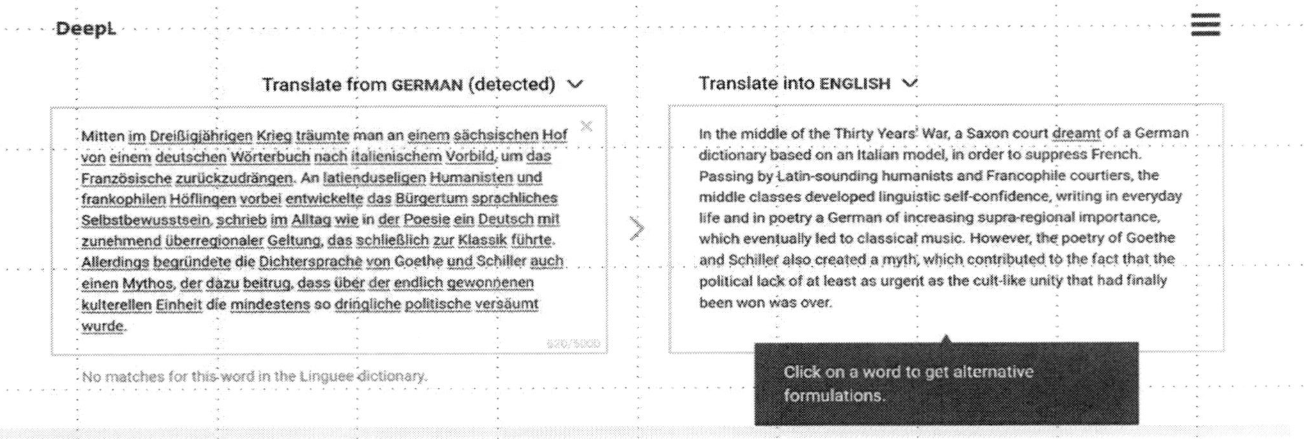

In the middle of the Thirty Years' War, a Saxon court dreamed of a German dictionary based on an Italian model in order to suppress French. Ignoring Latin-crazy humanists and Francophile courtiers, the bourgeoisie developed linguistic self-confidence, writing a German of increasing supra-regional importance in both everyday life and in poetry. To be sure, the poetic language of Goethe and Schiller also established a myth that contributed to the fact that although they finally achieved cultural unity, political unity, which was at least as critical, was neglected.

What is Happening to Tools?

- Probably little MT for
  - Tasks where there are needs for very low risk, high visibility, or extensive cultural context
  - Languages & domains with little demand
- In other areas, there is a need for translators to monitor the translations
  - Less surface editing
  - More checking for match with source text in content, completeness, and cultural context
  - Use of tools to facilitate that checking
    - Perhaps using predictive translation
    - Using confidence measures (e.g., match with terminologies)
    - Using quality assessment
    - Perhaps marking which sections have been evaluated
    - Perhaps also using automatic identification of different translation engines and translators
    - More sophisticated tools to check for negation, completeness, and subject area

What is Happening to the Translator Workforce?

- Discussion at the ATA Conference centered around different kinds of translation requirements
- Different source documents and requirements result in different tasks for translators
- Some of these tasks may be different
  - Question raised by David Rumsey, ATA President, at the 2017 Translation and Interpreting Summit:
    - Are we recruiting and training translators for the kinds of translation they have done in the past or for the new kinds of translation they will be doing in the future?
- Increasing focus on
  - Annotating data
  - Evaluating MT output for completeness, accuracy, context
  - Using tools and training others how to use tools

References

- K. Grace, J. Salvatier, A. Dafoe, B. Zhang, and O. Evans (May 2017). *Will AI Exceed Human Performance? Evidence from AI Experts.* Downloaded 13 February 2018 from Cornell Library site: *arXiv:1705.08807v2 [csAI} 30 May 2017.*

- Systran (3 November 2018). Neural MT Workshop, Washington D.C.

- S. Wright (27 October 2018). How to Future Proof. *New Options for Translators, Interpreters, and Project Managers in the Artificial Intelligence-Driven Future of Language Work*. American Translators Association Conference, Washington D.C.

- Z. Ostrega, Old and New Practices at State Department. *New Options for Translators, Interpreters, and Project Managers in the Artificial Intelligence-Driven Future of Language Work*. American Translators Association Conference, Washington D.C.

Image Permissions

Scribe, by unknown artist is licensed under CC by 4.0.

C3PO y R2d2 by Vansquell-Shinomori is licensed under CC by 3.0.

Raising the Bar by unknown artist is licenses under CC BY-NC-SA.

*The author's affiliation with The MITRE Corporation is provided for identification purposes only, and is not intended to convey or imply MITRE''s concurrence with, or support for, the positions, opinions or viewpoints expressed by the author.
Approved for Public Release; Distribution Unlimited. Case Number 18-0367

PEMT for the Public Sector
Evolution of a Solution

Konstantine Boukhvalov and Sandy Hogg

ManpowerGroup Public Sector, Inc

ManpowerGroup

ManpowerGroup Public Sector

- **25+ years** supporting commercial and government clients around the world
  - Translation and l10n, transcription, interpretation, tech support, linguist placements, intel analysis and reporting

- Uniquely positioned to observe **language technology pain points for both clients and vendors**

- Developed a **universal TMS implementation procedure**
  - Advise and support **client TMS implementations**
  - Deploy and manage **SaaS TMS** for our clients
  - Provide client and vendor **TMS training**

Presentation Objective

- Data protection concerns and knowledge of how to implement a practical HLT solution that delivers meaningful value have historically prevented public sector clients from using MT, CAT, and TMS

- We will show how our team successfully addressed data protection and client objectives to develop a practical, domain-specific PEMT solution to a public sector client who is now transforming how they use HLT

Key Takeaways:
- How to develop a customized PEMT solution for public sector
- How to build and optimize TM corpora for statistical MT training
- How to gauge technological and procedural efficiencies for overall program success and scalability

Historical HLT Challenges with MGPS PS Client Base

- **Limited HLT use due to various contract constraints**
  - No co-mingling data, no data in cloud
  - TM/TB corpora destruction
  - CONUS resources with citizenship, various clearance levels
    - HLT use still not widespread among PS linguist base (freelance)

- **No process automation**
  - Longer production timelines
  - Project-based translation

Early Steps

- Secure isolated **IT infrastructure**
- Dedicated **enterprise-level CAT** setup
- **Centralized TM/TB**
- Resource requirements, e.g. **CAT-trained linguists/project managers**
- **TM/TB corpora** included as a deliverable

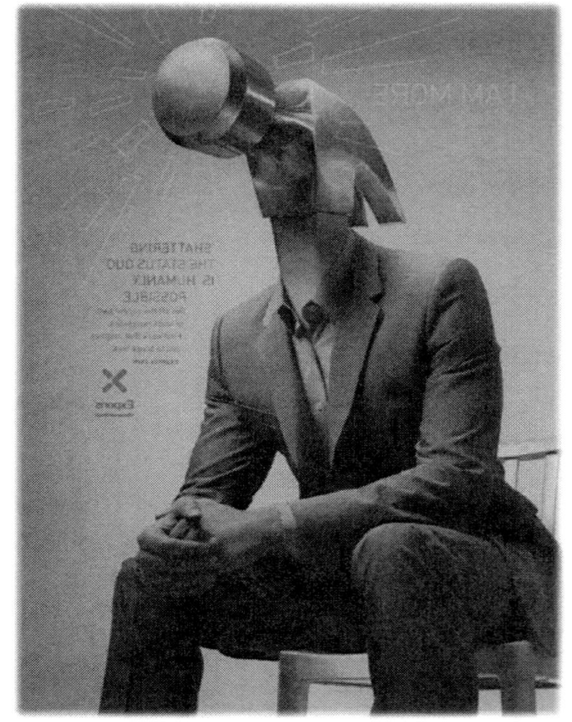

248

ManpowerGroup

Case Study

- **Objective:** Translate multiple domain-specific content streams with more automation and increased speed
- Large-volume legacy material alignment
- Geographically dispersed workforce of up to 120 participants in 3 continents/time zones
  - ➢ MGPS
  - ➢ Client stakeholders
  - ➢ Client linguists

ManpowerGroup

Program Requirements

- Centralized Globally Accessible HLT Resources
  - Projects
  - Integrated Domain-Specific Machine Translation
  - Translation Memories/TermBases
  - Tech Support
- Integrated Project Management
- Data and Personnel Security
  - Dedicated HLT resource instance
  - Controlled human access (US Citizen only)
- Continuous MT improvement cycle
- Process automation
- Seamless integration of cloud and local-install HLT solutions

250

ManpowerGroup

ANSWER?

Post-Edited
Machine Translation

MT

CAT

TMS

…Talent

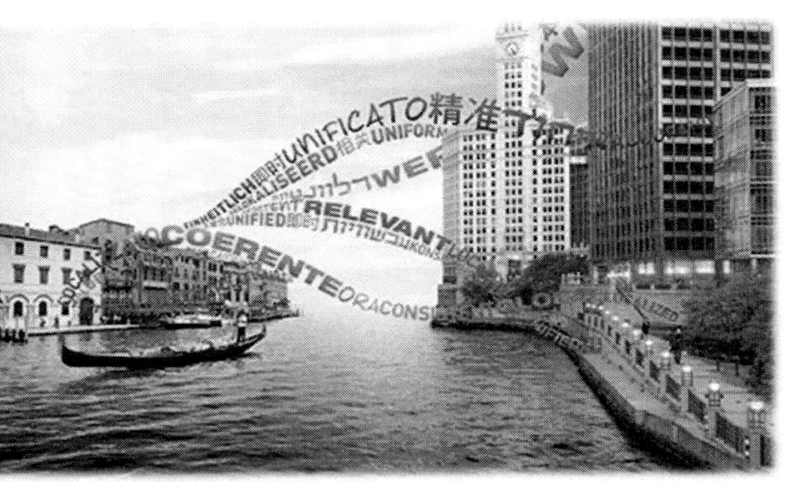

ManpowerGroup

Define Stakeholders and Budget

- Dedicate a representative team of production experts – include the client!
  - Get early buy-in from the future production team
  - Start building the TMS operations culture
  - Let the production-side stakeholders define a business case and the best solution
- Align Budget and HLT options
  - Define Scope and Level of Effort - manage budget and expectations
  - HLT costs (CAT/TMS/MT)
  - IT setup (local install vs. SaaS)

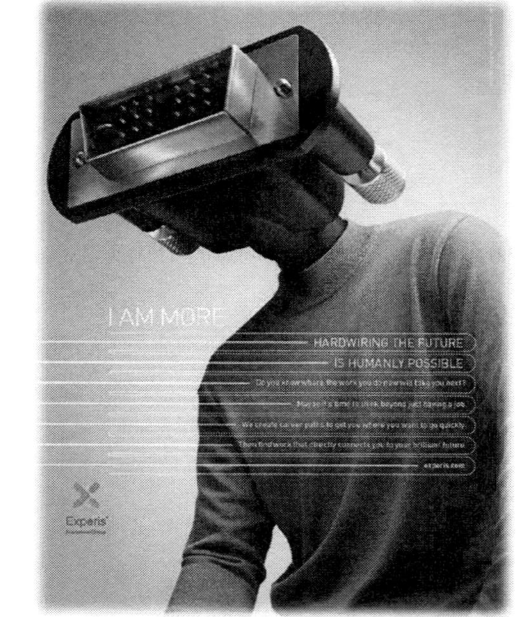

ManpowerGroup

Challenge

There are a growing number of strong HLT solutions. How do you select the right one, and how do you implement effectively?

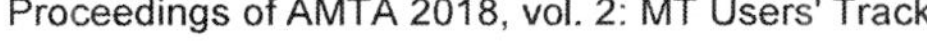

ManpowerGroup

Choosing/Validating the Right Solution

- Perform preliminary research
  - *What do I need?*
  - *What are my options (commercial/custom/open source)?*
  - *What are my community peers saying?*
- Choose solution candidates
- Set up orientation calls with solution developers
  - *Identify dedicated contacts for technical and contractual questions*
  - *Explore data security options for data and support*

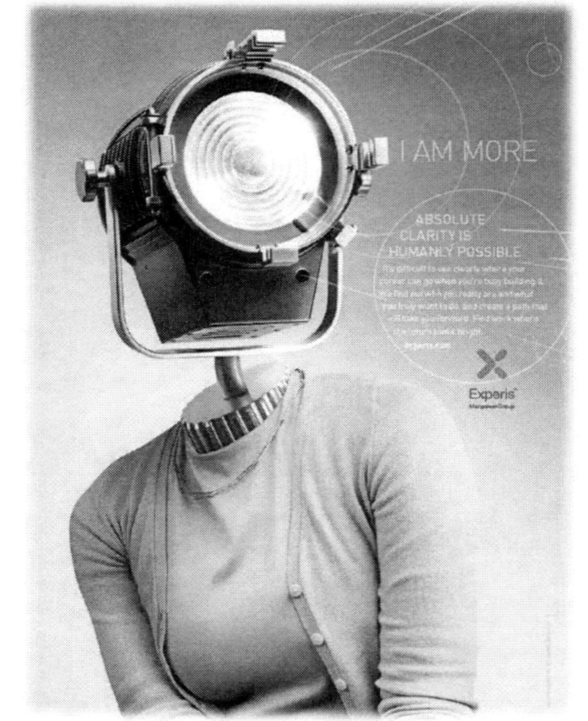

ManpowerGroup

Choosing/Validating the Right Solution (cont.)

- Create evaluation matrix
  - *Evaluate all products with the same criteria*
  - *Standard criteria include:*
    - Key features
    - Benefits
    - Shortcomings
    - Technical and contract support
    - Deployment options
    - Costs

PUT THE DATA ASIDE – TIME FOR WHITEBOARDING!

Whiteboard Your Workflows

- Define and document/update existing production processes
- Do *not* adjust workflows based on the solutions' limitations
  - *If it doesn't fit, it's not right for you*
- Generate a master workflow that addresses the variations
  - *Define production steps as "required" or "optional"*
- Whiteboard other business requirements/expectations
  - *Manage expectations*

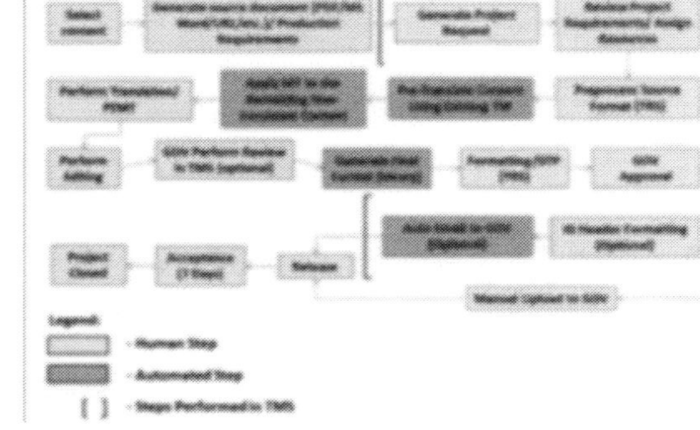

257

ManpowerGroup

See What "Fits" – Select and Acquire

- Combine the research with the master workflow and business requirements
- Identify the solution that provides the most value
- Generate TMS/MT Selection Report:
  - Fund the acquisition and deployment
  - Maintain technology knowledgebase
  - Validate your decision
- Finalize the deployment plan
- Minimize the time between the acquisition and production deployment

ManpowerGroup

Initial Configuration

- Master production workflow
- Sample business rules
- Sample linguistic resources (TMs, TBs, baseline MT)
- Optional/custom components and workflow steps (forms, fields, etc.)
- Production pilot
  - ➤ *Test the workflow, not just the filters*

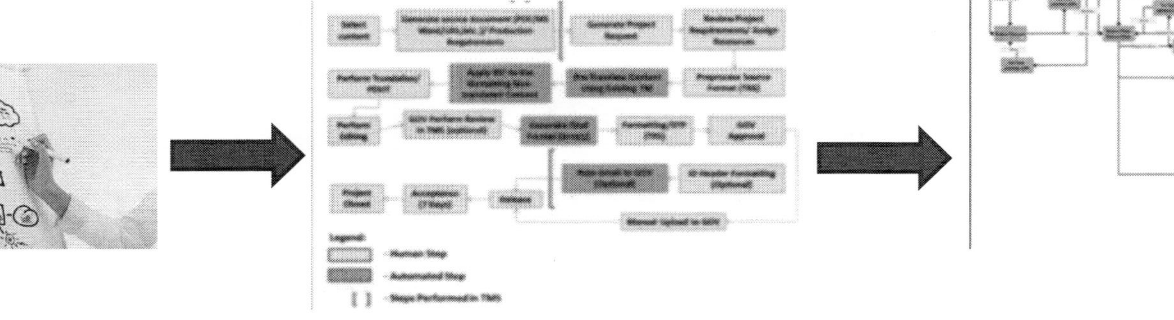

Document TMS/PEMT Production Procedures – Role-Specific Instructions

- Project Managers
  - *Production*
  - *Offline procedures*
- Linguist users
  - *Production*
- Client users
  - *Portal access/request*
  - *Production*
- Other production roles (as applicable)

Develop and Implement Training

Client stakeholder participation and buy-in is key to project success.

- Develop reusable curriculum
- Provide general system overview
- Provide role-specific training

Production Deployment

- Configure and deploy client portal and other auxiliary components
- Align legacy content
- Optimize TM corpora for MT training
  - Segmentation
  - Markup
- Perform initial training of Domain-Specific MT engines/language pairs
- Perform first automated and human evaluation of MT – start the measuring

ManpowerGroup

Start PEMT!!!

- Start production for the selected programs/projects

- Adjust configuration, procedures, and documentation, as applicable
  - *Deliver the updates to the appropriate parties*

Continuous MT Improvement Cycle

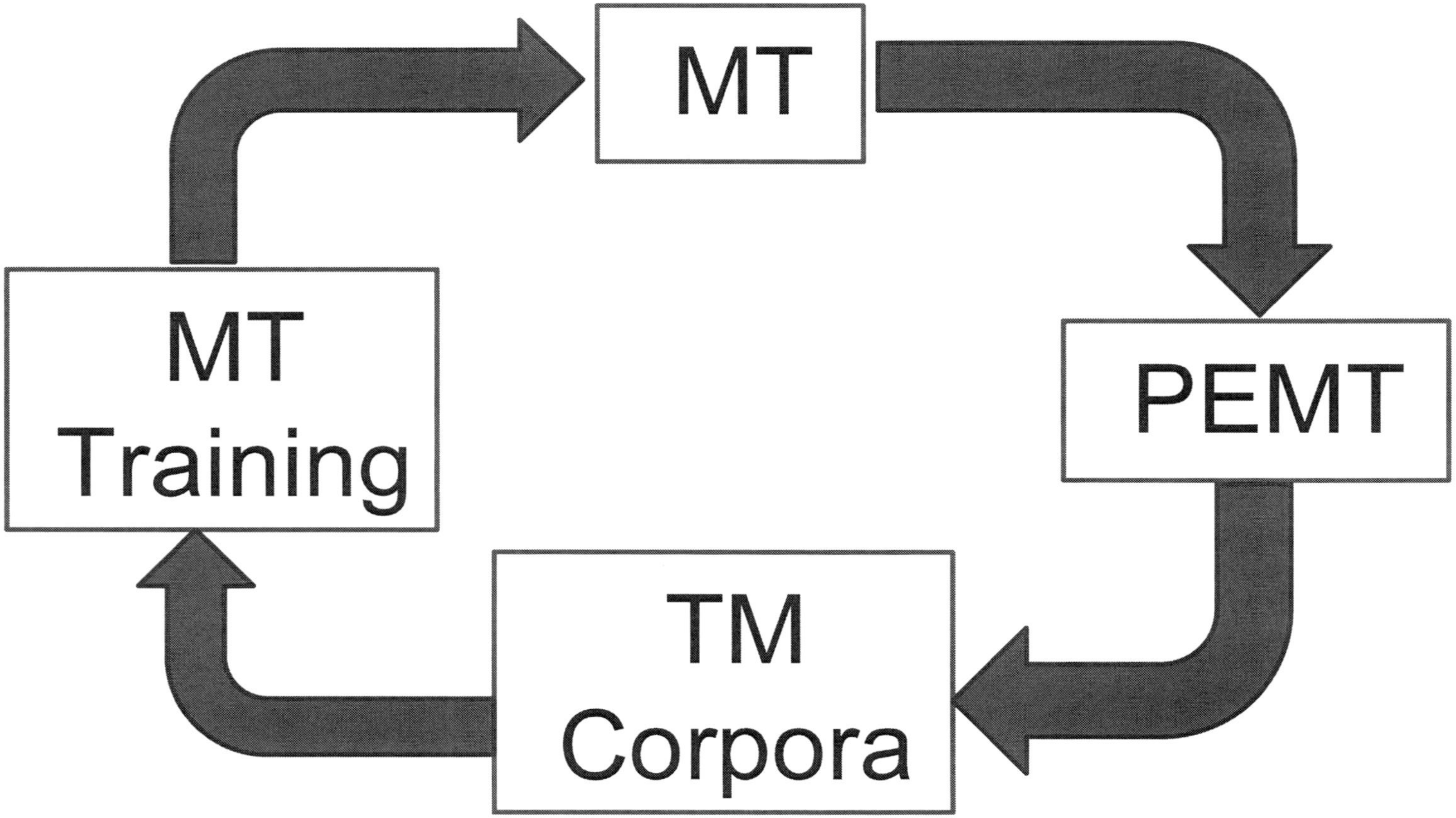

Proceedings of AMTA 2018, vol. 2: MT Users' Track

Additional Automated Workflow Options

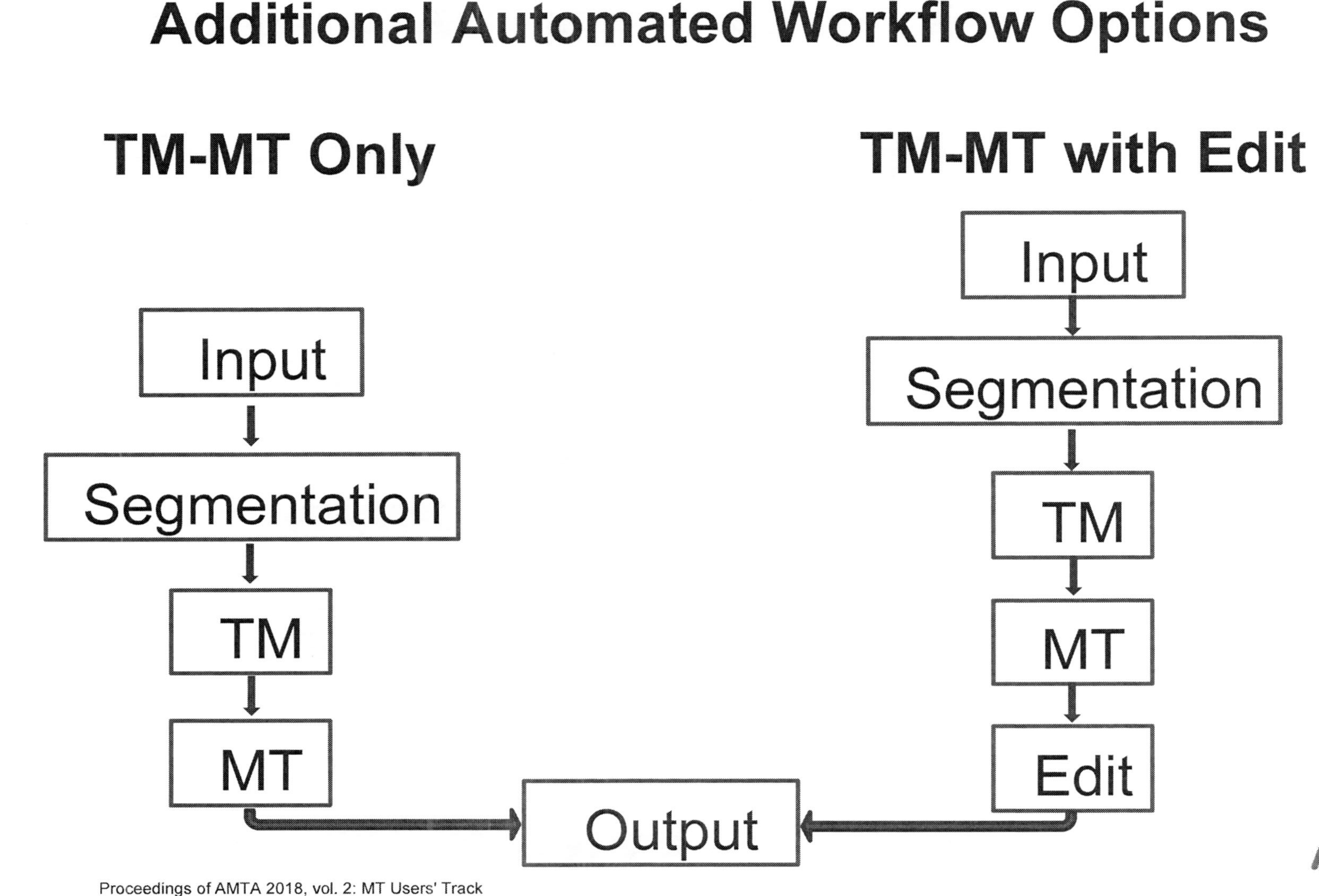

ManpowerGroup

Program Launch

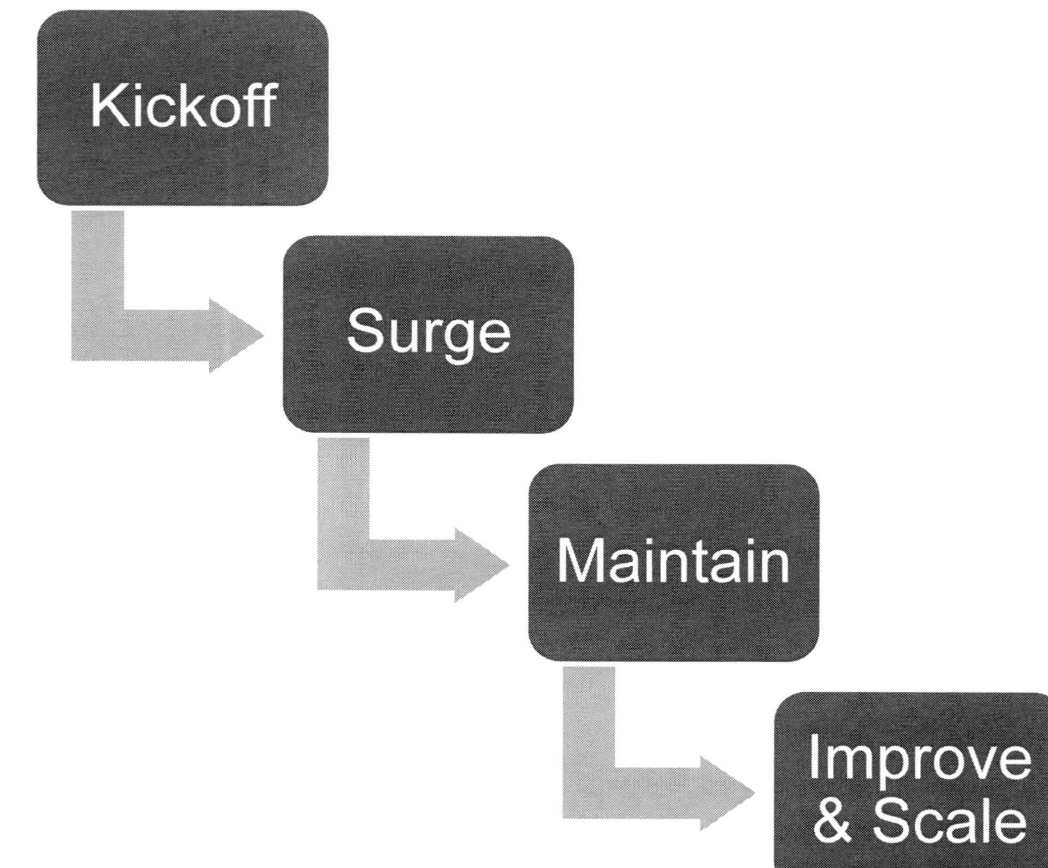

Kick Off

- **Review SOW**
  - ➢ Clarify parameters and assumptions at kickoff meeting with stakeholders
- **Inform Stakeholders – before, during, after kickoff!**
  - ➢ How to "engineer for success" with source selection, MT training corpus
  - ➢ Manage expectations for productivity, timeline
- **Set Goals and KPIs**
  - ➢ Linguist productivity
  - ➢ Tool effectiveness

ManpowerGroup

Surge

- **Build a Team**
  - ➢ Linguists, Engineers, PM
  - ➢ Success factors: full-time dedicated resources; native speakers, US citizens, tech-savvy; ability to handle breadth of subject matter domain
- **Baseline**
  - ➢ Translate sample set of material (larger = better) outside of PEMT environment to gauge productivity sans HLT
- **Track Everything!**
  - ➢ Client queries, client feedback, adjustments made to workflow
  - ➢ Technology data: MT training corpus size and details, BLEU
  - ➢ Project data: word count, TM leveraging, subject matter, time spent

268

Maintain

- **Prioritize Knowledge Share**
  - Training materials, lessons learned
  - Meet regularly

- **Monitor, Report, Adjust**
  - Provide reports and recommendations monthly
  - Metrics

- **Review client level of engagement**
  - Client involved too much or too little?
  - Client requests within contract scope?

Improve & Scale

- **Monitor technology developments and provide recommendations as necessary**
  - Raise questions/issues to software developers as needed
- **Evaluate MT output monthly; experiment and make adjustments as needed**
  - Capture qualitative and quantitative data
- **Communicate success stories and lessons learned**
  - Continually demonstrate ROI
- **Scale with additional domains and locales**
  - Ensure HLT solution can accommodate growth

Recap

- **Historical challenges with MGPS PS client base**

- **Early steps toward HLT culture**

- **Case Study Success Factors**
  - Client buy-in
  - Customized HLT solution -- one size does not fit all
  - Documentation for reusability and scalability
  - Talent development through training
  - Clear KPIs to evaluate success
  - Continuous improvement

ManpowerGroup

Future Enhancements

- Neural MT
- Adaptive MT/Augmented Translation
- Substring tokenization
- Integrated speech-to-text supported by TMS/CAT/MT
- Multilingual Redaction Database (MRD)

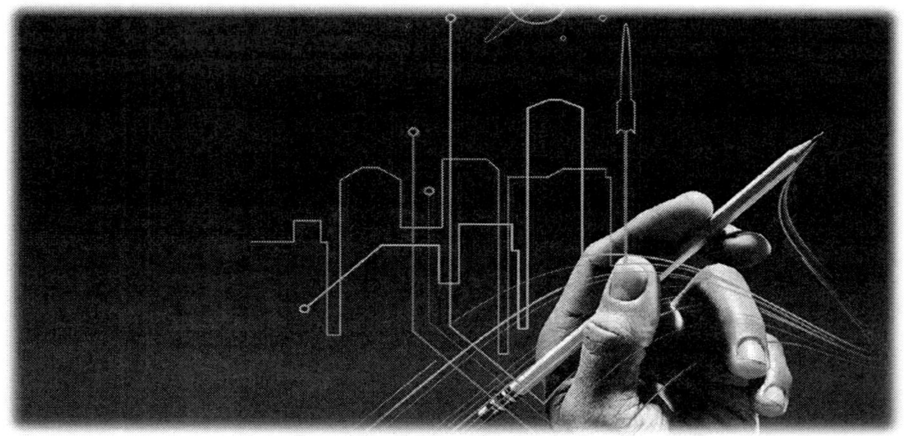

ManpowerGroup

Thank you

Konstantine G. Boukhvalov
Operations Manager, Engineering
ManpowerGroup Public Sector
703-245-9372
Konstantine.Boukhvalov@Experis.com

Sandra Hogg
Deputy Program Manager
ManpowerGroup Public Sector
571-358-7671
sandra.hogg@manpowergroup.com

Appendix

Acronym	Expansion
BLEU	Bilingual evaluation understudy
CAT	Computer-assisted translation
CONUS	Contiguous United States
HLT	Human language technology
KPI	Key performance indicator
l10n	Localization
MGPS	ManpowerGroup Public Sector
MT	Machine translation
PEMT	Post-edited machine translation
PM	Project manager
PS	Public sector
ROI	Return on investment
SaaS	Software as a service
SOW	Statement of work
TB	TermBase
TMS	Translation management system

ManpowerGroup

Embedding register-aware MT into the CAT workflow

Corey Miller
The MITRE Corporation, McLean, VA 22102   camiller@mitre.org
Danielle Silverman   danielle.c.silverman@nvtc.gov
National Virtual Translation Center, Washington, DC 20535
Vanesa Jurica   vjurica@mitre.org
The MITRE Corporation, McLean, VA 22102
Elizabeth Richerson   liz@mitre.org
The MITRE Corporation, McLean, VA 22102
Rodney Morris   rodney.d.morris@nvtc.gov
National Virtual Translation Center, Washington, DC 20535
Elisabeth Mallard   Elisabeth.d.mallard@nvtc.gov
National Virtual Translation Center, Washington, DC 20535

Abstract

As machine translation (MT) improves, the possibility for it to translate different registers appropriately becomes more possible. This capability is particularly relevant when confronting non-standard varieties such as are common in social media and chats. Register-sensitive MT, coupled with advances in register detection, opens up new possibilities for the enhancement of computer-assisted translation (CAT) tools.

1. Introduction

Many translation style guides say something like the following: "A translation is not just a transcription from one language into another. It needs to render not only the meaning of words and sentences but also the context and, more subtly, what is sometimes described in stylistic manuals as the register of the source text—its level and style of language." (World Bank 2004). It should be noted that such advice is also proffered to interpreters: "From the standpoint of the user, a successful interpretation is one that faithfully and accurately conveys the meaning of the source language orally, reflecting the style, register, and cultural context of the source message, without omissions, additions or embellishments on the part of the interpreter" (Federal Coordination and Compliance Section, 2011).

If such advice is to be adhered to, it will of course be most challenging to those translation departments whose work spans a wide range of registers, from slangy/chatty to scientific/formal. After discussing the nature of register and the motivation for advising its conveyance from source to target, we seek to establish ways in which computer-assisted translation (CAT) software can aid translators in this process. In particular, we explore the role of both termbases and translation memories (TMs) in recording register information. Within that context, we consider the possible role of automatic register detection. Finally, we discuss work on register in machine translation (MT) and how this may ultimately facilitate a register-enabled CAT workflow.

2. Register

Ability to effectively translate register variation is relevant to all spheres of translation, whether governmental, corporate or literary/creative. Government organizations must translate from a variety of sources, possibly ranging from social media to diplomatic communications and businesses produce communications variously targeted for customers and partners. Perhaps register variation is most obvious in the creative domains, including subtitling and fiction. In all of these domains, even literary ones (Francisco 2015), CAT usage is becoming more prevalent.

Failure to convey register in translation can have real-life consequences, even in "translations" within a given language. Jackman (2017) describes the case of Warren Demesme, who said "just give me a lawyer dog" in the course of his police interrogation in Louisiana. The Louisiana Supreme Court decided that this utterance did not constitute an invocation of the right to counsel. As pointed out by Green (2002), *dog* or *dawg* is a term of address used by African American males, "without negative import", a detail neither the interrogators nor the court seems to have taken into account.

Steiner's (1998) register-based analysis of original English and subsequent German Rolex advertisements indicates that adherence to register across languages may have business consequences. From this analysis, it appears that the effectiveness of the advertisements may be compromised by a failure to convey source language register to the target language in certain cases.

2.1. Definition

While at first glance, register might seem to simply include stylistic variation, we feel it may be useful to explore whether what is intended in recommendations to convey register from source to target might really include the full range of sociolinguistic variation. In addition to style, sociolinguistic variation can include language differences associated with geography (from nation to neighborhood), age (from youth to old), as well as social, ethnic or religious affiliation.

The notion of markedness proves useful in this discussion. While the notion of "standard" language is somewhat fraught, it seems fairly straightforward to say that a given expression is marked for a particular sociolinguistic category. For example, while a word like "money" might be considered neutral in most, if not all, varieties of English, a word like "dough" in the sense of "money" seems marked for informality. In the same way, "elevator" is markedly American (and perhaps beyond) and "lift" is markedly British (and perhaps beyond).

First, it will be helpful to assess whether register covers all the sociolinguistically-relevant information we might want to convey. Halliday (2002) focuses on functional (diatypic) registers, i.e. the language differences encountered across domains. Yu (2017) has a wider conception, including the range of language from vulgar to elevated, and the possibility both of several registers in a given domain, and the preponderance of certain registers within certain social groups.

Dialect or locale introduces another axis of sociolinguistic variation that is hard to dissociate from register, and its conveyance from source to target is not straightforward. For example, while "pop" and "soda" are two locale-specific ways of referring to carbonated beverages in American English, how or should one convey this in a French translation? Hanes (2012) discusses the rendering of Southern American English into Brazilian Portuguese subtitles and finds a variety of available strategies, many of which could benefit from a more structured approach to this problem.

Finally, we consider the sociolinguistic approach to style variation. Labov (2006) offers the notion that style is correlated with attention paid to speech, and work in this tradition explores a range of styles from casual to formal based on the task at hand, e.g. conversation vs. reading word lists. Bell (1984) offers a slightly different perspective, viewing style as "audience design", thus shifting the focus from attention to accommodation to interlocutors. We find that both perspectives on style variation are useful here.

For our purposes, the attentional view of style provides insight into the kinds of deviations from neutrality that often perplex translators: typographical errors, disfluencies, malaprops, and in the case of non-native speakers/authors, false friends (Chamizo-Domínguez 2008). At the same time, the audience-focused view of style is relevant when we consider for whom the translation is intended.

While we will not go into further detail on this topic here, we feel a proper analysis of how such displays of lack of attention (or education/experience/training) should be conveyed in translation is a proper part of register analysis and conveyance. While treatment of such "errors" are often handled by a diverse set of tools from use of the term *sic* to subtle correction in target language translations, it is clear that each of these devices carries baggage, whether by impugning the source author/speaker or masking/"upgrading" the source author's intent and characteristics.

3. Terminology Management

Termbases are a natural repository for register information. ISO/TC37/SC3, "Systems to manage terminology, knowledge and content" includes ISO/CD 12620, "Terminology and other language and content resources -- Data category specifications" whose current data categories are described at http://www.datcatinfo.net. The register, dating and frequency data categories shown in Table 1 provide a starting point for considering the extent to which dialect and register issues can be dealt with through terminology management.

Dating	Modern
	Old
Frequency	Commonly used
	Infrequently used
	Rarely used
Register	Bench-level
	Dialect
	Facetious
	Formal
	In house
	Ironic
	Neutral
	Slang
	Taboo
	Technical
	Vulgar

Table 1. Register data categories in ISO/CD 12620

While fairly extensive, this list is not exhaustive. For example, age grading, i.e. the use of terms by certain age groups and not others, sociolects and dialect/locale need to be (more finely) addressed. So, in contrast to simple data categories, these could allow more complex data types.

4. Translation Memory

TM metadata is another potential repository for register information, but a survey of the relevant standards (e.g. TMX, XLIFF) and literature indicates that it is not common to characterize translation units (TUs) beyond their date, translator, status and domain. Moorkens (2013) indicates the usefulness of date metadata, since more recent TUs may benefit from having been corrected and feature the latest vocabulary. However, even if register information were made specifiable in TMs, analogous to that proposed in the standards for terminology, it remains to be established how and whether this could be made useful for translators in conveying register into the target language.

In our imagined scenario, source and target variants of translation units in a translation memory would have the same metadata elements available to them, but they would not necessarily match between source and target. For example, while elements such as "frequency" or "slang" might well match, if further sociolinguistic detail is provided, such as "Southern United States" for the American English variant of a TU, this cannot be expected to have the same value as the equivalent in another language.

At this stage, we are agnostic as to whether separate TMs should be maintained for register. Given the potentially large dimensionality of register information, it seems that such an approach would prove cumbersome. At any rate, it seems that a register-sensitive TM search should not be greatly affected by the choice to use single or multiple TMs.

4.1 Automatic Register Detection

Assuming that register information can be captured in a TM, the question arises as to what extent this can be done automatically as new TUs are added. Lapshinova-Koltunski & Vela (2015) and Biber (2014) discuss automatic identification of registers. Salloum et al. (2014) discuss sentence-level dialect identification in service of MT; this seems like a promising approach to apply in the case of identifying register in source materials, since it can shift multiple times over the course of the document. Once enhanced with register information, TUs could be compared for register across languages, resulting in a way for translators and reviewers to identify register mismatches warranting further attention. Register detection could also enhance content optimization tools' capabilities with respect to style checking.

5. Machine Translation

Since MT can help fill in the gaps in TM, it is worth exploring whether it too can be made sensitive to register. Niu et al. (2017) describe initial attempts at imbuing MT with the ability to control register. In cases without a suitable TM match, MT register control could be exercised on source language TU variants in order to produce target variants with the appropriate register.

6. Discussion

How might all of this work in practice? Let us imagine a workflow including a CAT tool of the future which we call Register CAT. Register CAT provides both terminology management and translation memory both enhanced with register metadata, and the translation memory is enhanced with register detection capabilities. The translation memory backs off to machine translation that can output various registers on demand.

At this stage, we imagine that an input source text for Register CAT is segmented into sentence-sized segments as is common in today's CAT tools. While it is clear that register can vary within documents, it is not clear whether a different kind of segmentation would serve register conveyance better, and indeed, as will be seen below, individual segments can exhibit register variation as well.

The source language part of the translation unit can then be submitted to a language-specific register detector which can fill in register metadata information. This can then be used to search the translation memory, which has also been annotated (either by hand or by a register detector) for register. We leave the theory and mechanics of the factoring in of register information to TM match scoring to further research, but for now, we assume that better register matches will score higher than otherwise equally matching target language variants.

As the translator sets about modifying the translation memory match, the termbase will provide guidance by presenting register-matched target terms highest in the list. Once the translator is ready to commit the translation unit, the opportunity will be made available for her to modify the translation unit metadata in case the automatically generated register information requires it. In those cases where there is no suitable translation memory match for the source language segment, register-enabled MT will provide a target language segment best matching the source language register specifications.

Let us work through an example based on an American English news report from Oklahoma (https://www.youtube.com/watch?v=ydmPh4MXT3g). For the sake of this example, we will assume that the audio has been transcribed into the source language orthography and that the transcript is what constitutes the source side presented in Register CAT that needs to be translated into a target language, e.g. French.

> (Announcer) One resident describes her horrifying experience when she first realized the complex was on fire.
>
> (Sweet Brown) Well, I woke up to go get me a cold pop…

The announcer's utterance displays no marked properties and could well be described as register-neutral. In contrast, Sweet Brown's utterance displays two features that can be considered marked with respect to American English: "go get me" and "pop". The use of "me" in the phrase "go get me" is an example of a personal dative which Horn (2008) ascribes to "dialectal (Southern and Appalachian) U.S. English". The use of "pop" vs. "soda" (among other variants) has been a longstanding discussion among American English dialectologists (von Schneidemesser 1996). According to popvssoda.com, an internet survey project by Alan McConchie, "pop" is the lead variant in Oklahoma County, where the broadcast emanates. In fact, the state of Oklahoma appears to be one of the southernmost regions for "pop", whose main bastions appear to be the Northwestern and North-central regions of the United States.

Whereas the personal dative in "go get me" has a vernacular flavor, "pop" seems to be more of a geographical rather than a stylistic variant. In termbase metadata, we could indicate the stylistic and geographic features of each expression:

"go get me": informal, dialect:Southern/Applachian (US)
"pop": neutral, dialect:Northwestern/North-central (US), including Oklahoma

However, when considering how to indicate the metadata in the TM for the entire segment "Well, I woke up to go get me a cold pop…", we propose to take the union of the register features exhibited by the expressions it contains. Indeed, one segment could certainly contain both informal and formal words, or words with different geographical affiliations. Therefore, it is important to allow the metadata to accommodate this, perhaps by quantifying the number of expressions in a segment containing each relevant feature. This creates a situation where some utterances will have stronger sociolinguistic marking than others. For the expression in question, this could look something like this:

"Well, I woke up to go get me a cold pop": informal (1), Southern/Appalachian US (1), Northwestern/North-central/Oklahoma (1)

Now when considering a translation memory search for a target language, say French, equivalent for this phrase, we confront all of the sociolinguistic variation of that language. In this case, the personal dative, as in "Je me prends un petit café", literally "I take me a little coffee" (Horn 2008) does not seem to be markedly informal as in American English. In the case of "pop", French has a number of terms of its own, as shown in Table 2.

boisson gazeuse	Formal
liqueur[1]	Canadian, Informal?
soda	Informal?

Table 2. French equivalents for "pop/soda"

While mapping register properties like "formal" and "informal" between languages may seem at first straightforward, we are confronted by the lack of register parallelism (at least with respect to vocabulary) between languages. So, if "go get me" is informal in English, and the equivalent with a personal dative is not marked in French, must we try to find an informal way of expressing that? If "pop" is regionally marked in English, is our translation best served by seeking a regionally-marked term like "liqueur" in French? We do not offer solutions to these problems here, but they are discussed elsewhere (e.g. Berezowski 1997).

It is hoped that this outline specifying ways in which the CAT workflow can be fortified to accommodate register information will provide researchers and developers a path forward for a forthcoming generation of CAT tools which will make it easier for translators and reviewers to maintain and assess register fidelity.

References

Bell, Allan. 1984. Language style as audience design. Language in Society 13, 145-204.

Berezowski, Leszek. 1996. Dialect in Translation. Wydawnictwo Uniwerytetu Wroclawskiego.

---

[1] Thanks to Miguel Jetté for Canadian French consultation.

Biber, Douglas. 2014. Using multi-dimensional analysis to explore cross-linguistic universals of register variation. Languages in Contrast 14:1, 7-34.

Chamizo-Domínguez, Pedro J. 2008. Semantics and pragmatics of false friends. Routledge.

Federal Coordination and Compliance Section. 2011. Commonly Asked Questions and Answers Regarding Lim-ited English Proficient (LEP) Individuals. https://www.lep.gov/faqs/042511_Q&A_LEP_General.pdf [last accessed 25 September, 2017].

Francisco, Reginaldo. 2015. CAT tools em tradução literária: para quê? VI Congresso Internacional de Tradção e Interpretação da ABRATES.

Green, Lisa J. 2002. African American English: A Linguistic Introduction. Cambridge University Press.

Halliday, M.A.K. 2002. The construction of knowledge and value in the grammar of scientific discourse: With reference to Charles Darwin's The Origin of Species. In Jonathan J. Webster, editor, Linguistic Studies of Text and Discourse, Volume 2, Bloomsbury, pages 169-192.

Hanes, Vanessa Lopes Lourenço. 2012. Norms in the Translation of Southern American English in Subtitles in Brazil: How is southern American speech presented to Brazilians? Translation Journal 16(3). http://translationjournal.net/journal/61southern.htm [last accessed 25 September, 2017].

Horn, Laurence R. 2008. "I love me some him": The landscape of non-argument datives. In O. Bonami and P. Cabredo Hofherr, editors, Empirical Issues in Syntax and Semantics 7, pages 169-192.

Jackman, Tom. 2017. "The suspect told police 'give me a lawyer dog.' The court says he wasn't asking for a lawyer." Washington Post, November 2. https://www.washingtonpost.com/news/true-crime/wp/2017/11/02/the-suspect-told-police-give-me-a-lawyer-dog-the-court-says-he-wasnt-asking-for-a-lawyer.

Labov, William. 2006. The social stratification of English in New York City, Second Edition. Cambridge.

Lapshinova-Koltunski, Ekaterina and Mihaela Vela. 2015. Measuring 'registerness'in human and machine translation: A text classification approach. Proceedings of the Second Workshop on Discourse in Machine Translation, pages 122-131.

Moorkens, Joss. 2013. The role of metadata in translation memories. In Valerie Pellatt, editor, Text, Extratext, Metatext and Paratext in Translation, Cambridge Scholars Publishing, pages 79-90.

Niu, Xing, Marianna Martindale and Marine Carpuat. 2017. A study of style in machine translation: Controlling the formality of machine translation output. Proceedings of the 2017 Conference on Empirical Methods in Natural Language Processing, pages 2804-2809.

Salloum, Wael, Heba Elfardy, Linda Alamir-Sallou, Nizar Habash and Mona Diab. 2014. Proceedings of the 52nd Annual Meeting of the Association for Computational Linguistics (Short Papers), pages 772-778.

Steiner, Erich. 1998. A register-baed translation evaluation: An advertisement as a case in point. Target 10:2, 291-318.

von Schneidemesser, Luanne. 1996. Soda or Pop? Journal of English Linguistics, 24(4): 270-287.

World Bank. 2004. World Bank Translation Style Guide, Version 1.0. http://sitere-sources.worldbank.org/TRANSLATIONSERVICESEXT/Resources/Transla-tion_Style_Guide_English.pdf [last accessed 25 September, 2017].

Yu, Jing. Translating 'others' as 'us' in Huckleberry Finn: dialect, register and the heterogeneity of standard language. Language and Literature, 26(1): 54-65.

Challenges in Speech Recognition and Translation of High-Value Low-Density Polysynthetic Languages

Judith L. Klavans   judith.l.klavans.civ@mail.mil
John Morgan   john.j.morgan50.civ@mail.mil
Stephen LaRocca   stephen.a.larocca.civ@mail.mil
Jeffrey Micher   jeffrey.c.micher.civ@mail.mil
Clare Voss   clare.r.voss.civ@mail.mil

Multilingual Computing and Analytics Branch, Army Research Laboratory,
Adelphi, Maryland 20783, USA

Abstract

The focus of this paper is on setting out a framework for experiments on using the latest machine learning techniques over speech and text data collections of highly complex languages. We are in the process of creating comparable and consistent databases with associated processing technologies of some of the world's most challenging languages, polysynthetic languages, i.e. those where one long word can express the meaning contained in a multi-word sentence in languages like English. We present an end-to-end system for Automatic Speech Recognition (ASR) and Machine Translation (MT) involving Artificial Intelligence approaches of machine learning (ML). The ML framework uses deep learning since the networks we are sharing are deep in nature; this deep variant of Multi-Task ML (MTML) embodies human-like AI abilities to learn a language with small amounts of input thereby achieving a degree of AI. We explore recurrent neural networks (RNNs), long and short term memory network (L-STMs), bidirectional LSTMs (BiLSTM) and convolutional NNs (CNN) to compare and evaluate results.

1. Motivation

The government and military have to respond to and communicate in languages that present themselves in the field – whether for humanitarian aid, intelligence or other operational requirements. Currently, the government and military have many language requirements, ranging from interacting with coalition forces to public affairs to on-the-ground soldier interaction with foreign citizens to intelligence. To quote a current Program Manager at DARPA[1] in the Information Innovation Office (I2O):

> *"We do not know what language will be next in line for military and national defense needs. Thus, we need to be prepared with technology to handle any language of any complexity, and we need the capability to ramp up with small amounts of data."*

---

[1] Dr. Boyan Onyshkevych, personal communication.
[2] https://www.nytimes.com/2017/10/04/world/africa/special-forces-killed-niger.html

Increased globalization has led to an urgent need for even more and varied language capabilities than in the past. As Army Chief of Staff, Gen. Mark Milley said in response to the gap in intelligence leading to the recent ambush against US troops in Niger:

> *"We are training, advising and assisting indigenous armies all over the world. And I anticipate and expect that will increase not decrease in years to come,"*[2]

This paper presents strategies for addressing the computational and linguistic challenges posed by such complex languages. We address specifically the areas of automatic speech recognition and MT research and development in government and military settings.

2. Research Goals

The focus of this paper is on setting out a framework for experiments on using the latest machine learning techniques over speech, text, and data collections of highly complex languages. We are in the process of creating comparable databases with associated processing technologies of some of the world's most challenging languages, those where one long word can express the meaning contained in a multi-word sentence in languages like English. These are called polysynthetic languages. To illustrate, consider the following example from Inuktitut, one of the official languages of the Territory of Nunavut in Canada. The morpheme *-tusaa-* (shown in boldface below) is the root, and all the other morphemes are synthetically combined with it in one unit.[3]

(1) **tusaa**-tsia-runna-nngit-tu-alu-u-junga
    hear-well-be.able-NEG-DOER-very-BE-PART.1.S
  'I can't hear very well.'

Kabardian (Circassian), from the Northwest Caucasus, also shows this phenomenon, with the root *-še-* shown in boldface below:

(2) wə-q'ə-d-ej-z-ɣe-**še**-ž'e-f-a-te-q'əm
    2SG.OBJ-DIR-LOC-3SG.OBJ-1SG.SUBJ-CAUS-**lead**-COMPL-POTENTIAL-PAST-PRF-NEG
  'I would not let you bring him right back here.'

Polysynthetic languages are spoken all over the globe and are richly represented among Native North and South American families. Many polysynthetic languages are among the world's most endangered languages,[4] with fragmented dialects and communities struggling to preserve their linguistic heritage. In particular, polysynthetic languages can be found in the US Southwest (Southern Tiwa, Kiowa Tanoan family), Canada, Mexico (Nahuatl, Uto-Aztecan family), and Central Chile (Mapudungun, Araucanian), as well as in Australia (Nunggubuyu, Macro-Gunwinyguan family), Northeastern Siberia (Chukchi and Koryak, both from the Chukotko-Kamchatkan family), and India (Sora, Munda family), as shown in the map below (Figure 1).

---

[2] https://www.nytimes.com/2017/10/04/world/africa/special-forces-killed-niger.html

[3] Abbreviations follow the Leipzig Glossing Rules; additional glosses are spelled out in full.

[4] In fact, the majority of the languages spoken in the world today are endangered and disappearing fast (See Bird, 2009). Estimates are that, of the approximately 7000 languages in the world today, at least one disappears every day (https://www.ethnologue.com).

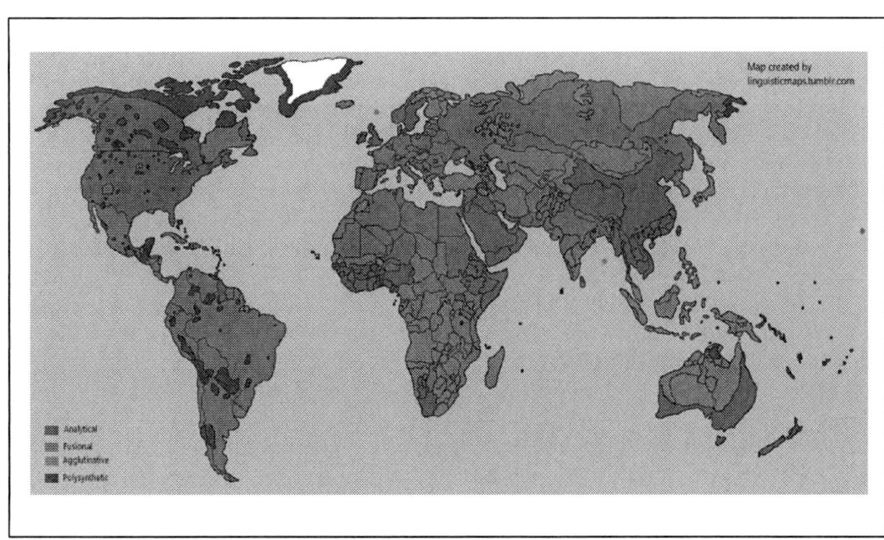

Figure 1: Polysynthetic Languages[5]

Although there are many definitions of polysynthesis, there is often confusion on what constitutes the exact criteria and phenomena (Mithun 2017). Even authoritative sources categorize languages in conflicting ways.[6] Typically, polysynthetic languages demonstrate holophrasis, i.e. the ability of an entire sentence to be expressed in what is considered by native speakers to be just one word (Bird 2009). In linguistic typology, the opposite of polysynthesis is *isolation*. Polysynthesis technically (etymologically) refers to how many morphemes there are per word. Using that criterion, the typological continuum can be represented as follows:

(3) isolating/analytic languages > synthetic languages > polysynthetic languages

Adding another dimension of morphological categorization, languages can be distinguished by the degree of clarity of morpheme boundaries. If we apply this criterion, languages can be categorized according to the following typological continuum:

(4) agglutinating > mildly fusional > fusional

Thus, a language might be characterized overall as polysynthetic and agglutinating, that is, generally a high number of morphemes per word, with clear boundaries between morphemes and thus easily segmentable. Another language might be characterized as polysynthetic and fusional, so again, many morphemes per word, but so many phonological and other processes have occurred that segmenting morphemes becomes more challenging.

---

[5] http://linguisticmaps.tumblr.com/post/120857875008/513-morphological-typology-tonal-languages. Map by Rodrigo Pereira.

[6] For example, the article in the *Oxford Research Encyclopedia of Linguistics* on "Polysynthesis: A Diachronic and Typological Perspective" by Michael Fortescue (Fortescue, 2016), a well-known expert on polysynthesis, lists Aymara as possibly polysynthetic, whereas others designate it as agglutinative (http://www.native-languages.org).

So far, we have discussed the morphological aspects of polysynthesis. Polysynthesis also has a number of syntactic ramifications, richly explored in the work of Baker (Baker 1997; 2002). He proposes a cluster of correlated syntactic properties associated with polysynthesis. Here we will mention just two of these properties: rich agreement (with the subject, direct object, indirect object, and applied objects if present) and omission of free-standing arguments (pro-drop).

Polysynthetic languages are of interest for both theoretical and practical reasons, as discussed more fully in the next section. On the theoretical side, these languages offer a potentially unique window into human cognition and language capabilities as well as into language acquisition (Mithun 1989; Greenberg 1960; Comrie 1981; Fortescue 1994; Fortescue et al. 2017). On the practical side, they offer significant obstacles to accurate linguistic analysis as well as to computational modeling.

3. Some Computational Challenges of Polysynthetic Languages

Polysynthetic languages pose unique challenges for traditional computational systems (Byrd et al. 1986). Even in allegedly cross-linguistic or typological analyses of specific phenomena, e.g. in forming a theory of clitics and cliticization (Klavans 1995), finding the full range of language types on which to test hypotheses proves difficult. Often, the data is simply not available so claims cannot neither refuted nor supported fully.

One of the underlying causes of this difficulty is that there are many languages for which a clear lexical division between nouns and verbs has been challenged; these languages are characterized by a large class of roots that are used either nominally or verbally, and many of these languages typically have polysynthetic features (cf. Lois & Vapnarsky 2006 for Amerindian, Aranovich 2013 for Austronesian, Testelets et al. 2009 for Adyghe, Davis & Matthewson 2009, Watanabe 2017 for Salish). Without a clear definition of what counts as a verb and what counts as a noun, there is no reliable way to compute significant correlations. Thus, a deeper understanding of polysynthetic phenomena may well contribute to a more nuanced understanding of cross-language comparisons and generalizations and enable researchers to pose meaningful and answerable questions about comparative features across languages.

On the practical side, many morphologically complex languages are crucial to purposes ranging from health care,[7] search and rescue, to the maintenance of cultural history (Fortescue et al. 2017). Add to this the interest in low-resource languages (from Inuktitut and Yup'ik in the North and East of Canada with over 35,000 speakers, and all the way to Northwest Caucasian), which is important for linguistic, cultural and governmental reasons. Many of the data collections in these languages, when annotated and aligned well, can serve as input to systems to automatically create correspondences, and these in turn can be useful to teachers in creating resources for their learners (Adams, Neubig, Cohn, & Bird 2015). These languages are generally not of immediate commercial value, and yet the research community needs to cope with

---

[7] For example, the USAID has funded a program in the mountains of Ecuador to provide maternal care in Quechua-dominant areas to reduce maternal and infant mortality rates, taking into account local cultural and language needs (https://www.usaidassist.org). Quechua is highly agglutinative, not polysynthetic; it is spoken by millions of speakers and has few corpora with limited annotation.

fundamental issues of language complexity. Finally, many of these understudied languages occur in areas that are key for health concerns (e.g. the AIDS epidemic) and international security. Consequently, research on these languages could have unanticipated benefits on many levels.

Recent research (e.g. Micher 2016) has applied neural nets to one polysynthetic language towards creating a feasible model for machine translation. As for speech recognition, longer words are generally less prone to error (Shinozaki & Furui 2001); this accounts for the fact that under 70% word accuracy is useful for keyword spotting, as shown in the IARPA Babel project[8]. On the other hand, if a language has only very long "words" encompassing all the nouns, verbs, clitics, affixes and particles, then these languages might not conform to established principles. At the same time, morphological and syntactic processing of polysynthetic languages pose specific challenges due to the blur between the more usual morphology-syntax distinction (Baker 1996). On low-resource language speech recognition, based on our experience with a range of language types, we hypothesize that the most effective units of recognition might be morphemes, although many of these morphemes might have a variety of possible surface forms. Because of the sentential nature of words in these languages, they can constitute a number of unique forms, raising intriguing speech recognition challenges.

4. Ongoing Language Research at the Army Research Laboratory

This paper provides an overview of one aspect of multilingual language research at the Army Research Laboratory, presenting the approaches used in polysynthetic languages. Figure 2 below shows which aspects of the project are being addressed. In the presentation, we will discuss technical details of each component and discuss further the novel methodological contributions of the research.

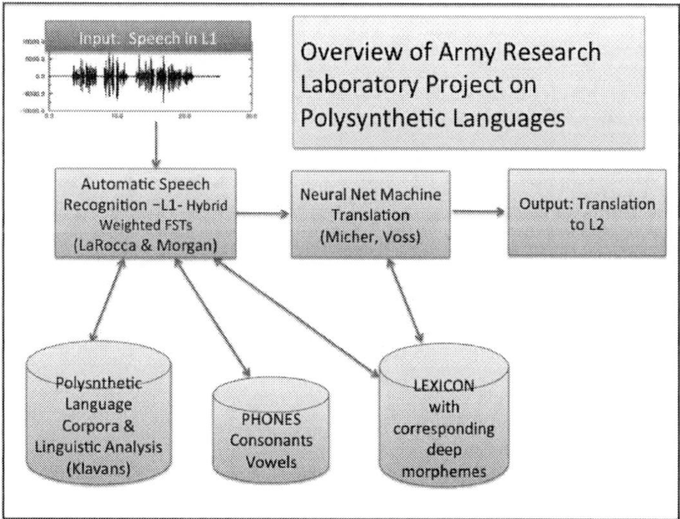

Figure 2: Overview of Speech-MT Polysynthetic Language Architecture

[8] https://www..gov/index.php/research-programs/babel

ARL has demonstrated leading technologies in the field with critical expertise. We are planning on developing systems, capable of performing speech translation. We are applying machine learning techniques using neural network approaches e.g. segmental recurrent neural networks (Kong et al. 2015, Micher 2017) and byte-pair encoding Sennrich, Haddow, Birch 2015) to several challenging problems for polysynthetic language analysis and processing. For ASR, we have implemented adaptive learning for iterative ASR, incorporating principles from the Kaldi toolkit[9] with modifications as required by different workflows and tasks.

5. Corpus Collection - Electronically-available resources

Only recently have researchers started collecting well-designed corpora for polysynthetic languages, e.g. for Circassian (Arkhangelskiy & Lander 2016) or Arapaho (Kazeminejad et al. 2017). There is an urgent need for documentation, archiving, creation of corpora and teaching materials that are specific to polysynthetic languages. Documentation and corpus-building challenges arise for many languages, but the complex morphological makeup of polysynthetic languages makes consistent documentation particularly difficult.

The more language data that is gathered and accurately analyzed, the deeper cross-linguistic analyses can be conducted which in turn will contribute to a range of fields including linguistic theory, language teaching and lexicography. For example, in examining cross-linguistic analyses of headedness, Polinsky (2012) gathered data to examine the question of whether the noun-verb ratio differs across headedness types across a wide sample of language types. However, she notes that:

> *"[T]he seemingly simple question of counting nouns and verbs is a quite difficult one; even obtaining data about the overall number of nouns and verbs proves to be an immense challenge. The ultimate consequence is that linguists lack reasonable tools to compare languages with respect to their lexical category size. Cooperation between theoreticians and lexicographers is of critical importance: just as comparative syntax received a big boost from the micro-comparative work on closely related languages (Romance; Germanic; Semitic), so micro-comparative WordNet building may lead to important breakthroughs that will benefit the field as a whole."* (Polinsky, 2012, *p. 351*)

In recent years, there has been a surge of major research on many of these languages. For example, the first Endangered Languages (ELs) Workshop held in conjunction with ACL was held in 2014 and the second in 2017.[10] The National Science Foundation and the National Endowment for the Humanities jointly fund a program for research on ELs.[11] The US government through IARPA and DARPA both have programs for translation, including for low resource languages.[12] The IARPA BABEL project focused on keyword search over speech for a variety of typologically different languages, including some with polysynthetic features.

---

[9] http://kaldi-asr.org/doc/pages.html

[10] http://www.acsu.buffalo.edu/~jcgood/ComputEL.html;
http://altlab.artsrn.ualberta.ca/computel-2/.

[11] https://www.nsf.gov/funding/pgm_summ.jsp?pims_id=12816;
https://www.neh.gov/grants/manage/general-information-neh-nsf-documenting-endangered-languages-fellowships.

[12] MATERIAL, https://www.iarpa.gov/index.php/research-programs/material and LORELEI,
http://www.darpa.mil/program/low-resource-languages-for-emergent-incidents, respectively.

Concomitant with the collection and cataloging of corpora, we are working with colleagues especially from the the NSF-funded EL-STEC Shared Task Evaluation Campaign project[13] on a future *shared task* in order to bring linguists and computational linguists together around the common area: accuracy in data analysis. We aim to formulate a shared task that meets the goals outlined in Levow, et al. (2017), namely, to "align the interests of the speech and language processing communities with those of ... language documentation communities....", guided by their design principles of realism, typological diversity, accessibility of the shared task, accessibility of the resulting software, extensibility and nuanced evaluation.

6. Future Research and Applications

Our next steps involve a two-phase approach, one on the ASR input and then one on the MT side (as shown in Figure 2.) On the ASR side, we plan to use Multi-Task Learning (MTL) (Caruana 1997), using corpora from multiple languages. Multitask Learning (also known as Multi-Task Machine Learning MTML) is an approach to inductive transfer that improves generalization by using the domain information contained in the training signals of related tasks as an inductive bias. It does this by learning tasks in parallel while using a shared representation; what is learned for each task can help other tasks be learned better. MTL is an established machine learning framework that has been applied to multiple domains.   The ASR problem, however, brings specific language problems to any machine learning approach. As noted in Hasegawa-Johnson 2017:

> To date, ASR has failed to achieve its potential, because successful ASR requires very large labeled corpora; the human transcribers must be computer-literate, and they must be native speakers of the language being transcribed. Large corpora are beyond the resources of most under-resourced language communities; we have found that transcribing even one hour of speech may be beyond the reach of communities that lack large-scale government funding. (Hasegawa-Johnson et al. 2017, p. 50)

This deep variant of MTML that we use embodies human-like AI abilities to learn a language with small amounts of input thereby achieving a degree of AI. We build on related techniques, widely used in the ASR community (Povey et al. 2011). The original contribution consists of using a range of conversational modalities (news, dialog, read speech) as sources of data in order to realize the potential for dissimilar input to contribute to more robust output. We hypothesize that the MTL technique can capture features characteristic of the target Low Resource language across dissimilar modalities and similar languages. Our approach is reported in LaRocca and Morgan 2018, to appear.

On the Machine Translation side, the research questions to be addressed in future work include methods to improve the performance of the existing Uqailaut morphological analyzer for the Inuktitut (Farley, 2009) making use of a variety of neural network approaches; improvements over a baseline statistical machine translation (SMT) English-Inuktitut system by using alternate subword units with a neural network architecture; diagnosis of which subword units yield the most improvement; determining how a pipelined English-Inuktitut translation

---

[13] http://depts.washington.edu/uwcl/el-stec/index.php

system, with deep morpheme translation plus deep-to-surface sequence-to-sequence model performs compared with the best subword system; and then exploring the use of hierarchical structures over morphemes in a novel approach to improve over the best subword system.

From an applications perspective, the outcomes of the research will be useful for a wide range of applications including collaboration with coalition forces and civil affairs requirements, in particular. From a theoretical perspective, we contribute to a deeper understanding of the effectiveness of neural network architectures which take context into consideration, for example, a recurrent neural network (RNN), a long- short term memory network (LSTM), a bidirectional LSTM (BiLSTM), or a convolutional neural network (CNN). We will reveal necessary modifications in order for successful low-resource ASR and MT. Finally, from the perspective of language revitalization and contributions to native communities, we explore tools that could be useful to teachers and language analysts as we reach the future goal of enabling a deep understanding of language across types and both their superficial and underlying features.

To conclude, we have set out a strategy and approach for an end-to-end speech recognition system along with machine translation that involves developing novel machine learning techniques and computational approaches for low-resource polysynthetic languages.

Acknowledgements: Thanks to Roland Kuhn and Anna Kazantseva, National Research Council of Canada who are part of the organizing committee for the upcoming workshop on Polysynthetic Languages to be held at COLING 2018, in Santa Fe, New Mexico on August 25, 2018. This workshop will be the first where both researchers and practitioners working on polysynthetic languages will discuss common problems and difficulties, and it is intended as the capstone to establishing possible collaborations and ongoing partnerships. We acknowledge Lori Levin, Carnegie Mellon University, for many helpful discussions on the nature of polysynthesis, and we are grateful to Maria Polinsky, University of Maryland, and Omer Preminger, University of Maryland, for enabling us to dig even deeper into some of the more fine-grained aspects of polysynthesis. All errors are, of course, our own.

References

Adams, O., Neubig, G., Cohn, T., & Bird, S. (2015). Inducing bilingual lexicons from small quantities of sentence-aligned phonemic transcriptions. *Proceedings of the International Workshop on Spoken Language Translation (IWSLT 2015)*. Da Nang, Vietnam.

Aranovich, R. (2013). Transitivity and polysynthesis in Fijian. Language 89: 465-500.

Arkhangelskiy, T. A., & Lander, Y. A. (2016). Developing a polysynthetic language corpus: problems and solutions. *Computational Linguistics and Intellectual Technologies: Proceedings of the International Conference "Dialogue 2016"*, June 104, 2016.

Baker, M. C. (1996). *The polysynthesis parameter.* New York: Oxford University Press.

Baker, M.C. (2002). *Atoms of language.* New York: Basic Books.

Bird, S. (2009). Natural language processing and linguistic fieldwork. *Computational Linguistics, 35* (3), 469-474.

Byrd, R. J., Klavans, J. L., Aronoff, M., & Anshen, F. (1986). Computer methods for morphological analysis. *Proceedings of the 24th annual meeting on Association for Computational Linguistics* (pp. 120-127). Stroudsberg, PA. Association for Computational Linguistics.

Caruana, Rich, (1997) "Multitask Learning." *Machine Learning,* Vol. 28, pp. 41-75, Kluwer Academic Publishers.

Comrie, B. (1981). *Language Universals and Linguistic Typology.* Oxford: Blackwell.

Davis, H., & Mattewson, L. (2009). Issues in Salish syntax and semantics. Language and Linguistics Compass 3, 1097-1166.

Farley, B. (2009). *The Uqailaut Project.* Retrieved from Inuktitut Computing: http://www.inuktitutcomputing.ca/Uqailaut/info.php

Fortescue, M. (1994). Polysynthetic morphology. (R. E. al., Ed.) The encyclopedia of language and linguistic, 5, 2600–2602.

Fortescue, M. (2016). Polysynthesis: A Diachronic and Typological Perspective. In M. Aronoff (ed.) *Oxford Encyclopedia of Linguistics.* Oxford, Oxford, England: Oxford University Press.

Fortescue, M., Mithun, M., & Evans, N. (Eds.). (2017). *The Oxford Handbook of Polysynthesis.* Oxford: Oxford University Press.

Greenberg, J. H. (1960). A quantitative approach to the morphological typology of language. *International Journal of Linguistics, 26,* 178–194.

Kazeminejad, G., Cowell, A., & Hulden , M. (2017). Creating lexical resources for polysynthetic languages—the case of Arapaho. *Proceedings of the 2nd Workshop on the Use of Computational Methods in the Study of Endangered Languages* (pp. 10-18). Honolulu: Association for Computational Linguistics.

Klavans, J. L. (1995). *On Clitics and Cliticization: The Interaction of Morphology, Phonology, and Syntax.* New York: Garland.

Kong, L., Dyer, C., & Smith, N. (2015). Segmental Recurrent Neural Networks. *CoRR*. Retrieved from http://arxiv.org/abs/1511.06018.

LaRocca, Stephen and John Morgan (2018, to appear) "Incorporating MT into a Bi-directional Speech Translation System for U.S. Army units", Paper to be presented at the Association for Machine Translation in the Americas conference (AMTA 2018), Boston, Massachusetts. March 17-21, 2018.

Levow, G.-A., Bender, E., Littell, P., Howell, K., Chelliah, S., Crowgey, J., et al. (2017). STREAMLInED Challenges: Aligning Research Interests with Shared Tasks. *Proceedings of ComputEL-2: 2nd Workshop on Computational Methods for Endangered Languages.*

Lois, X., & Vapnarsky, V. (2006.). Root indeterminacy and polyvalence in Yukate-can Mayan languages. In X. Lois, & V. Vapnarsky (Eds.). *Lexical categories and root clauses in Amerindian languages* (pp. 69-115). Bern: Peter Lang.

Micher, Jeffrey (2016) "Machine Translation for a Low-Resource, Polysynthetic Language" Presentation at AMTA 2016. Austin, Texas.

Micher, J. (2017). Improving Coverage of an Inuktitut Morphological Analyzer Us-ing a Segmental Recurrent Neural Network. *Proceedings of the 2nd Workshop on the Use of Computational Methods in the Study of Endangered Languages* (pp. 101-106). Honolulu, HI: Association for Computational Linguistics.

Mithun, M. (1989). The acquisition of polysynthesis. *Journal of Child Language, 16*, 285–312.

Mithun, M. (2017). Argument marking in the polysynthetic verb and its implications. In M. Fortescue, M. Mithun, & N. Evans (Eds.), *The Oxford Handbook of Polysyn-thesis* (pp. 30-58). Oxford, UK: Oxford University Press.

Polinsky, M. (2012). Headedness, again. *UCLA Working Papers in Linguistics, The-ories of Everything. 17*, pp. 348-359. Los Angeles: UCLA.

Povey, Daniel & Ghoshal, Arnab & Boulianne, Gilles & Burget, Lukáš & Glembek, Ondrej & Goel, Nagendra & Hannemann, Mirko & Motlíček, Petr & Qian, Yanmin & Schwarz, Petr & Silovský, Jan & Stemmer, Georg & Vesel, Karel. (2011). The Kaldi speech recognition toolkit. IEEE 2011 Workshop on Automatic Speech Recog-nition and Understanding.

Sennrich, R., Haddow, B., & Birch, A. (2015). Neural Machine Translation of Rare Words with Subword Units. *CoRR, abs/1508.07909*. Retrieved from http://arxiv.org/abs/1508.07909

Shinozaki, T., Furui, S., 2001. Error analysis using decision trees in spontaneous presentation speech recognition. In: Proceedings of the Automatic Speech Recognition and Understanding Conference. Trento, Italy.

Testelets Ya. (ed.). (2009). *Aspekty polisintetizma: Očerki po grammatike adygejskogo jazyka [Aspects of polysynthesis: Essays on Adyghe grammar],* (pp. 17-120). Moscow: Russian University for the Humanities.

Watanabe, H. (2017). The polysynthetic nature of Salish. In Fortescue, M., Mithun, M., & Evans, N. (Eds.). (2017). *The Oxford Handbook of Polysynthesis* (pp. 623-642). Oxford: Oxford University Press.

Evaluating Automatic Speech Recognition
in Translation

Evelyne Tzoukermann tzoukermann@mitre.org

Corey Miller camiller@mitre.org

The MITRE Corporation, 7525 Colshire Dr, McLean, VA 22102

Abstract

We address and evaluate the challenges of utilizing Automatic Speech Recognition (ASR) to support the human translator. Audio transcription and translation are known to be far more time-consuming than text translation; at least 2 to 3 times longer. Furthermore, time to translate or transcribe audio is vastly dependent on audio quality, which can be impaired by background noise, overlapping voices, and other acoustic conditions. The purpose of this paper is to explore the integration of ASR in the translation workflow and evaluate the challenges of utilizing ASR to support the human translator. We present several case studies in different settings in order to evaluate the benefits of ASR. Time is the primary factor in this evaluation. We show that ASR might be effectively used to assist, but not replace, the human translator in essential ways.

1. Introduction

Advances in deep learning have had a major impact on human language technologies and the results have been visible in Neural ASR and in Neural Machine Translation. As such, we can now reevaluate the benefits and challenges of using improved ASR systems to facilitate the translation of audio documents.

Translating audio documents involves the use of a media player specifically developed for performing transcription and translation; that is, a media player capable of going back and forth in the audio stream, looping over segments in order to listen and re-listen to unclear sections, and slowing down the audio in order to capture the content. These tools are for the most part available to government linguists. The problem lies in the nature of the incoming files which may be very noisy. Numerous factors can be the source of the noise in the audio files. Multiple conditions can be present, such as inside/outside noise, landline, cellular, and Voice over Internet Protocol (VoIP). Each of these conditions can in turn be associated with a diversity of noise, such as overlapping voice with other voices, music, street noise, static on the line, etc. As a result, government linguists who are given the task of translating audio files spend a considerable amount of time translating audio input[1].

---

[1] According to professional industry standards, for each minute of audio, an average of 4 times the length is required to translate. Thus, for example, for a short fifteen minutes of speech, one hour of transcription time is required. Furthermore, for noisy recorded audio, the same operation can take several more hours. See http://www.confidentialtranscription.co.nz/cost.htm.

Given this variability in recording conditions and incoming files, we have decided to isolate the problem of "noisy" files, and deal only with "clean" files or clearly recorded files in order to investigate the integration of ASR technologies in the workflow of audio translation. This reduces factors impacting performance so we can rigorously test without confounding factors.

The next section presents related research particularly as it relates to operational settings. Section 3 shows three different tasks on which we applied ASR and scoring. Section 4 shows the results of the experiments. We then conclude in offering recommendations for decision makers.

2. Related Research

Academic literature abounds in research and evaluation on ASR, speech translation, and all the applications that include speech recognition and machine translation (MT). However, there is less work addressing the issues that we are bringing up in this paper, which is the integration of ASR into the linguist workflow. From a research perspective, work on ASR for translation has been studied and presented within the lens of speech translation – that is, audio input in a given source language translated into text of a target language, or speech-to-speech translation, which is the same as speech translation but the target language output is spoken.

Stüker et al. (2007) describe the operational settings of the European Union where European Parliament speeches are translated in 21 languages, and the need for combining ASR and MT is required. Stüker et al. and Paulik et al. (2005) report on the benefits of smoothly coupling the two technologies and refer to a speech translation enhanced ASR system (STE-ASR). They demonstrate how the quality of ASR influences the overall quality of the output and how by adapting the ASR models to the task at hand, the Word Error Rate (WER) is lowered by 3% to 4.8%, providing more accurate results.

From a practical perspective, ASR offers a variety of advantages as well as challenges to translators. Ciobanu (2014) surveys the advantages and disadvantages of using ASR in translation services. The outcome of the survey demonstrates that the advantages outweighed the disadvantages and that "professional translators are essentially missing out by not engaging with such technologies more". In his later work, Ciobanu (2016) conducted research at University of Leeds Centre for Translation Studies to study the benefits of inserting ASR, and presented the challenges of ASR in the language services industry by concluding that "ASR has the potential to increase the productivity and creativity of the translation act, but the advantages can be overshadowed by a reduction in translation quality unless thorough revision processes are in place." (p.124)

Other academic research (e.g. Zapata 2012 and 2016) explores the benefits of interactive translation dictation, a translation technique that involves interaction with multimodal interfaces equipped with ASR throughout the entire translation process. In this work, Zapata demonstrates the range of interaction between humans and machines in translation processes and claims that a new turn in translation technology is needed, with the human translator as the central axis of investigation. Zapata's work provides a basis for well-grounded research on translator-computer and translator-information interaction, particularly for the design and development of interactive translation dictation environments. These interactive systems are expected to support professional translators' cognitive functions, performance, and workplace satisfaction.

In contrast, our current approach explores the extent to which resources should be expended at improving ASR transcripts prior to either human or machine translation. In the case of both speech translation and machine translation, we factor in the time that must be expended to correct its output. These measurements are considered with respect to three different possible workflows for combining ASR and translation.

3. Method

This section addresses the selection of languages and files, and explains the way audio files are processed, timed, and scored for accuracy. In addition, we describe the human particpants in our experiment.

3.1. Language Selection and File Selection

For this experiment, we selected the following languages: French, Spanish, and Serbian. We used two of the latest systems that are publicly available online: IBM Bluemix ASR[2] and Google Translate ASR[3]. For the French experiment, we selected excerpts from the speech that French President Emmanuel Macron delivered during his inauguration on May 15, 2017[4]. We downloaded the files from YouTube and used an online converter to convert the files into *.wav format. We then used Audacity open source software[5] for recording and editing and selected two speech segments of one to two minutes each. For the Spanish and Serbian experiments, similar political speeches by Mexican President Enrique Peña Nieto[6] and Serbian President Aleksandar Vučić[7] were selected and Praat software[8] was used to navigate and listen in order to make transcript corrections. As additional Spanish data, we used a television interview of the Bolivian Minister of the Economy, Luis Arce[9]. The files were originally recorded at a very clear high-quality stereo 44100Hz, PCM 16 bit, and this naturally yields better results. The experiments were performed by four linguists, one French, two Spanish, and one Serbian. Note that the Serbian linguist is a professional translator whereas the other three linguists are only fluent in the language.

3.2. Running and Analyzing ASR

For each of the tasks, files were run through an ASR engine. Each audio file was run through IBM ASR and Google ASR. Note that since Serbian is not available among the IBM ASR languages, the Serbian files were run only through the Google ASR system. While the IBM system allows file upload, the Google system does not. For the IBM system, we used the French and Spanish 16KHz broadband models. The Google Translate system provides a microphone icon that one can click in order to provide live audio input via a microphone, rather than typing text in. We employed a software package called Virtual Audio Cable 4.5[10] that allowed us to redirect file-based audio through the microphone so that it could serve as input to Google Translate. Note that when providing audio to Google Translate, there are two outputs: on the left side

---

2 https://speech-to-text-demo.ng.bluemix.net/ (as of February 2, 2018)

3 https://translate.google.com/ (as of February 6, 2018)

4 https://www.youtube.com/watch?v=K8Ea_RXktgg

5 https://www.audacityteam.org/

6 https://www.youtube.com/watch?v=qUeqwMl-_U0

7 https://www.youtube.com/watch?v=kGz9diiTV-M

8 www.fon.hum.uva.nl/praat/

9 https://www.youtube.com/watch?v=pxqw4TaqK1A

10 http://software.muzychenko.net/eng/vac.htm

is the ASR output in the source language, and on the right side is the translation in the target language; what we are calling "speech translation".

Figures 1a and 1b below show a sample of IBM ASR and Google ASR output for French. Overall, both transcriptions are of good quality in that the reader can get a gist of the speech. Both transcriptions are close to each other. The main differences in Figures 1a and 1b are highlighted in yellow. Note that the figures show the raw output of the recognition, and thus contain errors, such as agreement errors, erroneous words, missing words, substituted words, etc. The IBM system differs from Google in generating sentence boundaries, and as a consequence, adds punctuation and capitalization. In the IBM system, sentence boundaries appear to be based essentially on pauses and since Macron's speech is well articulated, the program adds too many periods, such as "L'audace de la liberté. Les exigences de l'égalité. La volonté de la fraternité." As a reference and comparison, Figure 1c shows the official transcript of the president's speech. One can notice the differences in orthographic realization (also mentioned in Section 3.3) with the representation of numbers, such as "*sept mai*" and "*7 mai*".

<table>
<tr><td>

L'audace de la liberté. Les exigences de l'égalité. La volonté de la fraternité. Or depuis des décennies la france doute d'elle-même. Elle se sent menacée dans sa culture quand son modèle social dans ces croyances profondes et les doutes. De ce qui le fait. Voila pourquoi mon mandat sera guidée par des exigences. La première sera de rendre aux français. Cette confiance en eux. Depuis trop longtemps a faibli. Oh je vous rassure. Je n'ai pas pensé une seule seconde. Quel sera instauré comme par magie le soir du sept mai. Ce sera un travail long. Exigeant. Mais indispensable. Il appartiendra de convaincre les françaises et les français que notre pays.

</td><td>

l'audace de la Liberté l'exigence de l'Égalité la volonté de la fraternité or depuis des décennies la France doute d'elle-même elle se sent menacé dans sa culture dans son modèle social dans ses croyances profondes elle doute de ce qu'il a fait voilà pourquoi mon mandat sera guidé par deux exigences la première sera de rendre au français cette confiance en eux depuis trop longtemps affaiblit oh je vous rassure je n'ai pas pensé une seule seconde qu'elle se restaurer comme par magie le soir du 7 mai ce sera un travail non exigeant mais indispensable il m'appartiendra de convaincre les Françaises et les français que notre pays

</td></tr>
</table>

Figure 1a. IBM ASR output of excerpt 1 from French President Emmanuel Macron

Figure 1b. Google ASR output of excerpt 1 from French President Emmanuel Macron

...l'audace de la liberté, l'exigence de l'égalité, la volonté de la fraternité. Or, depuis des décennies, la France doute d'elle-même. Elle se sent menacée dans sa culture, dans son modèle social, dans ses croyances profondes. Elle doute de ce qui l'a faite. Voilà pourquoi mon mandat sera guidé par deux exigences. La première sera de rendre aux Français cette confiance en eux, depuis trop longtemps affaiblie. Je vous rassure, je n'ai pas pensé une seule seconde qu'elle se restaurerait comme par magie le soir du 7 mai. Ce sera un travail lent, exigeant, mais indispensable. Il m'appartiendra de convaincre les Françaises et les Français que notre pays...

Figure 1c. Excerpt of the Official Transcript of French President Emmanuel Macron

3.3. Preparing files for ASR scoring

The object of ASR scoring is to establish a word error rate (WER) with respect to a given reference transcription and hypothesis transcription. We use NIST sclite[11] scoring software, which is a tool for scoring and evaluating the output of speech recognition systems.

In this project, we have two levels of transcript correction: basic and full, as explained in Section 3.4. For the purpose of ASR scoring, we have decided to focus initially on the basic correction.

---

[11] See https://www.nist.gov/sites/default/files/documents/itl/iad/mig/KWS15-evalplan-v05.pdf

The reason for this is that it can provide the most optimistic WER. For example, if ASR confuses two French homophones, e.g. *"parle"* and *"parles"*, we don't necessarily want to penalize the recognizer for confusing these. At the basic correction step, if we encounter *parles*, we also consider *parle* to be correct, since the two words are homophones and one is an inflectional variant of the other.

The scoring software compares the machine-generated transcription of audio segments to a human transcription of the same segment. Usually, the segments are aligned using time stamps associated with the audio file. Since Google ASR does not provide us with timing information, we added line breaks in the reference and hypothesis files corresponding to sentences or intonation units and tagged the lines in parallel, according to sclite's *trn* format. The purpose of separating the text into intonation units is to give the scoring mechanism, which is based on dynamic programming, a chance to reset and compare the same segments. This way, the exact boundaries do not matter[12], as long as they are consistent between reference and hypothesis.

We removed punctuation from both reference and hypothesis files. At this stage, punctuation accuracy is not scored. We also removed capitalization in both files. Theoretically, the output of step 1 (i.e. the basic transcript correction) for Google and IBM would be the same. However, in practice, there may be multiple cases where the orthographic realizations differ and thus, would require full normalization. For example, if Google outputs *50* and IBM outputs *fifty*, basic correction does not require this to be normalized. So, creating separate basic ASR scoring transcripts for Google and IBM was deemed the best way forward to ensure that neither engine is penalized for confusing things like *50* with *fifty*.

Table 1 shows the results of the IBM ASR and the Google ASR for French, Spanish, and Serbian. Note that since Serbian is not among the languages available in IBM ASR system, only the Google results are presented here.

	IBM ASR		Google ASR	
	Correct	**WER**	**Correct**	**WER**
French 1	87.2	12.8	96.7	3.3
French 2	82.0	22.3	93.9	6.1
Spanish 1	94.4	6.5	95.6	4.4
Spanish 2	80.3	22.2	81.7	18.3
Serbian	n/a	n/a	90.4	10.4

Table 1. Accuracy of IBM and Google ASR systems

Overall, the Google ASR system performs distinctly better than the IBM system. For the French documents, the results are on average 10% better with Google than they are with IBM. All the documents processed by Google are over 90% for Serbian and close to, or above 95% for the other languages. The difference in performance between the two Spanish documents has to do with their contents. "Spanish 1" is the Mexican president's speech, while "Spanish 2" is a television interview with the Bolivian economics minister. The speech is much more articulated and deliberate in contrast to the interview.

---

[12] We have noticed that using particularly long sentences can result in higher WER, presumably as a side effect of dynamic programming. This warrants further study.

We found that the performance of ASR is a strong indicator of how much effort will be required for humans to edit a document so that it is accurate. High ASR performance, e.g. low WER results, suggests that the human effort is minimized, even for more difficult transcriptions, such as the television interview. The following section shows the setup of the experiments where linguists correct the transcripts to prepare them for the follow-on processes.

3.4. Setting the Different Tasks

In order to measure the benefits of integrating ASR in the linguist's workflow, we designed three different task scenarios where each of the task components is measured in time. Each of these tasks represents a different possible workflow for combining translation and ASR.

Task 1. **BASIC** – ASR followed by Human Translation: the linguist is given an audio document and the file is run through the ASR system(s). The task consists of (i) correcting the ASR output, and (ii) translating the document into English. Note that correcting the ASR output at this level is time consuming. It involves using a media player, listening the audio, comparing it with the ASR output, and going forward and backward with the player to add, substitute, and replace words. At the same time, since the human will translate the ASR transcript, the output does not need to be perfectly accurate on sentence boundaries, capitalization, punctuation, and word agreement. However, the transcript should be accurate enough so that somebody using the resulting edited ASR transcript for translation purposes will **not** need to consult the audio file. This is the reason we call this correcting task "basic".

Task 2. FULL – ASR followed by Machine Translation (MT): the linguist is given an audio document as well as the corrected ASR output from Task 1. This task consists of fully correcting the ASR output after it has already undergone the basic level correction. Capitalization, agreement, and accents need to be corrected. Sentence boundaries need to be inserted for some systems, such as Google ASR and corrected for others, such IBM ASR. This stage consists of a complete and thorough transcript correction so that it is presentable to an MT engine. This is what we call "full" corrected output. This output is then submitted to Google Translate and the linguist times how long it takes him/her edit. This is a standard workflow in machine translation and is referred to as post-edited machine translation (PEMT).

Task 3. Speech to Text Translation: This step consists of using an end-to-end speech-to-text translation system, such as Google Translate, which takes audio input in our three selected languages and returns the text translated in English. The linguist takes the English output and times how long it takes them to edit and correct it. We refer to this operation as post-edited speech translation (PEST).

4. Results

Table 2 presents the time measurements (in minutes) of the transcription editing parts of Task 1 and Task 2, along with the word counts and the duration of each file. It is interesting to point out that it takes two to three times as long to correct the IBM transcript at a basic level as it takes to correct the Google transcript. For both IBM and Google ASR, and except for French 1, the time it takes to complete the full correction is minimal compared to the time necessary for achieving the basic level correction. Also, French 2 had more errors than French 1, yet it took less time to correct the errors—perhaps these results are attributable to priming effects since the linguist worked on French 1 followed by French 2.

The numbers in Table 2 clearly demonstrate that the quality of Google ASR is markedly better than that of IBM ASR in this use case. It also shows the correlation between ASR performance and the human time needed to correct the transcripts. As mentioned above, high ASR performance yields human time saving for transcript correction. At the same time, it shows that the overall timings exceed 4 times the duration of the cuts, as mentioned by industry standards. This is probably due to the experimental nature of the tasks (small amount of data) and to the fact that the linguists lacked experience in these particular tasks. More data need to be evaluated and run in similar experiments to understand these numbers in a clear fashion.

			Word count	IBM ASR			Google ASR		
Language	Doc	Time		Basic	Full	Total	Basic	Full	Total
French	1	1:22	180	20	16	**36**	7	3	**10**
	2	1:11	145	15	7	**22**	4	3	**7**
Spanish	1	2:42	343	18	5	**23**	6	5	**11**
	2	2:00	203	35	5	**40**	18	7	**25**
Serbian	1	3:30	516	n/a	n/a	n/a	16	6	**22**

Table 2. Times in Minutes for Correcting Basic and Full ASR Transcripts (Task 1 and Task 2)

Table 3 shows the time it takes to perform additional components of the Tasks. In Task 1, once the basic level of correction is completed, the linguist performs the manual translation of the file (Human Trans). For Task 2, once the full level of correction is completed, the linguist ingests the file into Google Translate, then checks and improves the accuracy of the machine translation by post-editing the document (PEMT). In Task 3, the linguist simply performs post-editing of the speech translation (PEST). Human translation is clearly the slowest of the three. Note that from a translation quality standpoint, PEMT is very reliable and very quick for French and Spanish.

Language	Doc	Word count	Human Trans (Task 1)	PEMT (Task 2)	PEST (Task 3)	Google Basic + Human-Trans (Task 1)	Google Basic + Full + MT + PEMT (Task 2)
French	1	180	12	**2**	3	19	12
	2	145	7	**3**	3	11	10
Spanish	1	343	13	**2**	5	19	13
	2	203	19	**4**	7	37	29
Serbian	1	516	n/a	**23**	33	n/a	45

Table 3. Times in Minutes for Human Translation, Post-Editing Machine Translation, and Post-Editing Speech Translation

The final three columns of Table 3 represent our three tasks or workflow scenarios, and the total time required to achieve a correct translation using them[13]. Task 3, using end-to-end speech to text translation, allows one to ignore the transcription correction process and proceed directly to post-editing the speech translation, and this seems to be the shortest way to a correct translation for the audio documents studied here. Task 1, ASR with basic correction followed by human translation, appears to be the slowest. Task 2, ASR followed by full transcript correction, followed by MT and PEMT, appears to be the second fastest method. The timing for Task 3 appears very competitive, which leads us to conclude that this approach is very compelling and promises to aid in creating more efficient audio translation workflows.

5. Conclusion and Future Work

In this paper, we addressed the challenges of using ASR to support the linguist translating audio files. Since there is large variability in incoming audio files, we experimented solely with clearly recorded files to control for extraneous variables and ensure reliable results. We implemented three different tasks where we measured the time it takes for linguists to achieve correct translations following different paths. We combined these timings with post-editing measures and we demonstrated that, except for the French documents generated by IBM ASR, there is a correlation between the quality of the automatic recognition and the amount of work that is necessary to edit the transcripts or a speech translation.

While it appears that time can certainly be saved by restricting transcription editing to a "basic" level, and that this is sufficient for subsequent audio-free human translation, we are not sure whether such a transcript is sufficient to generate reasonable MT or if would incur PEMT costs down the line. We need to compare PEMT on basic and full transcripts, since in this study we only measured PEMT based on the full transcript.

Based on these preliminary results so far, it appears that speech translation, coupled with PEST, may offer the fastest route to correct translation. The advantage to this approach is that it obviates the need for transcription correction. However, we need to examine this more closely and on more data in a variety of acoustic conditions, since the quality of speech translation is obviously especially sensitive to the quality of the input audio.

All in all, we can conclude that ASR has the potential to increase linguist productivity. This concurs with the outcomes of Ciobanu's survey. These results can be used as recommendations for decision makers who face the need to modernize their processes and increase the productivity of their workforce.

In future work, we are planning on making more extended tests and more fine-grained tests so that we can estimate the limitations of ASR in various domains and genres. Additionally, as research is making progress in the areas of adaptation and customization, we would like to explore how customized models for such domains and genres can improve recognition, and consequently reduce transcription adjustment time, leading to more efficiently produced translations of audio.

---

[13] Note that Serbian appears to be the language that is the most time consuming. The translations were processed by a professional translator as opposed to the other linguists who are fluent but not professional translators, and this possibly explains the discrepancy.

Acknowledgements

We thank Vanesa Jurica and Jason Duncan for their linguistic expertise as participants in this research.

References

Ciobanu, D. (2014). Of Dragons and Speech Recognition Wizards and Apprentices. Revista Tradumàtica, (12), 524–538.

Ciobanu, D. (2016). Automatic Speech Recognition in the Professional Translation Process. Translation Spaces, 5(1): 124–144.

Paulik, M., S. Stüker, C. Fügen, T. Schultz, Thomas Schaaf, and A. Waibel (2005), Speech Translation Enhanced Automatic Speech Recognition, in ASRU, San Juan, Puerto Rico.

Stüker, S., M. Paulik, M. Kolss, C. Fügen, and A. Waibel (2007), Speech Translation Enhanced ASR for European Parliament Speeches - On the Influence of ASR Performance on Speech Translation, in Proc. ICASSP, Honolulu, Hawaii.

Zapata, J. (2012). Traduction dictée interactive : intégrer la reconnaissance vocale à l'enseignement et à la pratique de la traduction professionnelle. M.A. thesis. University of Ottawa. Canada.

Zapata, J. (2016). Translators in the Loop: Observing and Analyzing the Translator Experience with Multimodal Interfaces for Interactive Translation Dictation Environment Design. Ph.D. thesis. University of Ottawa. Canada.

Portable speech-to-speech translation on an Android smartphone: The MFLTS system

Ralf Meermeier   ralf.meermeier@raytheon.com
Sean Colbath   sean.colbath@raytheon.com
Martha Lillie   martha.lillie@raytheon.com

Raytheon BBN Technologies, 02138 Cambridge, Massachusetts, USA

Abstract

For US troops on the ground in countries like Iraq and Afghanistan, one of the key objectives, "Winning the Heart and Minds" of the local population, presents a formidable challenge due to the language barrier involved. Employing human interpreters to address the issue has many of its own challenges, foremost availability of locals to willingly act as such. Because of this bottleneck, many of the Army's humanitarian missions are hindered as they require significant interaction between soldiers and the local population.

The Machine Foreign Language Translation System (MFLTS), a US Army project that originated out of DARPA's "TransTac" research effort, aims to address this bottleneck by equipping each soldier with a personal translation device running on a COTS Android smartphone. With it, soldiers can maintain basic free-form conversations with individuals in a turn-based "radio interview" style, with specific focus on topics such as checkpoints, information gathering and medical help. It can also be operated with optional peripherals that ease the interaction and improve the overall accuracy of the system.

1 Introduction

The paper is structured as follows: In Section 1 we outline the history of the MFLTS program, and in Section 2 we present the distinct challenges that have to be overcome when designing a speech-to-speech (S2S) Android application. Section 3 presents a conclusion that looks forward to where the application could go.

1.1 History of MFLTS

The MFLTS project's origins can be traced back to DARPA's "Translation System for Tactical Use" (TransTac) program, which aimed to spur research in the feasibility of running a full speech-to-speech system on a portable device. Partially in response to earlier systems that worked on the basis of choosing from a fixed set of phrases (and the limitations arising from that), the goal of the research project was to allow for free-form responses from both the soldier and the foreign speaker. Initial prototypes ran on full-fledged laptops which soldiers would carry in a backpack, but once cheap and powerful smartphones entered the market, specifically Google's "Nexus One" Android phone (a single-core 1GB ARM device with 512MB RAM), a push was made to transfer the system, and in turn its core technologies (speech recognition, mahchine translatrion, text-to-speech), to this platform.

In terms of language skill, the systems were desired to be at "ILR 1" level (*http://www.govtilr.org*), which corresponds to a person having a basic command of a foreign language, able to understand and pose pertinent questions. With a scale as notoriously difficult to evaluate as this, it is nonetheless the view of the authors that the system exceeds this basic level and is, when used to its full extent, better rated at ILR level 2.

The project had competing teams (BBN, IBM, CMU) build systems that were evaluated in regular intervals at NIST or MITRE (David Stallard, 2011).

Figure 1: Early S2S prototypes on the Nexus One

With the success of the TransTac project, the US Army subsequently created the MFLTS program with the intent of transitioning the research system into a fieldable system that would eventually get deployed in theater. BBN, a consistent top performer in the TransTac evaluations, was chosen to build this framework and reimplement its version of speech-to-speech in it.

The intent of the MFLTS program, however, has much broader scope: To avoid creating a one-off application that would tie the Army to one specific vendor, designing MFLTS as a framework allows easy writing of any application that wants to utilize natural language processing (NLP) components. An application makes a request to the framework for specific NLP components (ASR, MT, etc) and the framework instantiates these components for the app to interact with. The existing framework is massively parallel, adapting to the changing usage patterns, and even is "self-healing", i.e., it will replace crashed components as transparently as possible to the application in order to provide minimal downtime in possibly critical scenarios.

With this framework, the original S2S application is now just a specific app written for the framework. Not only that, but because MFLTS is required to support both Windows and Android operating systems, the same code can be used (with minor adjustments) to run the same application on those vastly different platforms. Another benefit is that the NLP components are designed to be plug-and-play, meaning any third-party vendor can provide new components; as an example, BBN recently replaced its old Byblos recognizer with the new "Sage" recognizer (Roger Hsiao, 2016) (Meermeier and Colbath, 2017) the application, however, has no knowledge of this and simply receives better ASR results. Just as easily, an application's voice output can be changed when a cheaper, or better, TTS provider wraps its engine using the MFLTS API.

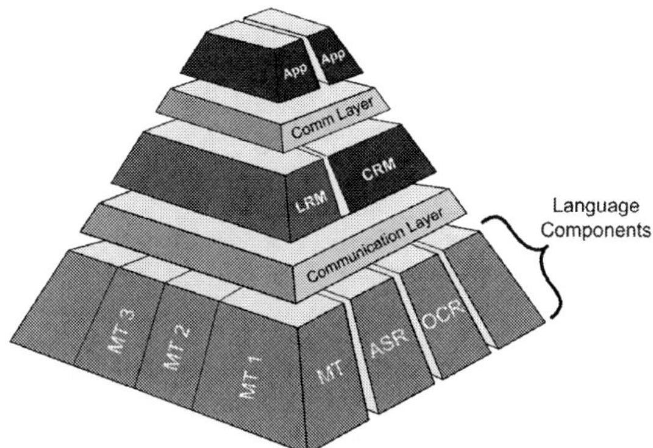

Figure 2: The MFLTS architecture: Apps are connected to NLP components by the framework

1.2 MFLTS S2S

(a) S2S mounted on vest, including peripherals

(b) Application main screen

Figure 3: The MFLTS S2S Android application

In general, the application works in an "interview-style" fashion where the soldier is the driver of the conversation. Initially he/she will start the conversation by speaking into the application, and then waiting for it to recognize, translate and output the translation via text-to-speech (TTS). All this happens close to real-time, with latencies from end-of-speech to begin-of-TTS on the order of 1000 milliseconds on the Android system. On the much more powerful Windows desktop system there is virtually no latency.

Depending on the conversation, the foreign language speaker ("FLE") might then be the one responding in turn, just as before speaking into the application and waiting for the translation. It is important to note that it is the soldier who signals through *body language* to the FLE that it is his turn to speak; not using the application to queue the FLE (e.g., with a TTS prompt) was a key realization that later became a design principle of the application.

In its current form, there are two ways to interact with MFLTS S2S:

- Smartphone only: The two text fields in Figure 3b also serve as buttons that, when pressed, start recording speech from the phone's internal microphone. Upon lifting the finger the translation starts.

- Peripheral: As seen in Figures 3a and 4, we created a peripheral microphone device that, alongside a battery-driven speaker, greatly enhances interaction.

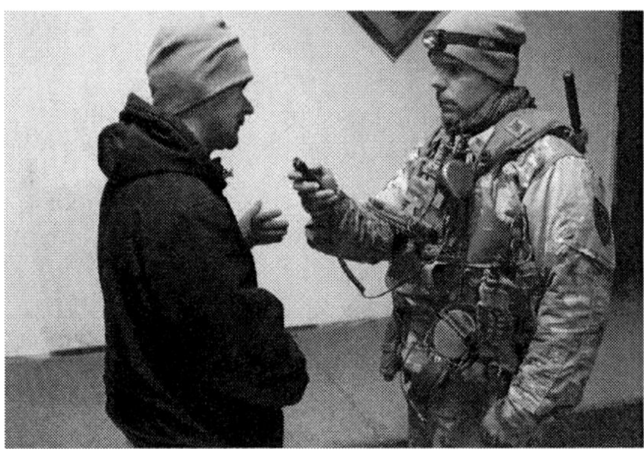

Figure 4: The application tested during a live exercise (AEWE)

1.3 Evaluation

When building a complex application such as an S2S application, it is not immediately obvious how to evaluate it in order to make improvements. The simplest way, and this was done in the early days of the TransTac program, is by evaluating the systems through their individual components' performance:

- Speech recognition: Word Error Rate (WER)

- Machine translation: BLEU (and others)

Because WER and BLEU scores are easily generated and compared, they are instinctively chosen for evaluation, but there is an assumption riding on using these low-level statistics, which is that an improvement in either of those scores translates to an improvement in the usability of the application.

What we found during the many iterations of the application is that, often that is not the case. In fact, minute changes in the user interface often would cause far more drastic improvements in user satisfaction. Because of this, later evaluations added the measurement of "High Level Concept Transfer": During an evaluation a soldier would be given a list of specific information he is trying to establish (e.g., "what days of the week do supply trucks come through this town?") by asking the FLE. Systems were then compared by how many concepts (i.e. pieces of pertinent information) they were able to transmit in a given time period. By the time of the MFLTS program, the software was being evaluated in mock exercises where it was being used (successfully) to gather actionable intelligence that helped soldiers achieve their mission objective.

1.4 The Right Flow

A key realization during the development was, for lack of a better description, the system's
"place in the conversation". Given such a powerful system, it is tempting to elevate its inter-
actions to the level of a human interpreter by having it inject itself into the conversation like
an interpreter would. As an example, an interpreter might ask for clarification from the soldier
("did you mean 'magazine' like the warehouse, or the gun magazine?"). This type of inter-
jection was in fact tested in more detail in a subsequent research project (DARPA *BOLT*), but
the problem that arises with this approach is that it essentially adds a third party into the conversation. Not only that, it also consumes precious time that the two parties involved have to
wait.

As a result, we followed the following guideline during design: **Any system output comes
at a premium**. This was a very consistent trend, as shown in three different aspects of the
application:

- English confirmation: The idea was to use English TTS to confirm what the system's ASR
  had recognized, with the expectation that the soldier would interrupt the system if the ASR
  was wrong. We found that soldiers rather preferred to deal with any ASR error during
  follow-up conversation than restarting the utterance. The flow of the interaction was more
  important than this additional checkpoint.

- Backtranslation: Similar to English confirmation, but instead the foreign-language text
  was again back-translated to English, and then put out with TTS before the foreign TTS
  was played. Once again, the slowdown of the conversation was deemed too onerous over
  the additional piece of information.

- Abort: Innocuous as it may seem, the ability to quickly abort an ongoing translation dras-
  tically improved usability (initially the soldier had to wait out the translation before begin-
  ning a new one).

The key conclusion here was that both parties want the system "out of the way" of the
conversation. That is, in a heavily multimodal human conversation (facial expressions, body
language etc.) the system needs to facilitate information flow, not take it over or manipulate it.
In terms of Enfield's "conversation engine" (Enfield, 2018), the goal is to maintain the flow of
said engine as much as possible.

1.5 The Right Hardware

In a similar vein to the previous section, finding the right physical representation of the device
can either facilitate or hinder the interaction. For example, one of the devices that was tested but
ultimately rejected was a telephone receiver that allowed the FLE to listen to the translation and
speak into it, to piggy-back on the familiarity of people with a telephone conversation. However,
the necessary physical proximity to the soldier with this device was rated too uncomfortable to
both parties, as were the possible social implications of a foreigner "receiving a phone call"
from a US soldier.

Instead, we opted to emulate another interaction most people are familiar with: a TV
interview, where one person with a microphone interviews the other. Several aspects made this
way of interacting stand out:

- All devices are in possession of the soldier, and he/she can decide how far or close the
  microphone is to the FLE

- The act of physically pointing the microphone either at the soldier's mouth or at the FLE's
  mouth is an implicit queue of "it is your/my turn to speak". As mentioned above, this type
  of non-verbal communication is almost always preferrable to voice-based queueing.

1.6 The Right Person

A different, interesting realization was that the success of the application is as dependent on its software as it is on the person that uses it. We have consistently experienced vast ranges of user reports, from "this app hindered my attempts to communicate" to "this was almost like I speak the language myself". What we found is that in any given group, there will be people naturally predisposed to using the app: for these people, and it is astonishing to witness, the application becomes second nature, and they return to focusing on observing the FLE speaking, as if they were conversing in their own native language. Just as with any other tool, success of the application comes down to selecting a "Communicator" in the group who shows natural adeptness.

That said, the MFLTS program requires basic proficiency of the app by any soldier within one hour, which we achieved by an interactive training embedded in the Android application. Leveraging soldiers' innate familiarity with smartphone user interfaces, usually it is rather a matter of minutes after which they then start focusing on mastering the social subtleties of the application.

2 Conclusion

The MFLTS S2S application has shown its value as a translation application under real-life constraints, and development is ongoing. There are many avenues that should be explored:

- Hands-free: To return even further to the ideal of an unimpeded conversation, the system would not have to be told when, or who, is speaking at a moment. It should detect the spoken language, and present its translation at an opportune time.

- Even smaller: Powerful smartphones are ubiqitous, but their different usage profile demand a size that is not necessarily needed for a translation device. At the same time, single-board computers (SBCs) are upcoming that could be used to create even more integrated devices.

- Far more advanced: A major incurrence of conversation latency is the current requirement to wait until the person has stopped speaking before the translation can be spoken out, simply because there would otherwise be two people speaking. An advanced approach such as directional speakers might allow for truly real-time translation where partial translations are output while the person is still speaking. An exciting array of considerations (translation accuracy vs latency etc) arise from this.

As mentioned before, what must be used as the ultimate goal is the "absence" of the tool, i.e., the application. Humans are masters at conversations, and any translation application needs to strive to return to that realm.

References

David Stallard, R. P. e. a. (2011). The BBN TransTalk Speech-to-Speech Translation System. In *Speech and Language Technologies*, chapter 3. InTech.

Enfield, N. (2018). *How We Talk: The Inner Workings of Conversation*.

Meermeier, R. and Colbath, S. (2017). Applications of the BBN Sage Speech Processing Platform. In *Proceedings of Interspeech 2017*, Stockholm, Sweden.

Roger Hsiao, R. M. e. a. (2016). Sage: The New BBN Speech Processing Platform. In *Proceedings of Interspeech 2016*, San Francisco, USA.